The Linden tree, with its heart shaped leaves and medicinal flowers, grows in abundance in Europe. In the country of Slovenia , it is thought to be the witness of many generations and point the way to heaven. Four generations of Slovene ancestry are depicted in these pages. They experience adventure, passion, sorrow, love, and forgiveness.

You will learn what happens to vivacious Louiza, handsome Anton, sweet Rose and gentle Frank, when they immigrate to the United States. Their lives are affected by the historic events that occur in the first half of the twentieth century, World War 1, Prohibition, The Great Depression, and the beginning of World War II.

The main characters are Louiza and Anton Poncek and three of their seven children; Ivan, Stefan, and Theresa. Other main characters are Frank and Rose Koznar and four of their eight children; Josip, Beth, Katja, and Eddi. The two families intertwine and survive many adversities.

THE LINDEN TREE LEGACY

The Dawning

B.F. KNUDSON

authorHOUSE®

AuthorHouse™
1663 Liberty Drive
Bloomington, IN 47403
www.authorhouse.com
Phone: 1-800-839-8640

First published by AuthorHouse   05/03/2011

ISBN: 978-1-4520-9265-2 (sc)
ISBN: 978-1-4520-9267-6 (e)
ISBN: 978-1-4520-9266-9 (hc)

Library of Congress Control Number: 2010915928

Printed in the United States of America

FOR MY PARENTS

ANTON

In an army-camp, a few miles outside of Vienna, a soldier was writing a note to his fiancé.

My dear sweet Agnes,   August 1, 1905

I miss you so. The Image of kissing your soft lips and holding you in my arms, helps me to fall asleep at night. I recall the summer breezes tossing your lovely hair as we stood under the Linden tree and the sparkle in your eyes when you agreed to marry me. It seems like an eternity before we are together again. I hope the time I have left in this army will pass quickly. Love, Anton

Anton placed the note in an envelope addressed to Agnes Simic, Leskovo, Austria. His obligation of serving two years in the Austrian-Hungarian army would be over in a few weeks. The days crawled by.

While on leave six months earlier, he had asked his sweetheart to marry him. Their lives had intertwined since they were children going to school at St. Vitus, a place of learning, worship and social activity. They became more aware of each other in their formative years, exchanging guarded glances and a few words at Sunday gatherings. Their childhood friendship developed into a romance as they reached adulthood. Anton was enamored with Agnes's beauty and sweet demeanor.

The village of Leskovo in the province of Slovenia was only a couple of kilometers from Anton's home. He passed it often while walking to the large town of Skofia Loka. One summer afternoon a day after Anton's seventeenth birthday, he decided to join the men serenading the women at dusk in Agnes's village. "I won't be home for dinner. I'm going to Leskovo," he told his mother.

"Don't come home late. I worry," his mother said.

"I'll come home when I want to! You've never worried about me before," Anton said.

"That's unfair," His mother said, frowning.

"I'm going." Anton walked out the door.

It was the custom for unmarried men to gather at sundown around the legendary Linden tree to sing and woo the single women. Slovenia had an abundance of Linden trees, but the old one growing in the center of the village square had special significance. Long ago, leaders held council meetings underneath this special tree. It was the witness of many generations and believed to show the way to heaven.

Anton gathered with the men in the center of the village by the old Linden tree, just as the sun was setting. The tree was fragrant with its yellow flowers in full bloom.

"What are you doing here?" A familiar voice asked.

"Oh, it's you Jako. I forgot you lived in this village." Anton said.

Anton had known Jako in his grammar school days. During recess, Jako was always hanging around Agnes, but she ignored him, preferring the company of Anton. Jako would taunt and tease until Anton lost his temper and raised his fists. Jako would always run away, for he was small, and no match for the taller Anton.

"I came to see Agnes." Anton said.

"Stay in your own village," Jako snapped.

"There's no law that says I can't come here," Anton said.

The young men glared at each other. Anton moved away from Jako to avoid trouble. When the singing started, it attracted the unmarried women who stopped what they were doing to mix and flirt with the men. Anton scanned the maidens as they walked toward the chorus, finally seeing Agnes among them. Pleasure showed on her face when she spied him among the suitors.

"Hello Anton. I'm surprised to see you here," Agnes said.

Anton took her hand, squeezing it gently as they sang the last verse of the song together. "You are in my heart until we meet again."

The summer breezes carried the voices throughout the village, bringing back sweet memories of past summer nights to the older folks.

"I came here to see you. You look lovely." Anton said.

Agnes blushed, "Your words are sweet."

2

Thereafter, Anton came often to serenade Agnes and their affection for each other grew over several summers. They took walks away from the village after singing, to avoid Jako. The romance was interrupted when Anton was called to fulfill his obligation of serving two years in the Austrian army.

Anton was on leave from the army for a few days and talking with Agnes when she said, "I've thought of becoming a nun, but I'm not sure,"

This was his opportunity to say what he had been thinking for the last month. "We've known each other since we were children and I love you. Your place is with me, not in a convent. Will you marry me?"

"Yes, I was hoping you'd ask." Agnes raised her lips to his and they kissed. Anton wanted another but she pulled away, "We can kiss all we want after we say our vows. Come sit with me at Mass; I go every day."

"I'll join you this Sunday and every Sunday after we are married," Anton said.

Every morning Agnes sat in the same pew holding her rosary, concentrating on the charred crucifix, the only relic saved from the fire that destroyed the old wooden church a century before. The crucifix was at the center of the altar, flanked by marble statues of saints and the walls were painted with the Station of the Cross.

Anton looked forward to his final Sunday before returning to his army post. He sat next to Agnes and watched her lovely head bent in prayer; her golden hair shimmering in the sunlight streaming from the window above. She was his angel. The Priest started to say the Lord's Prayer and Anton joined in, comforted in knowing Agnes was repeating it with him.

At the beginning of Anton's conscription, he thought of making the military his career, but the glamour of being a soldier faded. The discipline and structured living was monotonous. However, he did like drinking, joking and singing with his fellow soldiers on Saturday nights.

With only one week remaining in the army and in the midst of training his replacement, he spied a familiar face walking past his window. It was Jako from Agnes' village of Leskovo. Opening the door, he yelled, "Jako! Jako! it's me, Anton."

"Hello," said Jako.

Anton stepped onto the path in front of Jako and said, "So, you're in the army now. Have you seen Agnes lately?"

"Ja. She was fine the last time I saw her with Martin," Jako said.

"Who is Martin?" Anton asked.

"He's visiting his sister who lives next door to Agnes. Martin is very cozy with Agnes. I saw them hugging and holding hands," Jako said.

Anton's face reddened and his hands clinched into fists, but he refrained from punching Jako's mouth for fear of military punishment. Without saying another word, he turned and walked into his office, slamming the door behind him. "Get out," he shouted to the intern. The young man jumped up from his chair and hurried out of the office. Anton watched the intern leave and opened a cabinet where he kept a supply of slivovitz. He slumped into his desk chair, opened a bottle, took a swig and proclaimed to the ceiling, "That Jako is an asshole."

He opened the bottom drawer of his desk and took out a revolver hidden beneath several army manuals. The metal gun felt cool and comfortable in his hand and he pointed it at the door. He pulled the trigger of the unloaded gun, returned it to the drawer and took another shot of liquor. The clear liquid stung his mouth until he swallowed it. When it reached his stomach, his anger subsided. The letters inked on his left arm hurt when he pressed them. The tattoo was only a day old and still sore. Last night he was a happy man drinking with his friends, celebrating the end of his army days and his future with Agnes.

The world seemed so rosy last night that Anton wanted to carry his beloved's name on his arm forever. He liked his friends' tattoos, so why not have one too. The tattoo shop did most of its business at night when the soldiers had too much to drink. Anton had staggered into the shop and had the name Agnes printed inside a red heart on his upper arm to show the proof of his devotion.

The euphoria of getting married died. After downing another jigger, his mind went to a painful place experienced in childhood. He should have known. It was foolish to think a woman could be faithful to one man. Agnes did not deserve his love or her name printed on his body, for she was a slut, as were all women!

The last week of army duty was a blur and dark thoughts of revenge whirled around in his head. He was in a foul mood as he packed his things and said terse goodbyes to his friends on his last day of army life. Anton's gloom abated as he noticed the colorful spring flowers lining the familiar path to his home of many generations. Neighbors, known since childhood, slapped him on the back, shook his hand and welcomed him back.

The aroma of food wafted in the air as Anton approached his home. He looked up at "Stevilka Devet," (number nine) etched in the headstone of the front door. The four-hundred year-old house had two rooms built of large square stones, had a thatched roof and an attached barn where pigs and cows were kept. In the backyard were a dozen plum trees, the fruit used in making slivovitz. In late summer the ripe plums were picked, pitted, crushed, and fermented in barrels. Every house had a supply of this liquor offered to all visitors.

Anton's mother was stirring a pot of soup when he came into the kitchen and she cried with joy as she threw her arms around him and kissed his face many times, saying, "It's so good to have you home again." His mother had a bright smile and beautiful face that was becoming etched with lines as she aged. He hugged her for a few seconds, backing away as memories of the past flooded his mind.

Young Boris appeared in the kitchen doorway and greeted his half brother with a hug, saying, "I-I-I a-a-am glad y-you're home." Boris had a speech problem, needing patience in listening to him. If hurried, Boris stuttered even more, became embarrassed and refused to say anything at all. P-pa, P-pa isn't home he went fishing.

"Too bad!" Anton said, his sarcastic tone lost on Boris. He never liked his stepfather and blamed him for Boris's stuttering and for everything and anything.

"Come and eat," his mother announced.

The dining table looked festive covered with a lace tablecloth and a vase of fresh flowers in the center. Anton's mother placed a large pot of Imocht (chicken stew) and freshly baked Kruh (bread) next to Anton, who took the first portion. For this special occasion, his mother made flancate (deep-fried cookies) dusted with sugar, a family favorite.

During dinner, his mother happily chatted about relatives and friends, anxious to tell her son the latest news. "You know, uncle remarried when your aunt was barely cold in her grave."

"He took care of her for many years and deserves some happiness," Anton said.

His mother changed the subject, "Your cousin went to America, got a good job and sends money home."

Anton became alert when he heard this news.

After dinner his mother said, "I'm tired, son, and need to rest. You and Boris have much to talk about." His mother kissed him on the cheek and went into the bedroom.

Boris asked. "W-what is it like to be in the ar-ar-army."

Anton exaggerated about the rigorous training and his army duties, trying to make Boris think what he did was interesting and important. When Boris went to bed, Anton hunted through the cabinets and found a bottle of slivovitz to steady his nerves. As always, drinking calmed him down. He drank until early morning and thought about his future until he fell asleep on the divan.

Awakening after a few hours, he looked at the tattoo on his arm and stared at the letters that branded him for life. He took a penknife out of his pocket and tried to scrape the ink off. Wiping the blood away revealed the ink still embedded in his skin, infuriating him. He slashed at the tattoo, carving cross strokes across the letters. He wrapped a towel around his arm, satisfied that he had removed the name Agnes from his body.

In the morning, Anton put on a long-sleeved shirt to hide his wounded arm and walked to Skofia Loka to look for work. He had no special skills, and jobs were scarce. Europe was in the throes of an economic slump, and thousands of men were unemployed. He spotted some friends, known since childhood; standing in front of Janez's Tavern and approached them."

"Anton! Welcome back!" his friends chorused.

"It's too bad we're not happier to see you. You're competition."

"Ja, I've heard things are tough," responded Anton.

The friends had many opinions.

"Let's all go to America, where there are jobs for everyone."

"We have to be sponsored by a relative already living there."

"We all have relatives in America."

"Anyone, even a peasant, can become rich there."

Crossing the ocean to seek his fortune was tempting and Anton felt he had found the solution to his problems. He would start a new life and forget about the cheating Agnes and his awful stepfather. Making a quick decision, he booked passage on a ship bound for the United States.

Anton returned home late in the day and told his mother about his plans to leave. She didn't try to dissuade him. She said, "You're a grown man and ready to be on your own. I also have something important to tell you. Agnes came to see you. She was upset. I did not know how to answer her questions. She wanted to know why you hadn't written her for two weeks and was surprised you were home. You must talk to her."

"No, I will not," Anton said

His mother threw up her hands. "You're making a terrible mistake. Agnes is a wonderful, sincere girl. I don't understand you."

Anton stared at her. He always had trouble talking to his mother. "I have to get ready for my trip," he said.

Early the next morning, before anyone was awake, Anton walked to the train station. He watched people gather as he ate the boiled egg and piece of bread he brought from home. He saw Agnes approaching and realized his mother probably told her about his leaving. He hid behind an abandoned boxcar until his train arrived and boarded just as it started its engine. He watched Agnes through the window as the train departed and saw the tears falling from her face. She lifted her arms with her palms opened toward him, silently asking why.

Anton watched her disappear as the train chugged away. He brooded throughout the ride to the Rijeka pier, where he boarded his ship. He was unfriendly and kept to himself on deck, watching the ocean. Occasionally storms occurred and he felt in tune with the turbulence, the crashing waves and the driving rain. On calm days, he sat in one of the deck chairs listening to people speak many different languages.

By the second week of the voyage, Anton's anger subsided and he decided to talk to someone. For several days, he noticed a man sitting alone on deck that he heard speak Slovenian in the dining room. He introduced himself.

"Dober Dan, [Good Day]. I'm Anton Poncek."

"I'm Frank Koznar. Kako si ti? [How are you]?"

They began a friendship and talked about their plans for the future.

"I'm thinking of looking for a job in either New York or Cleveland," Anton said.

"New York is too crowded and dangerous for a new immigrant. Cleveland is the best place for you to work. Many manufacturing companies are located there and need people like us. Did you know Rockefeller got his start in Cleveland?" Frank said.

"Who is that?" Anton asked.

"I'm surprised you never heard of the oil tycoon, John D. Rockefeller. He's the richest man in the world and very famous." Frank said.

"So what!" Anton retorted.

Frank changed the subject. "There's a section of Cleveland populated by Slovenes. It's a good place for you to get adjusted to America."

"Is that where you're going?" asked Anton

"No, my brother says I can get a job cutting trees in Virginia," Frank answered.

The new friends stood together as they entered New York harbor, cheering loudly with their fellow passengers as they passed the Statue of Liberty. Young, healthy, and with their papers in order, they easily passed all the Ellis Island tests and entered the city of New York through Battery Park. Frank gave his brother's address to Anton, hoping to keep in touch. After saying goodbye, Anton dragged his steamer trunk to the nearest train station and bought a ticket to Cleveland.

Anton reached the Slavic community and rented a room from a Slovene family. He applied for a job at the Cuyahoga Gas Company located a few blocks from the house. The company needed strong men to stoke the ovens, and Anton was hired. He learned that producing artificial gas was a continuous, unceasing process. After the gas was purified, it was mixed with iron ore and wood shavings. The mixture was stored in huge round tanks that floated in water. As the gas was piped to customers, the tanks gradually sank into the water and then rose again when filled.

The Slovene men gathered in the late afternoon to discuss news, politics, and jobs at Novak's Tavern located in the center of the community. The only females allowed in the bar were barmaids and cooks. Anton was always thirsty after stoking coke all day, so each afternoon he stopped at his favorite tavern before going home. It was his custom to order a jigger of bourbon and a glass of draft beer. Anton sat for hours at the worn oak bar discussing work and the latest news with his new friends. They quaffed enough liquor to numb their bodies and minds. The more they drank, the more they argued.

Milan, who usually sat at the bar next to Anton, liked to impress everyone with his knowledge of world events. "Did you know Germany, Italy, and Austria-Hungary formed an alliance?" Milan said.

"Ja. Did you know France, Russia, and Great Britain formed an alliance too? Anton fired back with a question. Each man was sparring with words.

"You know why the alliances were formed, don't you?" Milan said.

"Ja, I do. They're protecting mutual economic interests. Did you know Serbia and the Hapsburgs debate over control of Bosnia and Herzegovina," Anton said.

"I knew that! I just wanted to know if you knew," Milan said

The bantering continued for hours until words became slurred and gestures became exaggerated from too much liquor. The night ended when Anton and Milan's speech became so garbled, they no longer understood each other.

The next evening they argued whether President Theodore Roosevelt was doing enough for the working class. Anton gave Teddy Roosevelt's opinion on immigrants. "The President said immigrants should be treated equally with everyone else. He doesn't believe anyone should be discriminated against because of religion, birthplace or origin. Roosevelt said there can be no divided allegiance and that we should be loyal to the American flag, the American people, and speak English."

"The President doesn't want us to speak our native language?" Milan asked.

"He means we should learn English, so all Americans have a common language to communicate with each other. We must first understand each other before we can settle disagreements and become friends," Anton answered.

"What about this loyalty business?" Milan asked.

Anton was quiet for a while, thinking about the difficult question. "I love the beauty of Slovenia, but this is where I choose to live, a country of opportunity and beauty also. My loyalty is to America while I am living here," Anton said.

"I want to return to Slovenia when I've saved some money," Milan said.

"You won't go back; I'll make you a bet," Anton said.

"I want to see my village, the groves of Linden trees, the beauty of Lake Bled, and the majesty of the Alps again. When I have my return passage to Slovenia, I'll meet you in this bar and buy you a whiskey," Milan said.

"That day will never come," Anton said.

"Ja. It will," Milan said.

LOUIZA

Louiza stared out the cabin window at the Julian Alps, and remembered her mother loved the first snows of winter. The village, valleys, trees, and mountain slopes were covered with an endless blanket of white. The soaring mountains surrounding Louiza's ancient village in Southern Austria offered solace to some, but not to her. She felt imprisoned

It was the beginning of a new century, but Louiza felt stuck in the old one. Her dark brown eyes scanned the encircling peaks closing in on her. They would trap her if she didn't escape soon and she would never experience anything beyond them.

Visitors awed by the beauty of the snow-capped mountains enjoyed skiing and gazing at Mount Triglav, the most majestic peak of the Julian Alps. The skiers left when the weather warmed and the snow started to melt. Louiza wanted to go with them, to flee to freedom, to a life of privilege. She scratched the skin on her neck, pulling the collar away, wishing she could wear silk instead of wool. The cold landscape disappeared as she imagined being dressed in an elaborate silk gown, dancing in Vienna's royal ballroom, surrounded by admirers and servants. She started humming.

"You seem happy today." The voice of Andrew stopped Louiza's reverie, and she turned away from the window, giving her brother full attention.

"I was dancing at the palace," she explained.

"That's dumb," Andrew said in a muffled voice that had recently changed to a deeper pitch. He was munching on a piece of cheese.

"Andrew, I've told you a thousand times, don't talk with your mouth full."

Andrew snarled, "Aw, leave me alone. You're not Mati [Mother]."

Louiza fumed, "You make my life miserable. I can't cook enough to satisfy your hunger. I do everything around here and have no time for homework. Why don't you help me? All you think about is yourself."

"You're unfair. I take care of the animals." Andrew paused, then added, "You won't have to worry about feeding me in a few months."

"You're heartless. Maria is gone, and now you." Louiza said.

"When you're old enough, you'll leave too," Andrew said.

"You don't care what happens to me," Louiza said.

"C'mon, you know I care, but I have to focus on my future. Now who is being selfish?"

Louiza watched her brother carve a grape in the handle of a spoon made from Linden tree wood. She said, "You might get a krona for that one."

She studied Andrew's face as he created a cluster of grapes with his knife. He was two years older than she and it was the week of his sixteenth birthday. He had the blue eyes of their father and Mati's nose and mouth. Hair was sprouting along his jawline and his face had a few blemishes. He grew taller by the day and ate constantly, trying to keep his stomach full in his slender body. Affection for him overwhelmed her. Being close in age, they had played, teased and laughed together until Mati (mother) died. Now they quarreled often.

Louiza's lesson assignment was due tomorrow and her eighth grade teacher was a stern taskmaster. The nun disciplined errant students by making them balance books on their heads for hours, so it seemed. She obeyed all of the nun's rules, so she never had her hands slapped with a wooden ruler like some of her classmates. She needed to do her homework, but she also had to get dinner started. Gathering up the potatoes, she placed them in front of Andrew after pushing the half-carved spoon out of his hand.

"Here, carve potatoes instead."

"Aw, you're no fun." Andrew paused, then said, "I want to invite Mimi to my Birthday party. She's my second favorite person."

"Father will be upset, maybe Uncle too," Louiza said.

"Who cares what Uncle thinks? He's lucky to live with us. No one else would take care of him. Besides, it's my party and I can invite who I want," Andrew said.

"Go ahead and invite her, but you'll have to tell Father. I'm curious, who is your first favorite person?" Louiza asked.

Andrew threw potato peelings at her and said, "You'll have to guess."

Louiza ran her hands through his curly hair. "Since I'm your favorite, you won't mind cutting up the potatoes and boiling them for me. Here's the pan." Andrew sliced potatoes while Louiza did her homework at a small desk in the family room.

That evening during dinner, dark clouds gathered and the wind started to howl. "Looks like we're in for a big one," Father said.

"We're going to get more snow," Louiza said.

"The skiers love it," Andrew said.

"I hear a knock at the door. Who would come here at dinnertime?" Father asked.

It was their neighbor, Mimi. "Storms terrify me. My dear husband died in a storm like this. Can I stay here until the weather calms?"

"Of course! I'll get you a glass of wine, or would you like tea?" Louiza asked.

"Wine will calm my nerves." Mimi said.

As Louiza handed her the wine, she said, "I can't chat with you. I have to finish my homework. Father will keep you company."

During Mimi's oft-told story of her husband's accident, Father fell asleep. Uncle kept warm by the stove while Andrew was carving a fork to match the spoon he had finished. He looked up every so often, saying "uh, huh" to Mimi's many tales of woe. When the storm abated and she was about to leave, Andrew asked, "Won't you please come to my birthday party on Sunday?" Mimi's eyes moistened as she gladly accepted the invitation.

The swirling wind had stopped and light snow was falling when Louiza finally completed a brief history of the United States' Revolutionary War. She enjoyed studying about the young, vital nation and was determined to visit it some day. Her older sister Maria was already in America and Andrew would soon join her.

Louiza turned in her paper the next day and was happy not to have homework over the weekend. She could now concentrate on Andrew's party and finish knitting his gift. Wanting to keep it a surprise, she only worked on it when he was out of the house. The anticipation of Andrew's birthday celebration helped to brighten the gloomy atmosphere. Father's mood had been sour since Mati's death, but recently improved enough to curb his constant nagging and complaining. However, Uncle had become a pest, groping her whenever they were alone. In the past, the presence of Mati prevented his advances, but that protection was gone.

Louiza was responsible for the kitchen once her mother became ill. Cooking became easier as time passed, and now she wanted to bake something special for Andrew's birthday. She chose potica, a confection usually made only at Christmas and Easter.

Sunday was bright and sunny, a fine day to go to church. Louiza asked her father, "Won't you go to Mass with me on this important day?"

"No! And don't ask me again," Father said.

"How about you, Andrew? Mati would want you to go." Louiza said.

"Ja, I'll go," Andrew said.

Louiza did not ask Uncle.

Father was sitting in the kitchen, drinking coffee laced with schnapps, when Louiza and Andrew came home from Mass. He questioned them the minute they walked in the door. "You've been gone too long. What were you doing?"

"We talked to friends for a few minutes after Mass. You're so suspicious. I wouldn't do anything that you didn't approve." Louiza answered. Andrew avoided the unpleasantness by going outside.

Father watched Louiza preparing the potica and gave her directions. "You're over-mixing the dough. Make sure all the shells are off the walnuts. I chipped a tooth biting into one of those damn shells."

"Why don't you shell the nuts for me?" Louiza asked gently, fearful of angering him. Once he hit her across the face when she sassed him. The memory of that stinging slap always made her speak to him in a respectful manner.

"That's women's work," Father said as he limped out of the kitchen.

Glad to have Father out of the way, she continued making the confection by coiling the minced walnut-pasted dough into layers and cutting the long roll into shorter pieces. The potica was time-consuming, taking all morning to prepare. She began boiling the beef and chopping carrots for soup.

"Gosh, that smells good!" Andrew said as he walked into the kitchen.

"Andrew, I need you to take these pans to the ovens and bake them for an hour."

"You made potica? You're super. Ja, I'll do that, but I have to eat something first." He took a hunk of bread and slathered it with butter and went on his way. In the late afternoon, Andrew came back.

"You've been gone for hours. The ovens couldn't have been busy today. I bet you were talking to a girl." Louiza chided.

All Andrew said was "uh huh" as he laid the warm pans on the table and grabbed another hunk of bread.

The kitchen clock chimed four o'clock just as Mimi walked in the house without knocking. "Where is my darling Andrew? There you are, you handsome man." Mimi handed Andrew a bag of candy bought in Zavoj, the town at the bottom of the mountain.

"Thank you. You look nice," Andrew said to Mimi as she sashayed around the family room. She was dressed in her Sunday clothes; a bustled ankle length skirt with a high-collared blouse. Father, who was sitting at the table waiting for the celebration to begin, did not say a word to her. He scowled when Mimi sat next to him and then moved his chair a few inches away from her. Disappointment in Father's reactions showed in Mimi's face.

"Aren't you proud of your son? It's freezing outside. My, you're looking rested. " Mimi fired one sentence after another trying to make conversation. Father ignored her and opened a bottle of wine, pouring it into each glass on the table. Mimi never gained his friendship, though they had been neighbors for many, many years.

Uncle came into the kitchen, stamping his feet and clearing his throat. He was deaf and made odd sounds. Louiza acknowledged him by turning her head slightly, while putting noodles in the soup, paying scant attention to him. She stiffened when she felt his body press in on her, infuriating her. "How dare you!" she said. As she swung her arm to hit him, she knocked a metal platter of bread onto the floor, making a loud clatter. It didn't stop her from smacking him hard across his face.

"Ow," Uncle yelped as he retreated a few steps.

"If you do that again, I'll kick you where it really hurts, you creep," Louiza hissed. Uncle read her lips and backed into a corner.

Father heard the commotion and came into the kitchen asking, "What happened?" Uncle shrugged his shoulders to indicate he didn't know.

Louiza did not want the incident to ruin the party. "I dropped the platter. Uncle and I bumped each other trying to pick it up."

Father eyed Uncle with a doubtful look and then pushed him into the family room saying,

"Come on, say hello to Mimi."

Uncle sat down at the table with his hand across his cheek, hiding the telltale red mark Louiza had caused, and smiled at Mimi. Acting as if nothing had happened, Louiza placed bowls of food in the center of the table and sat down next to Andrew.

When Father finished saying grace louder than usual, he raised his glass of wine, signaling the others to do the same. "Here's to my son who is now a man. We'll miss him when he goes to America."

Louiza saw the elation on Andrew's face at being permitted to drink wine for the first time in front of his family. It was not his first sip. A few weeks ago, after dumping dirty water by the back step, she saw him drink wine from a bottle he had hidden in the barn. He tried to disguise his breath by rinsing with water and squirting milk from the cow's teat in his mouth. His secret had no importance now. Andrew grinned as he lifted the glass to his lips. This was the moment of his recognition as an adult.

All eyes focused on him as they raised their glasses, saying "Nazdravja."

Tears welled in Andrew's eyes as he said "To Mati" before he sipped his wine.

Louiza felt his pain, hoping the grief of losing their mother would soon ease with time.

As they filled their plates, Louiza silently wished Mati could have been with them to share in this important event. She remembered that, only a few years ago, all of the family had been together, their lively voices reverberating through the room. After appetites were satisfied, everyone was mute except for Mimi.

"Did you hear about the Priest's older brother marrying a fifteen year-old girl? He's too old to have a young wife, but he has money and owns a horse," Mimi said.

"She'll live well and won't see his face in bed." Father replied as he rolled his eyes and fidgeted in his chair.

Louiza hoped he wouldn't say anything mean to Mimi. The party needed cheerfulness, so Louiza grabbed Andrew's wrapped gift hidden in the kitchen cupboard and put it in front of him. "You have to guess what's in there before you open it."

Andrew shook the package and felt it with his fingers. "It's a pair of gloves, maybe a pair of socks." Impatient to open the gift, Andrew tore the paper open and lifted up the colorful cap for all to see. "This will keep my head warm!"

"I'm glad you like it," Louiza said

"Thank you, sister." Andrew kissed her cheek, put the cap on his head and started to dance, slapping his thigh to make rhythm for his feet.

Father picked up his accordion sitting in the corner of the room lying untouched for many months. Taking it out of its worn leather case, he set it on his lap, placed his hands on the keys and buttons and played a waltz in a slow beat. The next tune was a polka and feet began to tap to the fast beat.

"Come on," Louiza said as she clasped Andrew's hand and they began to twirl around the room. They circled the floor faster and faster. "Whoop, whoop," they shouted.

After a few minutes, they sat down and laughed. How good it was to laugh. Father played another waltz, and Mimi invited Uncle to dance with her. Though Uncle didn't hear the music, he felt the vibrations and danced in rhythm with his neighbor. He took advantage of the situation and moved his hand from Mimi's waist to her buttocks. Mimi did not protest, and Uncle did not move his hand back to her waist until he noticed Louiza watching him.

Andrew took a turn at playing the accordion so Father could dance with Louiza.

They moved slowly, not letting Father's dragging foot interfere with their fun. Uncle indicated that he wanted Louiza to dance with him. She took his hand, Mimi's hand, and Father's hand, making a circle, so everyone danced together. As the merriment continued, they all danced as if their grief for Mati would pound away through their feet.

Close to midnight, Father said, "enough" and put the accordion in its leather case. After drinking and eating too much and dancing until their legs ached, the weary group retired to bed and Mimi went home.

Early the next day, Louiza was making cornmeal mush for breakfast when Andrew came into the kitchen and said, "Funny. This morning I'm sixteen, no longer a boy, but nothing has changed."

"Listen, silly, becoming a man doesn't happen overnight. You didn't flirt with girls a couple years ago. I've seen you with Anchka."

"You've been spying on me. I think Anchka is the prettiest girl in the village. But I heard girls in America are beautiful too and free with their affection."

"That's hogwash! Now put on this scarf, it's cold outside," Louiza said.

"You're so bossy." With that remark, Andrew spooned the last of the mush into his mouth and went outside without putting on the scarf.

It was clear to Louiza that Andrew was establishing his independence and preparing for his break from the family. He complained, "There is nothing to do in this village but raise chickens, pigs and cows. I don't want to spend my life doing that and selling wooden spoons. Maria says there are all types of jobs available in America besides farming."

"Just think, you're going to have a job you like, store-made clothes and lots of money," Louiza said.

Father had a different opinion. "Don't go yet. Finish school. You're smart enough to become a priest or a doctor."

"I've got to leave this freezing place. There's a whole world out there and I want to see it. You just want me to stay to do the work," Andrew said.

"That's not true. No use telling you anything; you're gonna do what you want. You're gonna need money. Maybe that rich guy Hans will give you a job." Father said.

Sorrow

The year before Andrew's sixteenth birthday was the most difficult period of Louiza's young life. It was the year her mother died. Mati came down with a cold in February that would not go away. She tried to get rid of the congestion by placing a towel over her head and inhaling steam from boiling water. Her coughing became constant and she wheezed.

Father was worried. "Louiza go to Zavoj and get the doctor."

It was early spring and the snow was melting, forming rivulets of water, making the journey down the mountain slippery. Louiza slid down the slushy hill and was embarrassed by the mud covering her shoes when she entered the medical office. She ignored the three people sitting in the waiting room and rushed up to the white clad receptionist seated at a desk. "My mother is very sick. She needs the doctor. Please tell him."

"Yes, I will. I can tell you were in a hurry to get here. Here, child, wipe off the mud with this cloth." Louiza proceeded to clean her shoes when the receptionist went through the door behind her desk.

The doctor she had known since she was a baby, came out of the room and said, "Hello Louiza, you'll have to wait while I see the rest of my patients. It won't be long."

Louiza had no choice but to wait an hour that seemed like two. One by one, the patients entered the room behind the receptionist's desk. When the waiting room was empty, the receptionist said, "Go outside, the doctor is waiting for you in his buggy." Louiza was anxious and asked the doctor to make his mules go faster up the mountain.

"I have old mules and they are going as fast as they can," the doctor said.

Frank was standing on his steps awaiting their arrival when they pulled up to the house. "I'm so thankful you were able to come," he said. He ushered the doctor into the house and up the stairway into the bedroom where Mati lay looking pale and sweaty.

After listening to Mati's chest and feeling the heat of her face, the doctor said to her, "You have pneumonia and must stay in bed to rest. Take a swig of this medicine every four hours to fight the infection. You must keep wet towels on your forehead to reduce the fever and drink plenty of water."

The doctor only stayed for a few minutes, explaining that he had many other calls to make. Father was grateful for the medical advice and was generous by paying the doctor's fee with a chicken.

Mati did not like lying in bed due to the pressure on her lungs. "I can't breathe. Let me sit in the chair." The same chair Father sat in when he was a sick child. Mati gurgled and rasped while talking, even though sitting upright. The family had Mati drink plenty of water and kept cool towels on her forehead. She always had her favorite afghan wrapped around her.

One afternoon Louiza was alone with Mati and wanted her attention. She tapped her on the shoulder to awaken her. "Mati, it's me." Her mother opened her eyes in her thinning face, for she was losing weight. "I'm starting my monthly." At age thirteen, Louiza's body was maturing, and she wanted to discuss her concerns, aware of what was happening, but needing her mother's assurance.

In a whispery voice Mati advised, "Talk to Mimi. I'm too tired." She closed her eyes again. Mimi was Mati's best friend.

"How is your mother?" Mimi asked after she invited Louiza into her house.

"Not good."

"I pray for your mother every day." Mimi said.

"Mati told me to come here. She said you would help me."

"What kind of help?" Mimi asked

"I'm beginning to bleed down there." Louiza pointed toward her hips.

Mimi giggled and said, "That's natural honey. You've become a woman and that will happen every month. I have some extra rags if you need them. I have a book about the female body. My, my, where is that book. Oh yes, here it is." Mimi picked a book from dozens of others stacked neatly on a bookshelf. "My husband loved to read. I miss him so. He never had a chance in that storm."

Mimi's husband had gone down the mountain to buy needed supplies in Zavoj, the closest town five thousand feet below Gora. He was coming home, driving up the mountain with a wagon full of goods, when a sudden snowstorm overcame him. Trapped in a blizzard, he froze to death. Mimi's eyes misted for a few seconds. She refocused on her young visitor. "This is a tough time for you. Come here whenever you want."

"Do you like Uncle?" Louiza blurted out.

For the first time in years, Mimi was at a loss for words. Avoiding the question, she reached into the cupboard beside the hearth and took out a lidded tin. "Take these cookies home. I baked them today. Tell Mati I'll come see her tomorrow." She put her arms around Louiza and gave her a big hug.

"Thank you. You are kind." Louiza said and ate one of the cookies on the way home.

Mati's health worsened and the family felt helpless while watching her downward spiral. She had no appetite and breathing became more labored each day. Father held her hand, gave her sips of water, changed the wet towel on her forehead, and slept in the bed next to her chair. Mati acknowledged his loving care when she pressed his hand and attempted a smile.

It was difficult for Andrew to cope with his mother's condition. He kept his distance, avoiding her room and crying in the barn where no one would see him. His mother once was a warm, nurturing, and cheerful person, but now barely able to speak or move.

The family prayed with the the old Priest for a cure, but to no avail. Mati was too weak to sit in the chair any more and did not object when Father lifted her onto the bed. She was as light as a feather. Louiza placed blankets and pillows behind her mother's back so she could breathe. Mati motioned her daughter to come closer. With a great deal of effort, she said, "I'll visit you in a dream."

A few hours later, Mati stared up at the ceiling as if she were looking at something and in a barely audible voice said, "They are waiting for me."

The family surrounded Mati's bed as they watched her breath become shallow, then cease. Louisa imagined her mother surrounded in white light greeted joyously by relatives and friends who had passed on before her. It was the end of summer and the end of Louiza's childhood.

The blue jacket and skirt, worn only on Sundays, was the one Mati wore in her pine casket. Her black beaded rosary was clasped in her hands, as instructed. She looked so pale lying in her coffin sitting in the middle of the family room. During the following two days, the villagers came to see Mati, bringing food and offering condolences to the family.

At the wake the night before the funeral, the mourners filed past the open pine casket, making signs of the cross and kissing Mati's forehead in a gesture of love. The large amounts of wine and slivovitz consumed during the evening caused increased moaning and weeping as people lost control of their emotions.

Andrew sat near his mother with his head down and did not converse with anyone. Father greeted the guests at the door, leaning on some of them to keep his balance, for he had overindulged in wine. Noticing his slurred words, Louiza said, "Father, sit down for a while and rest. I'll greet our friends." Louiza thanked the people she had known all her life, for coming to see her mother and bringing food.

The visitors came to attention as Hans, the wealthiest man in town, entered the room. He took off his cap, and shook Father's hand saying. "I'm sorry for your loss," then said to Louiza, "I'm sorry you have lost your mother. Here is a gift in her memory." Everyone stared as he handed Louiza an envelope.

"Thank you." Louiza said. She was in awe of him and didn't know what to say, so she asked, "I love horses and heard you own several. How many do you have?"

"I have four horses Would you like to see them?"

"Ja, I would." Louiza said.

Hans approached the casket and kissed Mati's cold forehead. He patted Andrew on the back and said, "I was fond of your mother."

Andrew looked up and nodded, unable to say anything.

As Hans was about to leave, Mimi said, "Hello Hans," while fluttering her eyelashes.

"Hello Mimi. This is a sad occasion. I cannot stay for I have to ready the tavern for tomorrow. I only had a few minutes to pay my last respects to the kind lady," Hans said.

"Mati was my best friend. I'm going to miss her." Mimi said.

"It's difficult to lose a friend." Hans said.

The tears ran down Mimi's face again. She could not stop crying, constantly wiping her face with her best handkerchief only used on special occasions. A few men held back tears, but many wept openly. Showing sorrow was customary.

Anchka came into the house and every man took notice. She was fifteen and easily the comeliest of all the young women. When Andrew saw Anchka, he stopped his vigilance of Mati's body and said. "I'm so glad to see you." He lowered his head onto Anchka's shoulder and she put her arms around him. They stood that way for a long time.

The death announcement was sent to Maria, Louiza's older sister who lived in America. The card outlined in black included Mati's formal name, Theresa Lenko; date of birth, October 15, 1865; date of death, August 20, 1904 and the Bible's twenty-third Psalm.

On the morning of the funeral, the family awoke early after a restless night. They dressed in black clothing and skipped breakfast, for they were all taking communion. Andrew and several neighbors carried the coffin the short distance to the church in the center of town. The congregation viewed the body in the entranceway to the sanctuary. After the coffin lid was closed, the pine box was placed in front of the centuries old altar. During Mass, Louiza took communion, knelt and prayed for her mother's soul. At the end of the rituals, the old Priest dusted the coffin with incense and Louiza became nauseated.

After the church service, the mourners followed the priest and Mati's coffin to the gravesite, which was muddy from a light morning rain. The old Priest finished praying over Mati for the last time and the flowers were taken from the casket wreath as a remembrance. Sick to her stomach and lightheaded, Louiza held onto Andrew when Mati's coffin was lowered into the earthen grave. Father crossed himself, grabbed a fistful of soft earth and threw it on top of the coffin. Louiza, Andrew, Uncle and Mimi did the same, murmuring last farewells.

The mourners were tired from drinking at the wake the night before and limited their time at the home reception. Mimi was the last to leave.

The throb in Louiza's head had increased, so she flopped down in the old chair and curled up in Mati's afghan.

The day after the funeral, the family struggled to return to some type of normalcy. Everyone awoke early to the crowing roosters. Andrew was the first one to tromp through the mud to use the outhouse. Louiza prepared a large breakfast, but no one had much of an appetite. They tried to function normally, but the day dragged and the tears came.

Wondering why a loving God would not let Mati live, Louisa confided her perplexity to the old Priest, whom she had known since birth. He said, "Trust in the Lord, knowing your mother is without pain, crowned with gold in heaven surrounded by Angels."

"I imagine my mother with a sparkling tiara on her head, sitting on a cloud singing with the angels." Louiza said to the Priest. About a month later when the air had chilled, Mati visited Louiza in a dream, as she had promised. Her smiling face was mute, glowing and shimmering. The dream convinced Louiza that Mati was indeed in heaven.

Louiza's faith in an afterlife deepened, but it did not change the fact that she missed her earthly mother. Washing dishes with Mati after supper had been a special time when they shared events of the day, laughed and sang old village tunes. Usually Andrew added his nice baritone, producing three-part harmony and Father joined in with his button box accordion.

Now that Mati had gone to heaven, Louiza had endless work caring for her brother Andrew, her handicapped father and her deaf uncle. Making breakfast for everyone, going to school, then coming home and fixing dinner, cleaning and doing homework, was all so tiring. The men did very little, except for Andrew. He took care of the animals, and supplied the house with water, the somber house where no one sang anymore.

It was late summer, and the vegetables were ready for harvesting and she needed Uncle's help. "Uncle, could you help me pick the garden?" She used her hands to help convey her message. Able to read her lips and understand her gestures, he consented. While digging up the beets, he came close to her, sniffing her like a dog and put his hand on her buttock.

"You old goat," she said twisting around, kicking him in the groin and pushing him to his knees. He sat doubled up on the ground for a minute. He got up, avoided her eyes, brushed the dirt from his pants and returned to harvesting the garden.

The sun was setting and Louiza was still angry when Uncle tapped her on the shoulder while she was bending over, pulling up onions. She stood up with her fists clenched, ready to defend herself. Uncle backed away to let her know he meant no harm. To her surprise, he offered her a flower. As the days cooled, Uncle and Andrew gathered wood and dug up the garden while Louiza washed the bedding before the warmth of summer disappeared.

Uncle was not the only problem for Louiza, Father's disposition had changed since Mati's death. His wife knew how to soothe him by rubbing his arm, kissing him and making him laugh. Without her to calm him, he yelled at Louiza and Andrew often, shouting and ordering them around.

"Father has become difficult. I don't know what to do." Louiza confided in Andrew.

"He's depressed and he's crippled," Andrew said.

"Don't make excuses for Father. I don't feel sorry for him. He's mean and I don't feel sorry for Uncle either. He makes my skin crawl."

"I don't think he'll pester you any more. I've noticed he's been going to Mimi's house often and seems happier. If anyone can tame him, she can," Andrew said.

"You look like you're in a hurry to go someplace," Louiza said.

"Ja, Anchka works at Han's tavern and says the janitor is sick and cannot work. If I get there today, maybe I'll get his job. That's why I have to go there now," Andrew said.

Andrew ran as fast as he could and was out of breath when he reached the tavern. Hans Bern was busy with a customer and Andrew waited for him in the kitchen. Hans came into the kitchen carrying several dirty cups. This was Andrew's chance. "I need a job Mr. Bern. I've quit school and can work any time."

"I can use someone to clean up around here. I'll pay you one krona for two hours."

"Yes sir. When can I start?" Andrew asked.

"Tomorrow, at noon," Hans said.

Andrew was excited to tell his sister of his good fortune. "Louiza, I got the tavern job, but it only pays a few krona per day. I thought Hans would pay more." Andrew said.

"Not more than he has to," Louiza said.

THE TAVERN

The ski slopes only accommodated day sking and Han's tavern was a popular lunch stop before taking the trail down to Zavoj before dark. If the skiers lingered too long, they could easily lose their way on the trail, darkened in late afternoon by the huge mountains blocking the sun's rays. January was the busiest season at the tavern and Andrew had no time to chat with Anchka during his shift. Hans pressured his help when the tavern became crowded at noon, "You've got to work faster. Customers are waiting and I'm running out of clean dishes." He had a kinder tone when instructing Anchka.

The tavern was at its busiest when a handsome young man came in, sat at a table near the hearth, took off his ski gear and warmed himself in front of the fire.

"May I take your order, sir?" Anchka asked the dark curly haired man.

"Yes. I'll have a ham sandwich and a beer." The young man eyed Anchka's face and body as she wrote his order on a tablet. "Have you ever been to Trieste?" he asked her.

Anchka blushed and said, "Ne."

Andrew watched them. She never smiled at him that way.

The man continued to engage Anchka in conversation. "If you sit with me I'll tell you all about Trieste. It's not far from here."

"I have to keep working or the owner will be mad at me."

"He couldn't be angry with such a pretty girl." The young man said.

Anchka blushed again and gave him side-glances as she cleaned the tables. As she walked into the kitchen with her tray of dishes, Andrew said, "Be careful. That guy is smooth."

"Don't be jealous. I've known you all my life and your like a brother" Ancka said.

"Everybody here has known everybody forever. That's why this village is so boring," Andrew did not want to be regarded as a brother.

When the young man came for lunch the next day, Anchka paused in her work and said to him, "Do tell me about Trieste."

The man wet his lips and held her gaze. "My name is Romero. What's yours?"

Andrew watched them flirt with each other. When Anchka came into the kitchen, he said, "That Romero is a snake. Don't trust him." Anchka ignored him.

It was Friday and Andrew was running as fast as he could toward the tavern because he was twenty minutes late. He feared Hans would dock his pay for his tardiness or even worse, fire him. Anchka came rushing out of the back door of the tavern with a wounded look on her face and ran past Andrew without greeting him. He called her name, but she kept running. Hans glowered at him as he entered the door.

"Where have you been?" Hans demanded.

"I'm sorry. My cow was sick." Andrew lied.

"Don't tell me a lie. Do you think I'm a fool?" Hans said.

"The truth is, I was talking to a friend and the minutes flew by. I just saw Anchka leave and she seemed upset. What happened? " Andrew asked.

Hans said, "I don't know."

Andrew looked around the room. A large bag of flour lay open with most of its contents spread all over the floor. While Andrew cleaned up the mess, Hans uttered, "I think Anchka was raped."

Andrew was stunned. "What! Are you sure?"

"No, but I found her lying on the flour sack with her clothes in disarray and her bloomers about her ankles. She looked shocked. When I asked what happened, she did not explain and ran out the door."

"I left the tavern about half an hour ago to get needed supplies and thought you were going to be here in a few minutes. You've never been late before." Hans said. He pressed his hands on his temples. "I'm getting one of those pounding headaches. I knew she was attracted to that Romero. I never thought he would attack her."

"How do you know she was attacked by him?" Andrew asked.

"Who else could it be? He was here when I left the tavern and is not here now. I don't even know if Romero is his real name. Nothing like this could have happened, if you had been on time. Since I'm in charge of this tavern, I'll take the blame for leaving Anchka alone with the customers." Hans said.

"Customers? You mean there were other men in the tavern besides Romero?"

"Ja, two others." Hans said.

"They might have ganged up on her."

"I don't think so. They were old men engrossed in conversation and didn't pay any attention to Anchka."

"But, maybe they could tell us something." Andrew said

"They were strangers and I wouldn't know how to find them. The only way to get the truth is ask Anchka. I don't want the villagers knowing about this incident. Don't tell anyone. I'm closing the tavern for the rest of the day. My headache is worse. I'm going home to bed. Please lock up."

On the way home, Andrew passed the common ovens a few yards away and saw Mimi chatting with women waiting for their bread to bake. He was in no mood to talk to her, so he took an alternate path that avoided the ovens. When he entered the kitchen, Louiza was preparing a pork roast for dinner.

"What's the matter? You look miserable," Louiza said.

"Hans closed the tavern early today." Andrew said.

"Why would he do that?" Louiza asked. Andrew sat down at the table and cupped his hands over his head. With her hand on Andrew's shoulder, she said, "Tell me what's wrong."

He blurted out. "It's my fault. I was late getting to work."

"What are you talking about?" Louiza said.

"Hans went on an errand and left Anchka with three customers including Romero.

"Who is Romero?" Louiza asked.

"He's the guy Anchka's been flirting with the last couple of days. Hans thinks Romero raped her while he was gone. All I saw was Anchka's panicked face as she ran past me and the flour from a broken sack strewn all over the strorage room. The only one who knows the truth is Anchka.

I wasn't supposed to tell this to anyone." Andrew smashed his fist into the table. "Promise you won't tell anyone about this."

"I promise I won't tell anyone. Don't feel guilty, you did nothing wrong," Louiza said.

"I told Anchka she shouldn't flirt with Romero." Andrew said.

"Maybe she consented to his advances." Louiza said.

"Maybe," Andrew said.

Anchka came back to work after missing one day. She was quiet, her cheerfulness subdued. Andrew put his hand on her arm and asked, "Why were you in such a hurry the other day? You looked upset."

Anchka pushed his hand away and said, "I had to get home." She offered no further explanation and avoided Andrew. She sulked when not busy waiting on customers. Hans tried to talk to her too, but Anchka was evasive in answering his queries. After a few weeks, Anchka quit her job, claiming she was sick.

The town of Gora had little excitement except for the marriages, births and deaths of its residents. This year was different. Unfortunately, the unmarried Anchka was gaining weight and rumors about her spread like wildfire. The women who gathered at the ovens shared their opinions.

"Anchka's stomach is getting big. I bet she's pregnant."

"She's gotten cozy with someone."

"All the men like her."

"Hans might be the father."

"Ne. He's an ugly man."

"It could be anyone."

"Who knows what goes on in that tavern!"

Hans decided to go to Anchka's home upon hearing the nasty rumors. Holding a bag of candy, he knocked on the rough-hewn door. His welcome by Anchka's parents was cool, but polite. They accepted the candy and asked him if he would like to have a piece of strudel. It was the custom to be hospitable to all visitors, liked or not.

"No, thank you. I've come to see Anchka."

"She is too sick to see you," the mother said.

"I'm sorry she is ill. I have another gift for you." Hans took an envelope full of krona.out of his coat pocket and gave it to them. Her parent's faces brightened.

"May I come again?" Hans asked.

"Ja." How could they turn down a man who gave them money.

On the next visit, Anchka welcomed Hans into the parlor. "I'm glad to see you," she said.

"How are you feeling today?" he asked,

"The morning sickness is gone and I'm getting fat. I seldom go out. When I do, the townspeople stare at me." Anchka said.

"Don't worry about them. Here, I brought you this." Hans handed her a bag of cookies.

"You are kind." Anchka said while eating a cookie. "I've wondered why you came to Gora. I can't imagine leaving the excitement of Vienna."

"I'm an only child and have managed our jewelry business since my father died a few years ago. I needed a holiday and wanted to see the plot of land in Gora my father won in a high stakes pinochle game," Hans said.

"Is that the land the tavern is on?" Anchka asked.

"Ja, the lot was too rocky for farming, but close to the ski slopes. I thought of building a place where skiers could buy food and something to drink. I worked many hours planning and constructing the tavern and have made a success of it. It keeps me busy, but I miss seeing your lovely face every day. You are very special to me,"

"Hvala (Thank you.) What a nice thing to say. Why haven't you married?" Anchka asked.

"When I was young I almost married, but that is not important now." Hans gathered his courage, "I have a large house in Vienna. I can take care of you and help raise your baby just like it was my own. Let's get married. I'm offering you and the baby respectability. You may not love me now, but I am hopeful you will some day."

"You are a kind and gentle soul. Ja, I will marry you."

Anchka parents were relieved and grateful that someone, anyone, wanted to marry their tainted daughter. They were the only witnesses to the wedding performed by the old Priest in the side chapel of the church sanctuary.

Hans closed the tavern while he and his bride spent a week

31

honeymooning in Vienna. He took Anchka to his house to see his mother. After the surprise of her son's marriage wore off, Hans' mother expressed her pleasure in his choice of young woman that could bear children. She asked her new daughter-in-law, "Do you like it here, my dear?"

"Oh yes, madam. I've never been in a mansion before."

"Yes, I can tell you do. Why don't you come and live with me? The house is big enough for all of us. You are so pretty, Anchka. You will have a beautiful baby and I will hire a maid to help you with my grandchild. I'm so happy. I thought I would never be a grandmother."

Hans watched his bride's pretty face while his mother talked to her. He and Anchka agreed never to tell his mother the baby was not his biological offspring. She accepted the invitation to stay with Han's mother while he returned to Gora to sell the tavern. He received a fine offer from two local families that combined their money to buy the profitable business.

While waiting for the legal transfer of his property, Hans kept the tavern open. A couple speaking Hungarian dressed in expensive ski wear, came for lunch. Hans spoke several languages and asked in his best Hungarian, "How was the skiing today?"

"Great! The snow is perfect. Don't you agree Titania?" The man's companion smiled at him and nodded. "We'd like two steins of beer and two dishes of goulash," the young man said.

"Andrew, pour the beer while I heat the stew," said Hans.

Distracted by the snuggling and kissing of the couple, Andrew spilled the beer and had to refill the steins. After the couple had eaten and served coffee, they warmed themselves by the hearth.

"It is colder than usual today," Hans said.

"You have a German accent, where were you born?" Titania asked.

"In Vienna," Hans said.

"We were both born in Budapest and married two days ago," Titania said.

"Congratulations," Han's said.

Titania was telling Hans about the wedding, when her husband interrupted, "The sun is setting.We must be going,"

"You won't make it to Zavoj before it gets dark. The trail is dangerous at night and you may lose your way. Stay here. I have blankets and pillows and I'll make you breakfast. Leaving in the morning will be much safer," Hans said.

"The sun is still shining and the sky is clear. We are good skiers and like the bed at the Inn." The young man winked.

"I won't charge you for the night's stay," Hans said.

"That's very kind of you! Don't worry about us, we'll be fine," the husband said.

Hans was exasperated. "You're making a foolish decision."

He said a quick prayer for the couple's safety as they donned their coats and gloves and exited out the door. The sun dipped below the mountains just as Hans lost view of the couple racing down the hill. A few minutes after they were gone, dark clouds appeared over the mountains, blocking the last rays of sun. Sheathes of white flakes started falling and the storm added layers of snow to the path down the mountain.

A few days later, a middle-aged woman entered the tavern and asked in Hungarian, "I'm looking for my daughter Titania and her husband. They were on their honeymoon and came here to ski. Here is their picture. Have you seen them?"

Hans recognized the couple. He did not answer, but instead asked, "Would you like something to drink or eat? You look a bit weary."

"They were here, weren't they," the woman said.

Hans took a deep breath. "They came here for lunch and stayed until the sun was low in the sky. I told them it was dangerous to go down the mountain in the late afternoon. I even asked them to stay overnight without charge. They paid no attention to my warning."

"They never reached their hotel room that night and no one has seen them since." The woman's eyes were watering. Hans offered her slivovitz.

"No, I'll be going. Thank you for the information." The sad woman almost tumbled getting up from her chair and Hans steadied her by grabbing her arm. "I'm okay," she said as she pushed Han's hand away and went out the door.

Hans guessed the couple became disoriented in the snowstorm and wandered off the trail. Despite his concern about the disappearance of the young couple, Hans was content. He had a wife who was about to give birth, his mother was happy and to his delight, he had sold the tavern for a good price.

The Lessons

When father was a child, he was bedridden with Polio for a year and read away the hours. His parents spent the scant money they saved on books for their ill son. The world came to his bed and the pleasure of reading continued throughout his life. He had an incurable disease that attacked his muscles and lungs. His parents tried remedies such as ice packs, rest in bed and feeding him garlic-laden chicken soup, with little success. Eventually, the weakening of Father's body stopped, leaving his left side and leg impaired. He depended on his right leg and walked with a cane

Before Mati's death, Father shared his vast knowledge of history with his family during the cold months. After everyone was full of dinner, the family huddled around their ceramic stove for warmth, waiting for their nightly history lesson. Father sat waiting in his rocking chair and when all were quiet, began his lesson. He added drama to the story by softening or raising his voice for emphasis. Mati interrupted only if she thought Father forgot to mention something or disagreed with him. He almost, always discounted her suggestion.

The stories unfolded night after night. Uncle had difficulty reading Father's lips in the soft light. He watched the children's faces and the shadows made by the drying corn above the stove dance on the walls until he fell asleep.

Father showed his children where Slovenia was on a map of Europe and made them touch a finger on the small area in the Southern Alps. "From here," he said, "If you went west and crossed the Adriatic Sea, you'd be in Venice. North of us is Vienna and in the east is Budapest and in the south is Sarajevo."

Father repeated the history of Slovenia often, so no one would forget the past. He demanded their attention when he began his lectures. "We were once part of the Roman Empire, evidenced by their superb roads and aqueducts built centuries ago that still function. The Romans called our main city Emona, now named Ljubljana."

His voice had a proud tone as he continued. "After the fall of Rome, did you know Slovenia had one of the first systems of democracy in the world? A Duke was selected and he took an oath to be fair, preserve peace and defend Carantania (northern Slovenia) against all enemies. It is said that Thomas Jefferson was influenced by this early form of democracy while writing the Declaration of Independence for the American colonies."

The children heard all of this before and started to become restless.

"Be still," Mati said in a stern voice.

"Slovenia formed an alliance with Austria to help fight off the Avars, a marauding group that threatened this area for three hundred years. The Teutonic army helped defeat the Avars, then controlled the area by force and destroyed their democracy. They subjugated the people into serfdom. During the darkest years of enslavement, peasants were bought, sold and killed at whim. Couples were only allowed to marry with their lord's consent and he had the right to bed the bride the first night."

Louiza whispered in Andrew's ear, "I'd rather die than let that happen to me."

Mati had sharp hearing and retorted, "None of us would exist without our grandmothers tolerating the abuse."

"Shut up," Father said, wanting to get on with his story. "Marauders attacked Slovenia over the centuries. The aggressors plundered the land and slaughtered anyone who got in their way. Thousands of Slovenes were killed and hundreds of children were stolen."

Louiza was amazed her ancestors survived the tumultuous times in which they lived and wondered about the fate of the captured children. Had it not been for Austria coming to their defense, the Slovenes would have been annihilated and not exist today.

Father continued, "The Slovenes built churches high in the mountains, using them as sanctuaries and lookout towers. The bells rang in warning when the enemy approached. Gora was settled on this mountaintop because it provided good visibility in sighting marauders."

"By the fourteenth century, most of Slovenia's regions were owned by the Habsburg Dynasty. Our ancestors farmed the land owned by the Teutonic aristocracy, their lives controlled by them. The serfs yearned for freedom. They fought for independence many times but were no match for the Austrian army. In the sixteenth century, thousands of men from Croatia and Slovenia revolted against the Habsburg Empire, using farm tools to fight their adversary. They were no match for the well-armed soldiers."

Father's story of the fight for independence became more dramatic due to a howling wind blowing around the old log cabin, causing the windows to rattle and the timber to creak. The cold wind swept under the house making the animals, kept there at night for warmth, restless. The children took blankets off the beds and wrapped them around themselves, huddling and giggling while poking each other, much to the consternation of Father.

"Quiet down," Father yelled.

The children became still and Father started again, "The Slovene leader Gregoric was killed in battle. The Croatian leader Gubec was captured, and forced to sit on a burning wood stool, and then crowned with a hot iron wreath. The army rounded up the peasants to watch the torture, including the quartering of Gubec's body. This ruthless treatment was done to deter future rebellions. Even though the uprising ended and never attempted again, the hope of freedom remained in the hearts and souls of our people."

"How terrible," Louiza said.

"Don't fret. This happened long ago," Mati assured her.

That night the children had nightmares, waking Mati up in the early hours of the morning. She pleaded with Father, "Those stories are horrible. You are frightening our children. Talk about something else."

"They have to know what their ancestors experienced." Father said.

"You are so stubborn," Mati said.

Mati's opinion had influenced Father, because that evening he emphasized positive events. "Because of the remote location of our village, the black plague of Europe during the fourteenth and fifteenth centuries did not reach us. It was a devastating disease, wiping out half the population of Europe and affecting most of the known world."

"Could it happen again?" Maria asked

"I don't know," Father said and changed the subject. "Do you know how Slovenia was able to gain some independence?"

"No," the children answered in unison. No one dared say yes.

"We were fortunate the Catholic monks settled here in the sixteenth century because they taught our people to read and write. The value of learning has passed from generation to generation, preparing us to handle our own affairs when the opportunity came."

Father lit the oil lamp and read a passage from a history book. "Europe's political, social and economic climate started to change in the middle of the nineteenth century and the aristocracy's control weakened. The baronial estates were no longer profitable due to the industrial revolution that started in England and spread to Europe."

"The quest for nationalism, inspired by the French and American revolutions, quickly spread to parts of Austria and its domains. The intellectuals of Vienna organized political groups that demanded more representation of the provinces in the government. Due to this economic change and the bloodless revolution, Austrian laws were changed so that serfs could own land and have political representation. Because of the turmoil this caused, Austria's Ferdinand 1 abdicated, letting his nephew Franz Joseph rule in December of 1848."

"Nobody in his right mind would do that. Bet he was sick." Andrew said.

Maria added, "Old too."

"It must be stressful to run a country," Mati said.

"Alright, we've had enough history tonight. Go to bed," Father said.

The next night the Father continued. "The law change was the beginning of our independence, and land from the estates was distributed to the serfs that worked on them. Each family got one plot of poor soil and one plot of rich soil. Our ancestors tempered like steel from terrifying and difficult circumstances, surviving centuries of strife, were now landowners.

"When I was a child in 1867, Austria and Hungary united under the Emperor Franz Josef. The government allowed those who were unhappy with the new unification to immigrate to other countries. That is when our relatives started leaving Slovenia."

After the death of Mati, Father was no longer interested in teaching history. He was lost in a world of regret wishing he told his wife how much he appreciated her before she died. When they first met, he was surprised she was interested in someone with his handicaps, let alone wanting to marry him. She was a sweet and dependable woman and kept the household running. One by one, he was losing his family; Maria had gone to America, Mati had died, and now Andrew was leaving and soon Louiza would leave too.

Father was aware Louiza was unhappy, suffering from the lack of comfort and advice only a mother could give. He felt inadequate to cope with her emotions. Going to America and being with Maria, who was so much like Mati, was the best solution to his young daughter's misery.

THE JOURNEY

In late April, Andrew and Louiza joined neighbors in climbing to a lake not far from the tree line to cut big blocks of ice. The ice was needed for the communal icehouses to keep food from spoiling during the summer. It was a joy to see trees and meadows coming to life again as they climbed to the icy lake. After cutting and dragging ice blocks down the slopes, the group joked and laughed while covering the ice with straw. This method was used to keep the ice from melting too fast during the summer months. It was the first time the siblings had enjoyed themselves since Andrew's birthday party, and it felt good to laugh again. The grief from losing their mother was softening like the weather.

May came with flowers in bloom, green leaves and a change in the family. Andrew prepared to leave for America by obtaining his documents, passing the ship company inspection and buying a steamship ticket. On the day of departure, he said to his father and uncle, "I wish you good health."

Father embraced Andrew and said, "I see the excitement in your face. Your future is in your hands and I hope all goes well in America."

Louiza walked with her brother to the end of the village as tears gathered in her eyes. "Write as soon as you get to New York."

"Don't be sad. I'm sure we'll see each other soon. One more thing, when I told Mimi I was leaving, she was upset. Give her a hug for me."

"I will miss you," Louiza said. After kissing each other on the cheek, Andrew made his way down the mountain. Louiza watched him until the curve of the hill swallowed him.

A few weeks later, a letter from Maria arrived addressed only to

Louiza, which was unusual, the previous ones always addressed to the family. Louiza tore open the envelope.

Dear Louiza,

Erich and I have bought a bowling alley in Cleveland, which keeps us very busy. We need someone to tend the children while we work. Could you help us? If you agree, the money in this letter is for the steamship and the train to Cleveland. Andrew is living in New York, happy earning twenty-two cents an hour working for a restaurant. He will meet you after your inspection at Ellis Island. Greet Father and Uncle for me. Love, Maria

Louiza's dream of escape was becoming a reality. She read the letter twice and again to Father. He agreed by saying, "You'll become happy again being with Maria."

"I'll send money home as soon as I have a job. And with Andrew's money, you can hire a cook and someone to care for the animals. May I have permission to go to Ljupa's house to tell her the good news?" Father nodded and Louiza ran the short distance to her best friend's home.

Ljupa and Louiza had played and schooled together since they were toddlers. The girls were opposite in color and temperament; blond, blue eyed Ljupa was fair and Louiza had brown eyes and dark hair. Their divergent personalities were complimentary. Serious Ljupa was opinionated and energetic, while Louiza was congenial and patient. Ljupa was the second oldest in the family and responsible for three younger siblings, since her mother died two years ago. The oldest sister had left for America a year ago.

"Guess what?" Louiza said.

"I can't," Ljupa said.

"We can go to New York together! My sister sent for me, just like yours did." The teenagers screamed, laughed, held hands and jumped up and down.

"I can't wait to tell Papa. He's worried about me being alone on the ship," Ljupa said.

"Where is your Papa?"

"He's resting, tired from selling chickens and eggs. He comes home earlier and earlier every day and goes to bed. He can stop working when I get my job in America."

"Your sisters and brothers will miss you." Louiza said.

"They're now old enough to care for themselves." Ljupa said.

Soon it was midsummer and the apple orchards were full of ripened fruit. Louiza said to Ljupa, "If it's not raining let's meet early in the morning and pick apples." It didn't rain and the girls ran to the largest orchard just west of the village. "Wow, those apples look delicious."

Ljupa picked one apple and took a big bite, causing juice to run down her chin. "These are so good. More apples are on the top branches than on the lower ones."

"Let's get up there," Louiza said.

Filling the burlap sacks with apples was a welcome change from housework. It was too hot to wear bloomers, so the girl's lower anatomy was exposed as they climbed the tree. Louiza's sack was half-full when she called to Ljupa. "Hey, I hear voices! Pull your skirt down and sit on a branch. We don't want to be seen."

The huge leafy tree hid them well. A group of boys passed under the tree, unaware of them. "We know all of them," Ljupa whispered, her eyes as big as saucers.

Louiza watched the boy with the auburn hair. They had thrown mud at each other when they were five years old. He had put a worm down her back at a village feast and pulled her hair when he sat behind her in the fifth grade. Once, she saw him set a haystack on fire and snitch on him when the adults wanted to know the culprit's identity. Recently, the teasing had stopped and he became shy around her.

Louiza and Ljupa waited until the group was a few feet away from the tree trunk and threw apples at them. They broke into giggles when the group started running, trying to duck the hurtling fruit. When the boys were out of hitting range, the girls heard one of them say, "Let's go back and find out who's throwing the apples."

The leader of the pack said, "No, none of us got hurt. I have to get home and finish my chores." The boys walked toward the village, glancing in back of them.

The girls waited until they were sure the boys would not see them come down from the tree. They had finished filling their sacks with sweet ripe apples and skipped all the way home. They kept the incident to themselves and often giggled about it.

The warm days passed slowly as Louiza and Ljupa looked forward to their departure. They showed their documents sent from Vienna, to the steamship representative in Zavoj. The official scrutinized them, asking questions about their families, their destination and their intentions once they reached America. He said, "You both look healthy and I am giving you permission to board the ship."

On the departure day in August of 1905, Louiza tidied up the two small rooms of her house, placed her money, tickets and vouchers in a black valise. She put on her favorite babushka given to her by Mati. On the previous day, Uncle took two large burlap sacks of the girl's meager belongings to the stagecoach station in Zavoj.

Taking a last look around the log house, Louiza had a twinge of nostalgia for the happy life she once led when her mother was alive. Everything in the house was old and worn but clean. Mati had taught her children to keep the house spotless to keep diseases away.

The old clock on the wall struck six o'clock and the alpine figures of a boy and girl appeared above the face, making their hourly journey. The clock had ticked away every minute of Louiza's life and the wooden children had made hundreds of circles. Her eyes moved from the kitchen clock to Father and Uncle sipping the coffee she had brewed and eating the ham and eggs she had prepared. They would have to make their own breakfast and coffee now. She had mixed feelings, loving them and resenting them, all at the same time.

Macek, the family tomcat, sat near the stove, as he always did, staring at her. She lifted him into her arms, scratched the back of his ears, and stroked his fur. When he started to purr, she laid him down by the stove. Louiza kissed Father on the cheek and gave Uncle a pat on the back. "I promise to write and send money as soon as I can."

"Aw, someone is always leaving; that's how life is. I wish the best for you," Father said. His body trembled when Louiza hugged him.

She took one last look at Father and Uncle and said, "I'll pray for you. Adijo."

Their neighbor Mimi was waiting by the doorstep to say goodbye. She was wiping her eyes with her favorite handkerchief. She said, "Here is a gift for you. I hope when you wear it, you'll think of me. It has been in my family for years. You and your brother are like the children I never had." She handed Louiza a small leather pouch.

"May I open it now?" With permission from Mimi, Louiza took out a cameo broach from the pouch. "Thank you. It's lovely." She pinned the broach on her blouse, hugged Mimi, and made her way to the church.

Louiza plucked purple, white, and yellow wild flowers growing along the path to the old church. The many gravestones in the front yard of the church reminded her of her mortality. She met Ljupa inside the holy sanctuary and they sat in the front pew just in time for morning Mass. The girls prayed for their families, for safety, and for courage, during their long journey. They watched the old Priest as he recited the holy rite in Latin. He had baptized them and conducted all the sacraments in their families. After the service, the girls told him they were leaving for America.

"God bless you on your journey and in your new land. I will pray for you," said the old Priest.

The girls visited their mother's graves to say goodbye. Kneeling beside Mati's resting place, Louiza laid the wild flowers at the foot of the stone marker and said, "I miss you and love you with all my heart. Some day I will join you in heaven. But now I must leave or I'll suffocate here." She made the sign of the cross and touched the etched letters of Mati's formal name, Theresa.

The girls started down the mountain slowly, looking back every few steps, waving goodbye to all they had known. When the village disappeared from sight, they ran to the valley below. They were out of breath when they reached the small station in Zavoj where the stagecoach waited. After their luggage was tied on the coach roof, they jumped into their seats and the driver made the horses pull away from the station with a flick of his whip. The girls watched the changing scenery as the coach distanced itself from Zavoj and their mountain home.

The coach stopped in Ljubljana, where they transferred to a train heading south-west to the Dalmatian coast. Tired from the bumpy stagecoach ride, the constant rumble of the train lulled them to sleep. Excitement returned when their train stopped in the city of Rijeka, a seaport on an Adriatic inlet. After getting directions, they left the train station and walked a short distance to the pier. They emerged upon a large boardwalk along the sea, awed by a panorama of new sights, sounds, and smells.

On the east side of the boardwalk were tall buildings, and on the opposite side was the pier and the sea beyond. The breeze smelled of fish and salt. The harbor was full of all kinds of watercraft including sailing boats, fishing vessels, and one large steam ship. Hubs of men were loading heavy crates tied with thick ropes into the hold of the ship.

"There's our ship," said Ljupa.

"It's big," Louiza said.

Emblazoned on the side of the ship was the name "S.S. Emperor of the Sea." Ljupa and Louiza walked to the gangplank where an officer stood. "You have to wait behind that rope." He pointed to the left side of the ship where the steerage class was gathered. The girls obeyed and stood with the other peasants watching first-class passengers board.

"Look at that woman with the large hat. Have you ever seen such a fancy dress?"

"I bet that's her servant next to her. Look at all those trunks." The crowd oohed and aahed, admiring the wealthy. The first-class passengers disappeared into the ship, not seen again by the steerage passengers until the end of the voyage. Those who had paid the least to cross the ocean, boarded last.

Ship officials examined Louiza and Ljupa's documents, comparing them to the official passenger list. Cards, with their names and numbers coded to the manifest sheets, were used as their identification during the voyage and at Ellis Island. It seemed like forever before the uniformed man said, "Your papers are in order. Board the ship."

Louiza and Ljupa had to pass several criteria before considered for immigration to the United States. They had no communicable diseases, were mentally sound and had no criminal record. They also were apolitical. In 1903, after the assassination of President McKinley by a political dissident, a new rule was enforced: Anyone suspected of advocating the overthrow of the United States government by force, was denied admission to the country. If the steamship company transported a person with any of these problems, they paid a fine of one hundred dollars and returned that person to their place of embarkation.

The girls leaned against the ship rails as it pulled away from the Rijeka pier. Louiza said, "Let's take off our babushkas and wave goodbye to Austria." They waved until the pier disappeared behind a spit of land. They stayed on the deck until sunset, passing many islands as the ship steamed along the eastern coast of the Adriatic, going toward the Mediterranean.

Louiza and Ljupa found their cabin located near the boiler room in the bowels of the ship. They greeted the women sitting on the bunks in the windowless and overheated room. Only two of the six bunks were empty. "I guess those top bunks are ours," Ljupa said.

"You're young and can climb up there," The pregnant woman said.

"Ja!" said one of the mothers holding a baby. A little boy with round, rosy cheeks and inquisitive eyes squirmed out of his mother's arms to investigate the new roommates. He played with Louiza's shoelaces and she smiled, opening her arms to the receptive boy. He cuddled for a few seconds and then went back to his mother and started sucking his thumb. The baby started crying and stopped when his robust mother let him suckle her breast. After nursing for a few minutes, the baby fell asleep and the smell of a soiled diaper permeated the air.

The pregnant woman said, "I'm Helga from Bavaria."

"When is your baby due?" Ljupa asked.

"In about four months. My baby will be born in the United States." Helga said.

"How do you feel?" Louiza asked.

"Lightheaded. It's hot in here," Helga responded.

"It's stuffy too. Let's go on deck," Ljupa said.

"We'll go too, my son needs fresh air," the boy's mother said. She looked tired with dark circles under her eyes.

The sea air was refreshing and the women stayed on deck until mealtime. A map posted in the dining room showed the ship route to several ports before reaching England. Excitement grew as the ship rounded the tip of Italy and approached the island of Sicily, where black ash and steam could be seen spewing into the sky.

"My father told me that's Mount Etna. It's one of the most active volcanoes in the world," Louiza said.

"It's spectacular," Ljupa said.

The ship passed the island and headed southwest to Algiers. The sun seemed especially bright and the girls felt wonderful in the warm air of the Mediterranean. After anchoring, they watched a line of dark-skinned people, with baskets balanced on their heads, come to the ship.

They unloaded the contents of the baskets into a large container. The graceful movements and colorful dress of the Africans were impressive. Then the ship sailed through the Straits of Gibraltar heading north and passing the shores of Portugal, Spain, and France. The weather cooled and the sky became cloudy as the ship steamed toward England.

The "Emperor of the Sea" anchored at Liverpool, where a few passengers disembarked and a few came aboard, as coal was loaded on to fuel the journey across the vast Atlantic. The dirtiness of the boardwalk and poor condition of the shanties along the pier were shocking. Black soot covered everything and gave the city a gray hue, so unlike the clear air of Gora. "I wonder if New York is the same as this city?" Louiza said.

Not expecting an answer, Louiza was startled when a male voice said,

"I don't think so, Liverpool is much older than New York The fog, the shipbuilding industry, and chimney soot, cause the grayness. A few years ago, pigs cleaned the streets of New York and now they have a crew of men clean them." The voice belonged to the young man standing next to Ljupa. He introduced himself. "I'm Marko from Croatia."

"We are Ljupa and Louiza from Slovenia, Look! We're pulling away from the pier."

THE VOYAGE

The ocean became choppy as the ship emerged from the sheltered harbor, making the ship pitch and roll, causing some passengers like Helga to become seasick. Helga spent most mornings on deck vomiting over the ship railing and huddling in her blanket, preferring the cold damp weather to the smelly cabins. She was pale and thin which accentuated her growing abdomen.

Her cabin mates had great sympathy for her, but she filled the enclosed room with an awful smell and when added to the other odors, the cabin became unbearable. The women took turns emptying the chamber pots as fast as they filled and kept the cabin door open, trying to keep the stench tolerable.

One night, after being at sea for a week, Louiza was awakened by moaning coming from Helga's bunk. Tapping Helga's shoulder, she asked, "What's the matter?"

"I'm having painful cramps. Ow," Helga said as she grasped her abdomen with her hands. Her nightgown, blanket, and mattress were wet with water and blood. The other women awoke and surrounded Helga's bunk.

"I've helped with births before. She's in labor," one of the women said. Everyone took turns rubbing Helga's back and shoulders, trying to soothe her. "Hold back; don't push. It's too early to have the baby."

"I can't help it. It hurts! It hurts!" Helga cried out.

After about an hour of increasing pain, Helga had an intense contraction and ejected a dead fetus covered in blood and mucus. More blood exuded and nothing could stop its flow. Helga bled to death.

Helga and her tiny fetus, wrapped in the blood-soaked blanket, were carried to the deck where two other bodies lay. With heads bowed, the passengers listened to a brief prayer said by the Captain. They watched the bodies tossed into the ocean and disappear in the dark water. Deaths occurred daily from diseases such as cholera, smallpox, and typhus; the ship disease caused by poor food, lack of fresh air, and poor sanitation. The girls prayed for the souls of Helga and her baby.

"Our old Priest would be proud of us," Louiza said.

Needing to relieve their sorrow, Ljupa said, "Let's walk to the other side of the ship." The peasants were playing lively music on instruments brought from home. Louiza began singing with a group of Slovenes accompanied by an accordion. Disliking the foul air in their cabins, the steerage passengers came on deck as often as possible. The young people danced under threatening clouds and even when it rained. When the ship hit large waves or when it was stormy, the folk music stopped until the weather calmed, then began again.

The Italians sang the best harmony and listening to their beautiful voices made the difficult living conditions on the ship fade for a while. The young Italian Leonardo was everyone's favorite singer. He had a smooth voice, expressive eyes and thick dark hair framed his handsome face. Watching Leonardo talk to friends and flirt with girls was one of Louiza's favorite pastimes. His laugh sounded like it came from the bottom of his shoes and his bright smile showed his even, unstained teeth. He looked at her once or twice and she shyly smiled back at him.

The young people liked to flirt, and Ljupa was no exception. While walking on deck, she saw Marko coming toward her and purposefully bumped into him, pretending it was an accident. He put his hand on her arm, stopping her from strolling further and said, "I hoped we would meet again. But of course we would. It's written in the stars."

Ljupa was pleased her trick was successful and looked into his blue eyes. "Are you an astrologer?" She asked.

"If you meet me when the sun is setting, I'll show you the constellations." Marko said.

"That would be interesting. I want to find out what "constellation" means." Ljupa said.

They watched the sun disappear behind the curve of the earth, looked at the stars, and the moon through wisps of clouds. They became quiet when their hands touched. It didn't matter that Marko didn't know anything about constellations. Every night thereafter, they met on deck and found a nook where no one would see them kissing and fondling.

"Marko has the sweetest kiss. I want to kiss him again and again," Ljupa confided, not expecting this revelation to be disturbing to Louiza.

"Be careful!" Louiza warned. "Our friend Anchka met that seducing skier at Hans' tavern and you know what happened to her. She and her family were disgraced. Her parents were so embarrassed about her pregnency, they hid in their house for days. That skier never returned to the village and Anchka was marked for life. How many rosaries do you think the old Priest had her say for her sin? That rich old guy Hans married her and saved her and her child from a lifetime of ostracism."

Ljupa didn't want to hear the lecture, but Louiza's admonitions did remind her of the possible consequence of her amorous behavior. "My willpower is weak, and I do want to be a virgin bride. I can't be alone with Marko. You can help me by staying by my side."

"I'll protect your purity as best I can," Louiza said.

As a result, the three of them were always together during their waking hours. While on deck, they watched cloud formations, the changing waves, playful dolphins, and sighted whales spouting. Ljupa and Marko held hands, aware that Louiza hovered nearby, watching them.

Sitting together at meals, the trio served themselves from large bowls placed in the middle of oblong tables. On the first days of the journey, arguments broke out among the diners. "You took too much food. There's hardly a scrap left for me." The ones who got to the table first, took too much food, and those who were last, got the least food.

A man shoved another man for overloading his plate, causing food to spill on the floor, which resulted in a scuffle. Leonardo intervened and separated the combatants. Leonardo had everyone's attention and announced loudly, "Everyone take one scoop from each bowl and no more, so the food will be shared equally. Those served first at one meal will be last at the next. I will enforce this rule with the help of my friends." There were no more arguments over food.

One afternoon, an unfamiliar crescent-shaped fruit was given as a snack to everyone on deck. Never having seen the oblong yellow fruit before, Louiza and Ljupa watched people peel the skin before eating the soft center. They did the same and enjoyed their first banana.

Many ships and boats appeared as they neared New York Harbor. Sea lions hung on the buoys, seals cavorted in the water, and all kinds of birds flew by. The voyagers stood on deck, excited to be reaching their destination. Unknown to Louiza, Leonardo had made his way through the throng and stood next to her. "Those large birds flying in a vee formation are pelicans," he explained.

Louiza was surprised her idol was standing so close to her. Not knowing what to say, she responded, "Those birds are so graceful." It was the last day of their voyage and the first day they spoke to each other. They joined the crowd cheering the Statue of Liberty, larger than many envisioned, causing mouths to drop in awe.

"Before we say goodbye, I want to tell you that you are the prettiest girl on this ship," Leonardo said. He leaned toward her, kissed her on the lips, and then walked away with a grin on his face. Louiza's face flushed, for it was her first romantic kiss.

Ljupa, amused by the affectionate scene, said to Louiza, "If you had met Leonardo earlier, you would have been the one needing a chaperone."

When the ship docked at the Hudson Pier, quarantine officers came on board to record the number of passengers, the number of deaths, and the health conditions of the ship. After this was completed, the first and second-class passengers disembarked. The wealthy were immune to inspection, due to the government's belief they would not cause problems. The ship pulled away from the pier with the steerage passengers still on board and headed for Ellis Island.

"Is it possible we could be rejected?" Ljupa asked

"I don't think so. We're healthy and came to work," Marko responded.

"Stay close. We don't want to be separated," Louiza said.

Before they could disembark, inspection cards had to be completed. When this was done, the immigrants were formed into groups of thirty and taken to the island by barge. As the excited voyagers entered the first floor, they were directed to check their luggage and climb the steps to the Great Hall.

Upon reaching the Great Hall, Louiza, Ljupa, and Marko sat in cubicles with their group and waited. The first exam to determine a person's state of health began when the medical staff observed the ease or difficulty a person had climbing the stairs that led to the hall, where each person was individually judged. If there was a health problem, the coat or dress of the immigrant was marked with chalk to indicate they needed treatment at the island hospital. The doctors and nurses declared Louiza, Ljupa, and Marko to be healthy, and they advanced to the next phase. The second exam was verifying the information on the manifest and the inspection cards.

The authorities made sure each person had a relative or friend to greet them at the end of the examinations. They were especially concerned for the safety of the elderly, single women, and women alone with children. Immigrants were not released from the island without a sponsor for fear of unscrupulous people taking advantage of them. Those who gave false information or had a mental illness or an incurable disease were taken back to their place of embarkation at the expense of the steamship company.

When the paperwork was finished in the Great Hall and all questions answered satisfactorily, the immigrants were tagged according to their destination. Louiza, Ljupa, and Marko passed through immigration in only three hours. Sometimes it took days to go through the process due to overcrowding and exam complications. The three companions were ushered down the Stairs of Separation to the first floor, where their sponsors were waiting.

Louiza was exhilarated to see Andrew waiting for her. Ljupa scanned the crowd and called out her cousin's name loudly. Her cousin pushed through the crowd. "Ljupa, Ljupa, I'm here. I'm so happy to see you."

Marko spotted his brother and shouted with joy, "It's good to see you."

"Did you have a good trip?" Marko's brother asked.

"Ja. He pointed to Ljupa, ."This is Ljupa. Isn't she beautiful," Marko said.

When the excitement of greeting their relatives and introducing their friends had subsided and before they dispersed to their destinations,

Louiza, Ljupa, and Marko clasped hands, pledging to write to each other. Before Ljupa rushed off to catch a train to Minnesota with her cousin, she kissed Marko and whispered, "I will be waiting for you, my love."

THE NEW LAND

The numerous buildings, stores, and crowded sidewalks of New York City awed Louiza. The noisy streets were jammed with horse-drawn carriages, electric trolley cars, bicycles and venders pushing carts of vegetables and fruits. White-clothed men swept the streets and sidewalks. Pedestrians were dressed in all sorts of clothing and spoke a variety of languages. Some women wore fancy hats and gowns, and their daughters wore frilly dresses. Others wore babushkas and plain homemade dresses. Men wore topcoats or vested suits, or ethnic clothing and some were in rags. Boys wore caps and knickers, or clothing of another culture. Blue-suited police officers patrolled on horses. Boys stood on street corners peddling newspapers, calling out, "Extra, extra, read all about it."

The hustle and bustle in the city was fascinating, so different from Gora, Rijeka, or Liverpool. Louiza's mouth was beginning to dry from being agape viewing the myriad of sights. "I'm hungry," She said as her stomach started to growl

"We'll stop at a butcher shop and buy hotdogs," Andrew said. "Hotdogs are popular at Coney Island. They're similar to Klabase."

Andrew showed her how to put mustard and ketchup between the bun and the sausage, and demonstrated how to eat the hotdog. The wiener tasted good, having a smoother texture and a different taste than Klabase.

Louiza saw that Andrew was comfortable in the big city after only living in it for a few months. They walked along the majestic Brooklyn Bridge, with its double arched towers strung with thick cables. "Isn't it beautiful," Louiza said, admiring the architectural wonder. Below the bridge, she spied a most unusual boat that was spouting water from its nozzles. "Look, look, Andrew," Louiza pointed her finger at the boat.

"That's the most powerful fireboat in the world. It's used to douse fires on piers, ships, and boats," Andrew explained.

They walked to the center of Manhattan Island, stopping at the entrance to the newly built subway. "It's the first of its kind in all of America. We'll ride the subway tomorrow, but now we have to find someplace to sleep tonight," Andrew said.

The sun was setting on the busy city, and weariness was setting in. It seemed the siblings walked in circles before finding an affordable room for the night. After climbing several flights of stairs, they reached their tiny room. There was only enough space to get into the double bed. Louiza was so tired she lay on the soft bed fully clothed and closed her eyes. Still feeling the sway of the ship, she fell asleep next to her brother.

The next day Louiza and Andrew reached Cleveland by train and took the trolley to the Slavic Café & Bowling Alley. They walked into the small café, and Louiza was shocked to see Maria looking so much like Mati. Her oldest sister was a younger version of her mother. Tears spilled down her cheeks as she and her sister wrapped their arms around each other. Louiza was overwhelmed by the enthusiastic welcome of Maria's children. When the noise abated, she noticed Erich standing with Andrew, smiling. The happy sisters ate very little dinner, for they could not stop talking, trying to catch up on the past six years. Erich and Andrew were quiet, listening to the chatter. After closing the café, the family had dinner and after eating dessert, Andrew kissed his sisters and returned to New York on the evening train so he could work the next day.

"You will share a room with my daughter," Maria said to Louiza.

It was evident the child wasn't happy with the arrangement by her facial expression.

"Show Aunt Louiza your room," Maria said.

"Your doll looks so pretty sitting on your bed. Does she have a name?" Louiza said, trying to befriend the girl.

"Yes, her name is Dolly. Santa brought her."

"Why did you name her Dolly?"

"President Madison's wife was named Dolly, and she had a lot of fun."

"Can you tell me about her?"

"My mom can. I have a tea set. You want to play with me?"

"Oh, yes, I'd love to have a cup of tea."

"You're fun, just like Dolly." The doll sat in her own chair and had her own teacup.

"My brothers never want to play with me. I'm glad you do."

Her brothers were interested in playing ball, kick the can and wrestling and did not want to sit at a table pretending to have tea.

While Maria and Erich toiled in the bowling alley, Louiza took care of her charges, cooked, and cleaned. The children adored their aunt, even though she made them sit at the table until they ate everything on their plate. After tucking the children in bed one night, Louiza became restless. "Can I help you in the bowling alley while the children are asleep?"

"Of course you can. I thought you would be tired after caring for the children all day. I could use a break a couple of evenings a week. I'll stay with the children, while you take my place in the café."

So, Louiza learned how to be a waitress, and a good one too. She was friendly when greeting customers, cheering them up with her peppy personality and efficiency. She liked the tips she received. After living with Maria and Erich for a few months, she noticed a change in their attitudes.

"Running the café and bowling ally takes all our energy. We want an easier life, so we've decided to sell the business. Our children never knew their grandmother. Their grandfather is still alive and we want them to know him and see the beauty of Gora. To tell you the truth, I miss our little village." Maria said.

"I don't want to return. I like it here. The weather is mild and there are so many things to do and so many interesting people. It's exciting. I know Father will be happy you're going back to him," Louiza said.

The bowling alley had increased in value since Maria and Erich had bought it, and it sold at a very good price. While doing the dishes with Maria the night before the family was to leave, the sisters sang one of their mother's favorite songs.

"Adijo, pa zdrava ostani [Goodbye and stay healthy.] Podaj mi se enkrat roko [Give me once more your hand.] Pa name nikdar ne pozabi [And never forget me.]"

Within a few days after Louiza moved into the apartment of a friend, she aided her sister in packing the family belongings. The day of departing came and after full trunks were loaded into the horse-drawn cart, the family went to the station. The porters lifted the baggage onto the train bound for New York. After the announcement, "all aboard, all aboard," it was time to say goodbye and they all hugged and kissed. Maria, Erich and the three children got on the train. "Adijo. Give my love to Andrew." Louiza called to them as the train started puffing steam and slowly picked up speed. She waved her scarf until the train was out of sight.

Back in Slovenia, Father was happy Maria and her family were returning to Gora to care for him and Uncle. They were both sick, and he was comforted to know his daughter would care for them in their dying days. Their neighbor, Mimi, had become ill also, and Uncle, even though he was ailing, visited her every day, bringing her flowers and hot soup their housekeeper made. Uncle stayed with Mimi during the last hours of her life and mourned for days after her death.

Even though Father was never fond of Mimi, he changed his mind when Uncle showed him a letter in her handwriting, bequeathing the house to Andrew. He studied the letter a long time. It was not official because no lawyer or witness had signed it. He doubted Andrew would ever come home again, so why would he have to know the house was his? How perfect. Maria and her family could live in Mimi's house.

A letter arrived from Louiza asking him to send her the kitchen clock and included five dollars for postage. Father waved the money in front of Uncle, did a little shuffle and put the money in his pocket. Everything in his house was old, including the clock. He had no objections in sending it to Louiza. He could afford to buy a brand new one.

Father had to dismiss his housekeeper, a young, robust girl who kept him warm at night by cuddling his head on her ample chest. "I'm sorry, my pet, but I must let you go. My oldest daughter will be here soon. Here, I added an American dollar to the krona I owe you. I have a favor to ask of you. I'm sending this package to my youngest daughter in America. Could you mail it for me? Here is money for postage. You can keep the change."

The housekeeper thanked and hugged her bed partner and said "Adijo" "No one must ever know about us," Father called after her as she left.

ANTON AND LOUIZA

One night while joking with his cronies at Novak's bar, Anton noticed a new waitress as she emerged from the kitchen, carrying a large tray of food. His eyes followed the voluptuous figure around the smoky room. She laughed often and her youthful face radiated joy. "What is the new maid's name?" Anton asked the bartender.

"A lot of customers are asking that question. Her name is Louiza."

The next afternoon, Anton watched Louiza rush in and out of the kitchen, take orders, serve, and clean. He tried to be inconspicuous, but she caught him looking at her while she collected dirty plates from the tables. After a few days of exchanging glances, Anton sat at one of the small round tables away from the bar, so Louiza could serve him. She approached him with a smile, showing her white, even teeth, and said "Dober Vecer [Good evening.]"

When he responded, "Kako si ti [How are you]?" she said, "Dobra [Good]" and asked him, "What can I get for you?"

Her brown eyes were captivating. "I'll have a dish of goulash." He watched the sway of her hips as she walked away. He sat at the same table the next night instead of the bar and winked at Louiza as she approached him.

She asked, "How are you tonight?"

"Better since you are here," Anton said.

"Does your wife know you come here every afternoon?" Louiza asked.

"I don't have a wife." Anton said as he saw the manager hurrying toward them.

In a loud voice, the manager interrupted the conversation, "Louiza, you are spending too much time at this table. Other customers need you.

"We're getting to know each other." Anton said.

"You're a regular customer and I appreciate your business, but I'll lose other customers if they don't get waited on," the manager said.

Anton was annoyed. However, the manager gave him an idea. He said to Louiza, "Look, I don't want to get you in trouble. Why don't we meet someplace and talk when you aren't working?"

"The park is a nice place. I don't work on Sundays," Louiza responded.

The manager glared at them and said with a tinge of anger, "Louiza, get on with your work, making dates with customers is not permitted."

"Ja." Louiza moved to the next table to take an order.

Louiza met Anton at the park after she attended Mass. "I prepared a lunch for us, and I brought a blanket to sit on. There's a good spot over there." They sat under a large maple tree and ate meatloaf sandwiches and potato salad.

"The meatloaf is very good," Anton remarked as he sipped his beer.

"I'm glad you like it." Louiza said.

"I want to know all about you. Tell me about your village," Anton requested.

"I come from Gora, a mountain village in the Julian Alps. My family has lived there for generations. Gora is a small town and not very interesting. We used to raise pigs and had a few cows. Father sold the animals after my brother moved to New York and I moved here. Father's been crippled since he was a child and lives with his deaf brother.. My mother died last year."

"Sorry about your mother. Did you inherit her eyes? They are so beautiful." Anton said.

"Thank you." Louiza smiled and looked down at the grass. She said. "Tell me about your village."

"I'm from a small town a few miles from Skofia Loka. My mother lives with my half brother and my evil stepfather." Anton said.

"He's evil?" Louiza's eyes widened.

"A nasty guy," Anton said.

"Why do you say that?" Louiza asked.

"I don't want to talk about him."

"What about your real father?" Louiza asked.

"There is nothing to say."

Anton avoided any further questioning about his family by changing the subject and inviting Louiza to a dance the next weekend.

Anton is so captivated, he wrote the first of many love letters to the dark-haired Louiza, never signing his name. After going to Novak's bar, he left the letter in an obvious place where the bartender could discover it. He sat at a table and waited for Louiza to come out of the kitchen. When she emerged, the bartender called to her, "I have a letter for you."

Anton watched Louiza open the envelope and saw the pleased expression on her face as she read the letter. She remarked to the bartender, "This letter is from a mystery man. He's romantic and a good writer."

"Let me read it, then I'll tell you what I think," the bartender said. He read the letter. "This guy likes you a lot."

Anton took Louiza to the Slovene dance hall, where they stepped lively to polkas and glided to waltzes. They had a great time dancing, talking and laughing with neighborhood friends. During the last dance, Anton pressed Louiza against his chest and nuzzled the soft skin of her neck.

"Don't do that. You're embarrassing me. You behave," Louiza scolded.

"Okay, okay." Anton didn't talk much the rest of the evening and took Louiza home earlier than usual. He avoided the tavern for one week; too long for him to stay away. He slipped into the tavern by the back door to be unnoticed. He watched Louiza move about the room and watched men flirt with her. He wanted to protect her, to take her away from this place, away from the vultures. He sat at his favorite table. Did he see a tear in her eye when she spied him?

"What can I get you?" Louiza asked.

"I think I'll have a ham sandwich and a glass of beer." Anton grabbed her hand. "Won't you come with me to a picnic on Sunday?"

"Ja, I've missed you," Louiza said.

Thereafter, Anton wrote love letters to her every day and left them at the bar. They become constant companions, hold hands, hug, and kiss often. One evening, after going to a movie, Anton became aggressive. While embracing her, he kissed her and caressed her breast. His breathing intensified, and she sighed softly as he pushed his hips against hers. She gently pushed him away.

"Don't do that. I must wait until I marry."

Anton calmed himself and vowed to control his desire. Louiza was so young, pure and innocent. He was sure she had no intimate experience with a man; a perfect mate for him. An unpleasant image of the past flashed in his mind. Late the next evening, Anton took Louiza for a walk after she finished work. "How was your day?"

"I made good money from tips." Louiza said.

"What are you going to do with it?" Anton asked.

"I try to save as much as I can for a rainy day," Louiza said.

"I do to, but I so spend a lot at Novaks," Anton said.

It was time for Anton to make his confession. "I wrote those love letters."

"I thought so. I enjoy them," Louiza said.

"I love you and want you to be my wife."

"Ja!" Louiza said without hesitation. "We will have beautiful, children. I'm so excited, I'm going to write my family and tell them the good news."

A few weeks later, Louiza received a letter from Maria and read it to Anton.

"Dear Louiza, We are pleased that you are going to marry a fine man. Father is having mental problems, confusing me with Mati. He keeps asking where Uncle has gone and does not accept the fact he is dead. The children are well, and Erich and I are content here. Come and visit us with your new husband. We wish you much happiness and many children. Love, Maria"

Anton wrote to his mother and Boris telling them of his forthcoming marriage. He invited his New York cousin, and friend Frank Poncek to the wedding. Frank wrote a note congratulating Anton and said he couldn't attend the ceremony because he had to work.

Louiza, at age sixteen, and Anton, at age twenty-four, said their vows on a cold day in the winter of 1907 with Andrew and Alicia, the cook at Novaks, as their witnesses. Louiza looked lovely in a blue gown cinched at the waist with puffy long sleeves and a high lace collar. On top of her swept-up hair was a headdress made of little poufs of white netting in the latest bridal fashion.

Anton was dashing with his hair and mustache trimmed, wearing a black-vested suit with a stiff-collared shirt that fitted too tight around his neck. Because he was fore bidden to eat before he took communion and felt light headed, he hoped he wouldn't pass out during the Mass. No one fainted in the hour-long rites, however, the photo of Anton, Louiza, Alicia and Andrew, taken after the ceremony, showed four people looking unhappy.

As was the custom, the wedding party ate a large brunch, satisfying their hunger. Food never tasted so good. After the meal, they all went home to rest before the evening celebration. The owner of Novak's Tavern let the newlyweds use his spare room for their nap, making sure the double sized bed had fresh sheets on it.

As soon as they entered the small room, Louiza laid down on the bed. Anton had anticipated this moment for a long time and was so aroused he quickly lifted her skirts and consummated their marriage. His bride shrieked, proving to Anton she had no man before him. His whole body relaxed, knowing he had married a virgin and he fell asleep.

After sleeping several hours, the bride and groom reassembled their clothing and rushed to the reception just in time to greet their guests at the entrance of the Slovene dance hall. White crepe paper festooned the light fixtures and doorways and white cloth covered the numerous tables. The five-piece band set up their instruments, which included a bass, a drum, a piano, and the most important instrument of all, an accordion. Adjacent to the hall was the kitchen, where stout women wearing printed aprons prepared the wedding feast under the direction of the ample Mrs. Beck. Perspiration beaded the women's brows as they talked while preparing the food.

"The groom is so handsome. He could get any woman, anytime."

"No one could compete with such a young and pretty bride."

"Stop gossiping. Keep mixing the soup. Get that roast out of the oven before it's overcooked," Mrs. Beck directed.

The hall became crowded and noisy with the arrival of friends, neighbors and children in their finest clothing. These warm, hard-working people came to drink, eat, dance, and, oh, yes, congratulate the newlyweds. The band started up with a lively polka and everyone danced and drank for an hour, then ate dinner. After the first round of eating, the guests broke out in song, harmonizing the same way they did at sundown in their villages. They reconnected with their heritage, reminding them of loved ones still living in the old country. People danced with abandon, yelling out their joy as their feet moved to the rhythm of the music. Men danced with women, women danced with women, and the children danced with everyone.

Mrs. Beck marched up to the bandleader and said, "I'd like a drum roll please." It was time for the highly anticipated pillow dance to begin. The beat of the drum got everyone's attention. "C'mon now, form the circle so we can start." Mrs Beck shouted at the revelers. All but the very young and very old joined hands and formed a wide circle, with Mrs. Beck in the middle holding a pillow in one hand and a dish in the other.

Mrs. Beck gave the pillow to Louiza, who dropped it on the floor in front of Andrew. He put money in Mrs. Beck's dish, and the band played for a minute or two while the bride danced with her brother. After that round was over the procedure repeated, with Anton joining Louiza as the band continued to stop and start again until everyone in the circle had placed money in the dish and danced with the bride and groom. Mrs. Beck gave all the money in the dish to Anton. He said to Louiza, "Look, we've collected enough money to pay the band, the hall, the food and Mrs. Beck."

It was time for the couple to cut the wedding cake, topped with a miniature ceramic couple dressed in wedding clothes. Mrs. Beck watched the newlyweds taste the cake she had baked, covered with her special white frosting. Louiza scooped a bit of icing and put it on Anton's nose. He wiped it off with his finger and put it on Louiza's cheek then licked it off. "I can't waste this good frosting," Anton said. The wedding guests laughed, the cake was sliced, and served to everyone who wanted a piece.

The big moment of the evening was at hand. The clock on the wall pointed to midnight, and the band stopped playing, except for the drummer beating out a cadence that caught everyone's attention. The celebrants gathered around the bride seated next to Anton. Andrew stepped forward, raised his wine glass and said, "Louiza, you've been a wonderful sister. I hope you and Anton will have a wonderful life together."

The guests cheered and then quieted for the ages-old ritual that was quite serious.

Alicia, the cook, never came to the reception and was supposed to take the white veil from Louiza's head. Instead, Mrs. Beck had the honor of removing the veil, which represented purity. As this occurred, the men sang an old folksong about the sadness experienced in the loss of virginity and proclaimed the bride's old life was gone and her new life was beginning. The crowd cheered as the song ended and Mrs. Beck took the small white rose from Anton's lapel and pinned it in Louiza's dark hair.

Some of the babies and young children had fallen asleep in their mother's arms, while older ones fell asleep on the floor. The elderly went home. Everyone else kept the party lively by dancing and singing, including Anton and Louiza. It was early in the morning when they paid everyone who contributed to the reception and went back to the small room in Novak's bar. After changing into their bedclothes, they sat on the bed and Louiza wanted to talk.

"Isn't it strange that Alicia never showed up at the hall."

"Ja," Anton said while yawning.

"I'm mad at her, but hope she's alright." Louiza said.

"I don't want to talk anymore." Anton started caressing Louiza's body.

Anton was a zesty, powerful lover and after a few days, his bride was beginning to respond to him. After a few weeks of enjoying their physical intimacy, painful memories started flooding his mind, causing him to become distrustful of his new wife.

Moving into a second-story apartment was easy because the newlyweds had no furniture except for a new mattress. Anton was adamant about sleeping on a brand new mattress. "No telling who slept on a used one or what they did in it."

In spite of the old building needing repair, it seemed like heaven to the young couple. When Louiza got through arranging and rearranging two chairs, a rug and a coffee table bought from a secondhand store, the tiny parlor looked somewhat attractive.

A month after the wedding, an announcement outlined in black arrived; Anton's mother had died, and he was stunned. He loved her, even though she had shamed him, and he wept. After composing himself, he noticed another letter inside the envelope. It was from his half brother, Boris, expressing his sadness at the loss of their mother. He also congratulated Anton on his marriage and asked for sponsorship, for he wanted to immigrate. Anton told Louiza, "I'll sponsor Boris. He will have to live with us until he adjusts and finds a job. He can sleep in the parlor. My brother is a nice kid with a stuttering problem."

"Boris is welcome, after all he is your brother," Louiza said.

Anton had another concern; a large field of natural gas discovered in West Virginia was causing the gas company's coke ovens to become unnecessary. The managers decided to transfer the coal stokers to other jobs within the company. Anton was assigned as an apprentice to a blacksmith named Wolf Verner.

"Who are you?" Wolf said when Anton showed up at the shop.

"I'm your new assistant."

"I don't need assistant."

"The company sent me. You'll have less work with my help."

"You make horseshoes?"

"No, but I can learn."

"You listen; I don't explain twice."

Anton understood Wolf's limited English as well as his fluent German, for Slovenia had been part of Austria for centuries. German words and sentences were common in the Slovenian language.

Wolf was an irritable perfectionist, and Anton admired his skill in making metal horseshoes for the gas company. They were alike in temperament and both understood that Wolf was in charge and Anton was his apprentice.

"First step is to make fire in hearth. Put slab of iron on hot grate." Wolf increased the temperature of the fire by blowing air into it with a bellows (a big leather bag.) Wolf yelled when Anton pulled up the shade on a window and opened it to air the room. "Shut that damn window. Pull the shade. Gotta be dark to see metal." Anton did, as he was told. "Never do that again! See, metal is yellow-orange color, now soft enough to shape," Wolf said.

Learning to hammer metal on the anvil was the trickiest part of the process, and Anton needed practice to develop expertise. Wolf was not patient, and his angry voice increased in volume when Anton asked too many questions. By watching Wolf and keeping questions at a minimum, Anton became proficient in making horseshoes and other iron implements too. With Wolf's help, Anton made a frying pan for his bride.

"My, that food smells good," Anton said as he came into the apartment.

"What are you hiding behind your back?" Louiza asked.

"I've made something special for you." Anton handed Louiza the iron skillet.

"I love it." Louiza said as she ran her fingers down the smooth surface of the skillet. "It's a fine pan. After you wash up, we'll have dinner."

"I see you have shoes on. Where have you been?"

"I went to Novaks for a few minutes to find out if anyone had heard from Alicia. No one has, she's disappeared. I went shopping for groceries too. You sound suspicious."

"I just asked a simple question."

Anton filled the bathroom basin with water and lathered with soap, washing off the sweat from working in the over-heated shop. The young couple talked over dinner, made love and fell asleep in each other's arms. The next evening when Anton came home, Louiza made sure she was wearing slippers instead of shoes. She pointed at the old clock her Father had sent hanging on the wall above the kitchen table.

"That's a good place for it. We can always tell the time. I'm hungry."

"Dinner will be ready in just a few minutes."

While eating ice cream, Louiza gazed at the clock, the memento of her childhood. "Anton, I'm going to paste this poem I found in a magazine on the back of the clock. The author is unknown."

"I would like to hear it." Anton said.

Louiza read the poem.

"The clock of life is wound but once
But who has the power
To tell when the hands will stop
On what day or what hour

Now is the only time you have
So live it with a will
Don't wait for tomorrow
The hands may then be still."

Life was sweet, except for the mornings when Louiza felt nauseated. She told Anton, "I think I'm pregnant. We are blessed!"

Eight months went by and Baby Ivan emerged from his comfortable womb in a healthy condition, causing much celebration. Anton was thrilled to have a son, smiling ear to ear and as he swaggered down the street with a fistful of cigars, handing them to neighbors and pedestrians while announcing Ivan's birth.

Halley's Comet was in the sky when Ivan was born, and caused great excitement and concern. The newspapers were full of forebodings and people were buying gas masks to protect themselves from the comet's gas. "Rumors that the comet spreads poisonous gas in the air, is hogwash," Anton said.

"I think the comet has brought us good luck," Louiza said as she put her arms around Anton. Ivan was starting to whimper in his crib.

"Ivan sure has a big appetite." Anton remarked.

Louiza recovered quickly from the trauma of birthing and enjoyed nursing and holding her beautiful baby. Anton was proud of his new family and brought home a bouquet of flowers or candy for Louiza or a toy for Ivan every month. Life was good.

FRANK

Before immigrating to the United States, Frank Koznar lived with his ailing mother, brother Pavel, and twin sisters in western Slovenia. Shoemaking was the family business and he started mending shoes when he was eight years old. After his father died he, ran the business with his brother and his cousin, but did not like being a cobbler. His mother suggested selling the business to his cousin and become a Priest. In Europe, many oldest sons entered the seminary, but he had no interest in doing this.

Frank was slight of build with a curly mop of red hair, blue eyes and a pleasing face. His older twin sisters had the same coloring and were shapely at the age of fourteen. They had great affection for men and decided to profit from their suitors. Satisfying lustful males more than paid for their clothing, food, and their ailing mother's medical bills.

"Please come in. It's so nice to see you." The twins, wearing low-cut dresses, ushered men into the parlor while the rest of the family stayed in the kitchen. Frank and Pavel often sat close to the kitchen door, keeping it ajar to hear the voices in the parlor.

"Welcome. Have you brought a gift?" One sister said.

"Yes, I hope you like the wine." A male voice said.

Depending on the gift, the next question was "Would you like me to sit on your lap? Or maybe you'd like my sister to sit on your lap."

"I brought a bag of sugar and a jar of walnuts for you," yet another male said.

"What nice gifts. Would you like to come with me to the shed?" One of the twins said.

"Ja," the male voice said.

The man and one of the twins went to the shed while the other sister stayed in the parlor with the other customer. The shed was furnished with a mattress and large sacks of grain. Frank and Pavel often hid behind the structure, peeping through a hole in one of the boards to watch the foreplay However, they never saw anything more for their sister and her customer always dropped out of view.

"We could make the hole larger." Pavel said.

"Naw, then they could see us." Frank said.

The sisters' vocation was the talk of the village.

"Your sisters are whores!" the neighborhood boys shouted.

"You take that back, or you'll be sorry," Frank yelled at them.

If the confrontation resulted in a fight, Frank always lost. He was as thin as a reed and did not have the temperament of a fighter. He was tired of being bruised and stopped defending his sisters' virtue, since they had none. Brother Pavel didn't like the shame, so he went off to America. When the twins reached the age of seventeen, they left home to ply their trade in the large cities of Europe where money was abundant. Their mother died a few months later and Frank sold the house and shoe business to his cousin. Pavel wrote that all sorts of jobs were available in America, and Frank followed his brother to the land of infinite possibilities.

Frank's first job was cutting timber in the lush forests of Virginia. He lived in a boarding house with the other lumberjacks where women did the cooking and cleaning. He was attracted to one of the servants named Rose. She was serving dinner when one of the boarders asked Frank, "Where were you born?

"Slovenia," Frank said.

All of the men had left the table before Frank finished his dinner. While Rose was clearing the table, she glanced out the window and said, "Snek pada [Snow is falling],"

Upon hearing his native language, Frank said. "You're Slovenian?"

"Ja, I know you are too," Rose said.

From that day on, they were together as often as possible and learned their villages of birth were not far from each other. "Tell me about your family," Frank said.

"My father was forty years old when he died and we were penniless. I was a good student and became a governess after graduating from high school. My earnings were barely enough to exist on, even though my mother, sister and I lived sparsely. We were so poor we never had enough food and we saw no relief from our poverty. I heard there was no limit to the money a person could make in America," Rose said.

She continued, "My sister, Hanna, came to the United States after answering an advertisement for mail-order brides. She married a Virginian and offered to sponsor me if I chose to immigrate. I was thrilled. Mother didn't want me to leave, but understood my decision. I promised to write her every week. The day I left, she ran alongside my stagecoach, crying and waving goodbye. Hanna and I send money to her and want to sponsor her. Mother has been sick and is waiting until she feels better to visit us."

Frank liked listening to Rose's lilting voice and looking at her sweet face.

"What about your family?" Rose asked.

"There isn't much to tell. My parents are dead. My brother, Pavel, used to be a lumberman here in Virginia. He's married now and lives in Pennsylvania. I have twin sisters in Europe. I've lost touch with them."

"That is a shame. Do your sisters know you are here?"

"No," Frank said.

"That's odd. I would never lose contact with any of my family." Rose said.

"That's nice. My brother and I are close. He's a great guy."

Frank talked about his job felling trees and Rose told him about being a governess and her family. Within a few months, their friendship kindled into a deeper emotion. One evening, after the workday was over, Frank led Rose to the porch swing of the boarding house. The last rays of sun were fading against a clear sky causing the air to chill. Rose started shivering.

"You look cold," Frank said as he put his arm around her.

"I like your arm around me." Rose snuggled into Frank's chest and put her head on his shoulder. "I feel warmer now."

They watched the stars brighten as the sky darkened. The only sounds heard were men talking loudly about their pinochle game in the parlor and the creaking of the swing as Frank pushed it back and forth.

"I feel content sitting next to you," Frank said.

"I do too," Rose said, lifting her lips to him, and they kissed.

"Rose, will you marry me?" Frank asked.

"Ja, there is no better man than you," Rose said.

A week later, Frank lost his job. The lumber companies were ignorant of preservation methods and completely denuded the beautiful forests of Virginia, causing vast unemployment in the lumber industry. Brother Pavel wrote that he was getting good wages mining bituminous coal in Western Pennsylvania.

The coal companies lured workers by offering transportation costs to anyone who would work for them. Out of a job and needing work, Frank contacted Pavel, who recommended Frank work for the Westland Coal Company. Pavel was employed by them. Frank asked Rose to come with him, promising they would marry when they got to Pennsylvania. They took a train to Johnstown, where his brother was waiting for them. Rose easily recognized Pavel, for he had the same curly red hair as Frank.

"Welcome, welcome," Pavel's wife, Helena, said to Rose and Frank as they entered the house. "Please sit down. Can I get you some water or beer? I bet you're hungry."

"Yes, we are. Thanks so much," Rose said as she accepted the beer.

They ate a tasty meal of boiled beef and potatoes. Rose and Helena talked to each other as though they had been friends for years. After dinner, Frank explained, "Rose and I are not married, and we want to be wed as soon as possible."

"Weddings are so much fun. I'll help you. We'll start planning tomorrow, while you guys are working. Tonight Rose can sleep on this sofa. Frank, there's a cot on the porch for you. We don't have an extra blanket, but I have a wool coat you can use," Helena said.

It was cold on the porch and Frank stayed on the thin cot for an hour trying to keep warm. He thought freezing to death was possible, so he went back in the house and slept on the throw rug next to Rose, who was sound asleep on the couch.

The marriage ceremony took place at St. Steven's Church one week later, on a beautiful sunny day, with Pavel and Helena as witnesses. Rose wore a long blue skirt with a matching jacket over a high-collared lace blouse bought in Johnstown. On her head, she wore a hat of gathered netting with a long veil borrowed from Helena. Frank was dressed in Pavel's three-piece vested suit.

At the end of the ceremony Rose and Frank kissed, and introduced to the small audience as Mr. and Mrs. Kosnar by the Priest. The modest reception was held in the church basement. A dozen new friends toasted the newlyweds, ate ham, sauerkraut, and potatoes and danced to a lone accordionist. The party ended at midnight and the newlweds slept in Helen and Pavel's bedroom for the first night of their marriage. They had obeyed church edict by resisting intimacy before their union was sanctified by the church. It was a relief to express their love physically as man and wife.

Three important events happened the first year of their marriage. Rose became pregnant, and Frank learned to be a coal miner. The mining company provided housing to their employees at a low cost. The newlyweds were crowded in a four-room house with three families. The house had ill-fitting windows, a roof that leaked, and a musty odor. Most of the miners' earnings were paid in scrip, the remainder in valuable dollars. The scrip was only good at the Westland Company store, which kept the miners from doing business outside the company-owned town.

Frank was determined to live in a decent house and found an acre lot for sale on a hill overlooking the town, located just outside of Lodun's boundaries, an area not controlled by the coal company.

He was excited about the lot. "Rose, I never told you this, but I saved some money from my days as a lumberjack. I bought a plot of land overlooking the valley and traded some of my scrip for dollars to buy lumber. The lot is sloped and has a little brook that trickles through it. We need to sketch out a house plan."

"Oh Frank, I never thought we would have our own home. How wonderful! This house is awful. There soon will be three of us and we need more space."

In the short time Frank lived in Lodun, he made many friends. He told them if they would help him build his house, he would help them build theirs. Frank, Pavel, and several friends worked on the house in the evenings, and on days when the mines closed. The Kosnars wanted to occupy it before their first child was born. Rose walked to the site daily, watching the house take shape even though earlier in her pregnancy, she didn't feel like it. She was nauseated in the morning during the first months and very sensitive to odors. There were many offensive smells in the mining house.

The couple moved in it during the eighth month of her pregnancy. Rose said to Frank, "Pinch me. I must be dreaming. We have our own house."

The first floor of the house was, nestled against the hill and contained the kitchen, dining room, and a storage room with an underground water spring, ideal for keeping food cold. The second level looked on to the backyard and had three bedrooms. There was also a small parlor with a door that led to the yard. There was enough land for a barn, a smokehouse, a garden, two cows, some pigs, and a few chickens. Frank and Rose were thrilled to have such a place to live in.

BIRTHINGS

Not wanting to pay any more rent for a leaky, moldy, company house, Helena and Pavel bought a small home from a widow moving to Cleveland.

"Why haven't you had children?" Rose asked while helping Helena put pots, pans, and dishes into her kitchen cupboards.

"I don't know. It seems my role in life is to help other people with their children. My mother was a midwife and taught me to be one. When I was just a child and a birth was pending, my mother took me along to watch and trained me.

"I'm glad you'll be with me when I have my baby," Rose said.

"The emergence of new life is a wonder," Helena said.

She withheld the fact that, on occasion, either the baby or the mother died or both died. "Dr. Malvec relies on me to help deliver babies. He says he has enough to do tending the sick and injured. He thinks caring for pregnant women and delivering babies is a woman's job. I call on him when there are complications."

In the middle of her ninth month of pregnancy, Rose's water broke and she started continual contractions, signaling impending birth. As promised, Helena came and comforted Rose by rubbing her back and assuring her all was progressing well during her hours of labor. "You're doing fine. Relax. If you stiffen your muscles, you make the pain worse by fighting nature. Breathe deeply and try to relax when you feel the contractions coming. "

Rose began to sweat and groan during the contractions until they came one on top of the other, with no distinction between them.

"Push, push, push," Helena encouraged her as the baby's head crowned and was in the perfect position for birth. With a kitchen knife,

Helena made a small incision to ease the tearing of Rose's expanding vaginal canal. After a huge contraction engulfed her body, the baby came out easily. After snipping the umbilical cord, Helena slapped the tiny bottom, delighting in the baby's lusty cry. Cleaned and swaddled, she gave the baby boy to his exhausted, but happy mother. Rose cooed, "Little one, you are sweet."

Frank was waiting by the doorway and when he heard the baby cry, he came into the bedroom with a wide grin on his face. What could be better than having a son! He kissed Rose on the cheek, taking a long look at his firstborn in her arms. They counted their son's fingers and toes and named him Josip as they looked upon him with adoration.

"I have a perfect son," Frank said proudly to Pavel who was waiting in the parlor. He gave Pavel a cigar, and they smoked the stogies on the porch, shouting the good news to the valley and hills and each passerby.

After napping on and off for a day, Rose awoke and noticed Helena dozing in the rocking chair with Josip sleeping in his cradle. Helena stirred when baby Josip started crying. "Put him to your breast. His suckling will make your milk come in faster."

"You didn't tell me having a baby would be painful," Rose said.

"Your baby's birth was as smooth as any birth could be. Almost every mother goes through the same discomfort with the first child. The next births will be easier. You have a beautiful baby," Helena said.

Rose wrote her mother every week, telling her about Josip, and asking her to come to Pennsylvania. Arguments with her sister ended when their mother wrote she would live part of the year with each daughter, but not until she felt better. The hope of seeing mother ended when a letter outlined in black came, announcing her death. Rose wept for a week, comforted by cuddling her baby. "I wish your grandmother could have seen you before she saw God."

The best time of the day was after the evening meal, when Rose and Frank cleaned the dishes while talking and singing. Rose had a high soprano voice with perfect pitch, and Frank had difficulty keeping his low voice in tune. They shared whatever came to their minds, and kissed often. After the dishes were put away, they sat on the veranda with Josip nestled between them, watching the sunset, the beauty of the echoing hills, and the stars making their debut. When darkness fell, they went inside, lit the gas lamps, put Josip to bed, made love and went to sleep. The peaceful evenings did not last long.

Josip was starting to walk when Beth was born, Eddi was born two years later and Katja was born a year after that. There was no problem with the birth of Eddi, but Katja's was difficult. Rose's labor was longer than usual and Helena became alarmed seeing the baby's head and body facing toward the spine. This was a complication only Dr. Malvec knew how to correct. "Hurry, Josip, run as fast as you can. This is an emergency."

"Something is wrong. You've never sent for Dr. Malvec before." Rose said.

"Don't worry. He just needs to turn the baby so it can be born properly." Helena said. About twenty minutes later, Dr. Malvec came into the bedroom. Helena said, "I'm so glad you're here. The baby is breach. I gave whiskey to Rose."

"Good. Give her more. Hi Rose, you may feel uncomfortable for a minute or two." Dr. Malvec checked the position of the baby and took out the steel forceps from his black bag.

"Helena, hold Rose's arms," Dr. Malvec said.

As the baby was turned, the grip of the forceps on the baby's head slipped. The seriousness of the accident revealed, only after baby Katja fully emerged from the womb. The slash ran from the right lower eyelid to the corner of the lip. Dr. Malvec paled when he saw the deep cut. He swabbed and taped the wound.

"How awful," Helena exclaimed too loudly for Rose not to hear. Helena cleaned and swaddled the crying baby and then placed her in Rose's arms. Rose started to weep when she saw her baby's bandaged face.

Dr. Malvec said, "I can't do anything more for the baby. I'll get the Priest."

The Priest gave extreme unction to baby Katja, expecting her to die, but she didn't. She became stronger as the days passed. Rose kept the wound clean and taped and prayed for the gash to heal. She cradled and rocked her injured baby, giving her as much time as needed to suckle, keeping her stomach full of milk. A sling, made from an old blanket kept Katja next to Rose's heart at all times, except when she slept in a cradle at night. Whenever Katja cried, Rose cuddled her, calmed her, and prayed.

Frank worked long days at the mine, but he was never too tired to hold his newborn in his arms and tell her he loved her. Each day, Katja improved and as her jagged cut healed, it became a rough scar.

When Katja was old enough to talk, she often put her finger on her face and said, "Scaw." She couldn't pronounce scar yet.

Rose explained the jagged blemish the best she could, "When the stork delivered you, the bird accidentally dropped you on the stone steps at our front door, causing the cut. Think of it as a beauty mark." She didn't want shy Katja to be embarrassed about her face.

Rose was very fertile and became pregnant after she finished nursing Katja. The boy was born three months premature and died after living only an hour. The last sacrament was given and the tiny fetus was buried the next day. Rose and Frank grieved briefly, believing and that the baby was content in heaven.

The fall season occupied with preparation for winter, gave scant time for the children to play. However, Rose gave permission for Beth and Josip to play with the neighborhood kids between chores. They played hopscotch, jacks, kick the can, or jumped over ropes in the barn. Beth jumped higher than anyone, as high as six feet or more.

Josip loved teasing Beth, "You're not a girl; you're a boy."

Beth tattled on him, and in his defense, he said, "She hit me."

"Haven't I told you not to tease your sister? Beth you shouldn't hit anyone. I'm tired of your fighting." Their punishment was to not let them play for several days.

One afternoon while helping Rose hang clothes, Beth said. "Mama, I can jump higher than Josip or any of the other kids."

Rose said, "I know darling," and reached for another pair of wet pants to hang.

Beth yelled from the opposite end of the yard, "Look, Mom, look."

Beth took off at great speed toward the fence. As she lifted her right leg to clear the top, she landed on top of a pointed slat that broke the delicate membrane of her hymen, causing blood to stain on her bloomers.

"Beth, now look what you've done, sometimes you are so foolish,"

Rose said as she helped lift Beth off the top of the fence. Beth was crying and Rose said, "You're lucky the slat didn't pierce your stomach or your leg."

Josip had observed the accident from the barn and yelled to his sister. "You're a big show-off. You deserved what you got!"

"Go away," Beth told her brother. She put her arms around her mother and said. "Now I can't prove I'm a virgin to my husband."

"Don't worry about that honey, that's a long way off." Rose said.

Beth found a way to get even with Josip for his taunting. She was alone with Josip in the kitchen when, she pulled the chair out from under him as he was about to sit in it. He hit the floor hard and groaned "Okay, okay. You got even."

"That'll teach you. Hah!"

It would be fun to play the same chair trick on her mother too. Beth was helping her mother peal beets for pickling. Her mother got up from the kitchen chair to check the supply of canning jars. When she was about to sit down again, Beth took away the chair.

Rose landed with a thud. She uttered, "Hudic [Devil]," a word she rarely used.

Beth had made a terrible mistake and regretted the prank. "I'm so sorry, Mama," she said while helping her mother get up from the floor. "Why don't you lie down? I will make dinner."

Rose slowly climbed the stairs while rubbing her bruised hip and hanging onto the banister. She reached her bedroom, fell into bed and closed her eyes.

After the dinner dishes were cleaned and put back in the cupboard, Beth went upstairs to her mother." Oh, mother, I really am sorry. I shouldn't have played that trick on you."

Rose did not reproach her daughter, instead she said, "I know you are sorry and I forgive you."

Frank was not so forgiving of his daughter's harmful joke and swatted Beth's behind. He was a gentle man and the switching was light, causing no harm. Beth rarely saw her father angry, deeply regretting that she had upset him and her mother. She vowed never again to hurt her parents in any way.

THE UNEXPECTED

Rose could not read English, so Frank translated the disturbing front-page article. "The Archduke Francis Ferdinand, heir to the throne of Austria-Hungary, and his wife Sophie were assassinated in Sarajevo on Sunday, June 28. Gavillo Princip, a member of a secret society called The Black Hand, shot him and his pregnant wife as they rode in a touring car.

Austria was outraged, and declared war on Serbia after negotiations with that country failed. The Allied Powers (France, Russia and England) defended Serbia against the Central Powers (Austria-Hungary, the Ottoman Empire and Germany.) Global hostilities exploded and World War 1 began

The United States was sympathetic to the Allied powers and when a German submarine sank a British passenger ship (the Lusitania) off the coast of Ireland, killing fifteen hundred passengers, the angry United States government slid toward official involvement in the war.

Another incident that enraged the United States was the interception of the Zimmermann telegram, sent from Berlin to the Mexican government. Germany asked Mexico to become an ally in a war against the United States. In return, Mexico would reclaim Texas, New Mexico and Arizona. It was then, that President Woodrow Wilson called on Congress to declare war on Germany on April 6, 1917. U.S. troops were sent to join the Allied Powers in fighting against the Central Powers.

Lodun's immigrants had difficulty staying neutral, feeling anguish for their conscripted relatives and friends fighting and dying in Europe in the "war to end all wars." The hostility between Austria and the United States upset Frank, for he loved his new country. He had learned to speak, read, and write English and decided to show his loyalty by becoming a naturalized American citizen. He went to class in the evenings to study the United States' Constitution. He passed the citizenship exam, and took the oath of allegiance to America, which gave him the power to vote.

The fighting American doughboys needed armor. Since coal made the steel for the weapons, the demand for it increased. The coalmines stayed open every day of the week, except Sundays, making Frank and Pavel happy with their increased paychecks.

Frank's working day was not over when he came home from the coalmines. He prepared his own sausages from the pigs he butchered by stuffing the entrails with a mixture of spices and ground pork. He made three different types of sausages: blood sausage (Krvava), rice sausage (Rizeva), and smoked sausage (Krainske Klabase). He also made Zelodec by filling a pig's stomach with spiced ground meat and flattening it between two boards. He hung everything in the smokehouse to age with the brine-soaked ham. The cows, Bessie and Lizzie, avoided slaughter by providing milk, cream, and butter for the family.

Frank also made tasty sauerkraut out of the garden cabbage. With the help of Josip, he washed, and sliced the cabbage from the garden and threw it into a large wooden barrel. Frank jumped on the cabbage with clean, sock-clad feet and instructed Josip, "Now, Son, add some salt and then a handful of caraway seeds."

When Frank's legs became tired, he asked Josip to change places with him. "Make sure your feet are clean and got on clean socks." Josip was energetic, and liked pummeling the cabbage. When the cabbage was ready, it was put in a barrel with rocks on the lid to make sure it was sealed tightly. "Guess we're going to have sauerkraut by Thanksgiving." Frank said.

Besides cabbage, the large garden produced lettuce, carrots, tomatoes, green beans, and beets. Fresh lettuce was eaten all summer and Rose, with the help of her daughters, picked the rest of the vegetables and canned them for winter meals. Bedding was washed and dried in the summer sun. Once the weather cooled, the women sewed dresses, skirts, and blouses from cloth and bloomers, underpants, and slips from empty flour sacks.

Thanksgiving Day arrived and a light snow covered the ground. Late in the day, Rose placed a stuffed, roasted turkey in the middle of the dining table along with gravy and mashed potatoes. The aroma of the food drew the family to the table.

"Hold on everybody until we say a prayer." Frank started. "God, our Heavenly Father, this Thanksgiving Day we are gathered together to humbly thank thee for the food we are about to partake. We thank you for sustaining us in health and remain in your grace and good will. Amen."

The weeks flew by and Christmas Day arrived, celebrated with special foods such as potica, nuts in the shell, and crated oranges Frank ordered from Florida. The fragrance of figs and chestnuts roasting in the fireplace filled the house. Paper ornaments made by the children hung on the Christmas tree with a small candle on every bough.

Frank warned, "Watch the candles. Never leave them burning when no one is around. We don't want the tree to catch on fire and the house along with it." Beth and Josip make sure the little ones understood. "Don't leave the parlor when the candles are lit."

On Christmas Eve, a plate placed by the hearth contained a piece of coal, a pencil box, and an orange for Santa. Early the next morning, the children scrambled down the stairs and were happy to find the plate empty and a gift for each of them under the tree. "Santa came! Santa came!" they shouted.

After opening the presents, Frank and the children attended Christmas Mass. In the afternoon, Helena, Pavel, and friends stopped by. Rose was exhausted from preparing for the holiday and spent the day in bed. Her legs swelled from being on her feet for hours, working in the kitchen, and being pregnant again. Sometimes, an enlarged blood vessel in her leg would burst, and blood would pool into her shoes and spatter on the cupboard. She tried to stop the oozing by sitting on the floor, pressing her hands on the veins and taping them.

"Rose, you have got to get those stockings in Jamestown," Frank said.

"I don't want to spend the money," Rose said.

"It will be worth it, you'll see," Frank said.

Rose relented, for her veins were getting worse. Dr. Malvec advised her to wear thick rubber stockings that reached over her knees to the middle of her thighs. They cost twenty-five dollars a pair. Rose complained, "I could buy two-hundred-fifty loaves of bread with that money."

"Do the stockings help?" Frank asked.

"Ja, they do," Rose said as she kissed Frank.

Another child, a beautiful baby girl named Christina, was born to the Koznars. While Rose was recovering and busy caring for Christina, Josip babysat his siblings. He complained to Frank, "I can't wait for Beth to be old enough to take over this job."

"I know yard work suites you better, but your Mom needs you to watch your brother and sisters," Frank said as he put his hand to his heart. He was beginning to have chest pains.

The Lodun population celebrated when World War I ended. However, peace also had its cost. The need for coal diminished, causing the mines to close many days each month. The tactic was done to keep the supply of coal equal to demand and the price per ton from dropping. Besides the mines closing off and on, Frank's ill health kept him home many days too. Money was in short supply.

"We need to rent one of our rooms," Rose told Frank.

"It'll be too much work for you," Frank said.

"Beth is old enough to help now, " Rose said.

It didn't take long to rent the room. Beth called the new boarders Joe and Moe, because their real names were unpronounceable. They looked so much alike they could be brothers or cousins. The pair said they came through Ellis Island a few days earlier and communicated in German. Beth had the job of cleaning their room and emptying their spittoons and chamber pots. It was worse than cleaning the children's rooms, worse than washing out Christina's diapers. Beth protested. "Mom, I hate cleaning Joe and Moe's slop."

"I know, I know, but someone has to do it. Just hold your nose when you dump the waste. We need the rent money."

"All I do is work, work, and work," Beth said.

"I understand. Soon Christina will be out of diapers and your workload will be easier," Rose put on the expensive rubber stockings daily and she was pregnant again. It was difficult to get enough rest because there was always cooking, washing, and scrubbing to do. She carried the baby to full term and the birth went smoothly. The family welcomed baby Jenny.

Beth was overwhelmed taking care of boarders, helping her siblings, and going to school. There was no time to study and she was not getting good grades. One Wednesday morning, Beth had a sore throat and stomachache, a good reason to stay home from school. As usual, Joe, Moe and her father left early for the mines, and Josip, Eddi, and Katja went to school. Only she, baby Jenny and Christina were home with Rose. After lying in bed most of the day, Beth thought some milk would ease her upset stomach, so she went downstairs to the kitchen. Jenny was sleeping in her bassinet, Christina was napping on her blanket on the floor and her mother was on her knees washing the kitchen chairs.

"Mom, why don't you rest for an hour? You look so tired," Beth said.

"No, I can't, my sweet child. These chairs need scrubbing," Rose said.

Beth drank a glass of milk and went back to bed. She adored movie stars and often dreamed about movie heartthrob Rudolf Valentino, or imagined herself as a cowgirl, a princess, or throwing pies at Charlie Chaplin. Lodun did not have a silent movie theater, so going to the movies in Johnstown was a big treat. Beth begged her mother to buy a movie ticket every time they went to the large city. Money was scarce and to Rose, going to the movies was a frivolous expense. An expense Rose gladly tolerated to reward Beth for all the work she did.

Late in the day, Beth awoke feeling much better and went downstairs to help her mother. As she approached the kitchen, she saw her mother lift a large kettle of boiling water from the stove. It seemed water was always boiling for either cooking or washing. A pair of her father's bibbed overalls lay halfway out of the washtub and a dozen pealed potatoes lay on the table next to the tub. Christina was playing with a kitten near the table.

The kettle full of steaming water was very heavy, and her mother struggled to move it to the kitchen table, not realizing the kitten was directly beneath her. She might have been steadier in shoes, but her swollen feet were more comfortable in slippers. She moved slowly, her shoulders bent forward from carrying such a heavy load.

The water in the kettle was bubbling, and steam was rising up in front of Rose's eyes. She was moving toward the kitchen table not noticing that Christina and the kitten were directly below her. She lost her balance as her right foot stepped on the cat, and the heavy pot tilted, spilling the boiling water all over her hip and leg. Rose screamed as the boiling water scalded her skin and splashed over Christina and the cat. Rose couldn't hold on to the kettle.

"Mama, kitty," Christina cried just before the iron kettle hit her head.

Beth lunged forward when her mother started to fall and could not get to her fast enough. The distance from the living room door to her mother was only a few feet, but it seemed like miles. Rose, Christina, and the kitten were lying in a heap on the floor. Her mother's face contorted in pain as she grabbed Christina and embraced her. Beth sat on the floor with her arms wrapped around her mother and little sister. They swayed back and forth, moaning. After a few minutes, Beth looked at Christina's burnt face, realizing the toddler was not breathing or moving. She shook Christina and her head swung unnaturally to one side. Her neck was broken.

Rose cried out, "Oh, no! Oh, no!" sending shivers through Beth's body, the cry reverberating in her head. The three of them sat on the floor, locked in a tight embrace. Rose and Beth sobbed, holding the dead Christina between them. The dead kitten lay nearby.

Looking through her tears, Beth saw Katja and Eddi standing next to Josip who was staring at them with a puzzled look. He said, "What's going on?"

Rose did not respond. Beth said, "Christina is dead." Katja and Eddi started to cry, so Josip pushed them gently outside the door and picked up baby Jenny. "I'm taking them to Helena's house. I'm getting Dr.Malvec."

Frank, Joe, and Moe returned from their day at the mines and came in the house followed by Dr. Malvec. It took them a minute or two, to realize something was very wrong. The sobs had quieted. Frank put his arm around wife and daughter, trying to comfort them. They sat on the floor with their arms wrapped around each other, with Christina in the center. Frank let go of Beth and put his hand to his chest.

Dr. Malvec brought out a bottle of whiskey from his black bag and made Rose take a big swig, hoping it would calm her. Frank gently pulled Christina from Rose's arms, kissed his beautiful baby girl, wrapped her in a blanket, and laid her on the kitchen table. He pulled Beth up from the floor and held her for a long time. Dr Malvec examined the severe burns on Rose's hip and leg, saying she had to go to the hospital in Johnstown.

Beth tried to comfort her distraught mother while waiting for Dr. Malvec's wagon. After helping her mother into the horse-drawn wagon and wrapping her in blankets, Beth sat with Rose's head in her lap and stroked her thick hair until they reached the hospital. Frank signed the necessary papers for Rose's hospital admittance, and he and Beth waited while Rose's burns were treated. A doctor approached them after they had waited about an hour.

"Are you Mr. Koznar?"

"Yes."

"Your wife has been seriously injured, but she will survive. The burns will heal.

"I understand," Frank said.

"Did you know your wife is two months pregnant?"

"No."

"We will be keeping her here for a few weeks," the doctor said.

Frank and Beth sat by Rose's bed, watching her restlessness in her half-conscious state, until a nurse shooed them out of the room. Exhausted from their trauma, father and daughter started their journey home. The creaky wagon and the snorts from the horses masked the soft sound of Beth's weeping.

They were halfway home when Frank asked, "How did the accident happen?"

Beth sadly related the incident and said in a low voice, "Instead of napping, I should've been helping Mama."

Her father held the leather straps guiding the horses with one hand, holding Beth's hand in the other and said, "It's nobody's fault. It was an accident."

Beth was relieved her father did not blame her for her sister's death.

"You will have to do the cooking from now on. .Your Mama will need to rest when she comes home."

"Oh, yes, Papa. I'll do the best I can," Beth said.

AFTERMATH

The undertaker took Christina's body away and Josip buried the cat in the backyard. He went to Pavel's house where Eddi and Katja were engrossed in a tag game in the yard. Helena was rocking baby Jenny, but could not stop the increasing volume of her cry.

"Something awful has happened. Christina is dead." Josip blurted out.

Helena and Pavel were stunned. "How awful! What happened?"

"I'm not sure. I think it was an accident. When I came home, Mom and Beth were sitting on the floor holding Christina. Water was all over the floor." Josip said.

"We'll help in any way we can. First, I have to take Jenny next door. She is very hungry. My neighbor is nursing her own baby and has plenty of milk." Helena dashed out of the house with Jenny in her arms.

"How will I tell Eddi and Katja about Christina?" Josip asked Pavel.

"Don't worry about that now; you're needed at home. We'll take care of the children." Pavel said.

Josip went home to mourn the terrible loss of Christina with his sister and father. Early the next morning, after a sleepless night, Josip grabbed an ax and snuck out of the house. He walked a long way into the woods and sat against a huge pine tree. He said a prayer for Christina's transition into heaven and envisioned her smile, her giggle and her lovely blond hair. He thought about his sad, sad mother lying in the hospital with her burns.

Feeling helpless and outraged, Josip took his ax and chopped viciously at the trunk of the old pine tree, his sorrow and anger flowing from his body through the ax into the tree. After fifteen minutes of chopping ferociously, he put down the instrument of destruction, laid down next to the maimed tree, and wept. After a while, he stood up and looked at the damage he caused. "I'm sorry." He put his arms around the tree.

Christina's body lay in a small white coffin on top of the premature baby's coffin, in a graveyard full of crosses. Old Father Rupnic said a final prayer, assuring the mourners that the soul of this baptized child was in heaven. Sweet Christina was one of many children who died that winter in Lodun.

Joe and Moe watched the burial rites from a distance. Joe said, "It's time we leave. We ain't makin' no money diggin' coal."

"Where are we going?" asked Moe

"To Cleveland, where folks have dough," said Joe

"Yeah, let's get outta here," said Moe.

"I know a fast way to get to Johnstown." Joe said as he directed Moe toward Dr. Malvec's horse and buggy parked at the side of the road.

Dr. Malvec could not believe someone would be brazen enough to steal his buggy while he attended the burial of a child. It didn't take long to suspect Joe and Moe when they never returned to the Koznar house. A friend recognized the horse and buggy sitting beside the train station in Johnstown and brought them back to Lodun. Dr. Malvec was so happy, be paid the man a dollar.

Frank visited Rose in the hospital as often as possible and tried to soothe her guilty conscience. "Christina is safe in heaven with her baby brother. You must get well for the sake of our other children and me too." Frank searched his wife's face for a response. None came.

"Don't worry about Jenny; Helena is taking good care of her. The children send you love and kisses, hoping you'll be home soon. They go to school every day and Beth feeds them good meals. She's learned to cook the way you do. You've been a good mother, Rose."

Rose listened, nodded her head, and did not speak. She had always been quiet but never so silent, which bothered Frank. He tried to make her smile. "Joe and Moe, moved out. They stole Dr. Malvec's buggy and left it at the train station in Johnstown." Rose just stared with glazed eyes and did not respond.

While Rose was in the hospital, Frank and Josip helped Beth clean up after dinner. One night when drying dishes, Frank began to sing a popular song. There hadn't been any singing in the house since the awful accident. Beth joined him, lifting her father's flat notes into a recognizable tune.

"Some fellows look and find the sunshine. I always look and find the rain. And, some fellows make a winning sometime, and I never even make a gain. I'm always chasing rainbows, waiting to find the little bluebird in vain."

Rose's burns had healed enough for the hospital to dismiss her. Two weeks after the accident, Frank brought Rose home to a family grateful to have their mother back. Everyone tried to be cheerful, but the grief from Christina's death lingered in the house. Helena visited almost every day to check the progress of Rose's burns forming wide scars on her arm, hip and ankle. Rose's sorrow caused her to stare blankly for long periods, as if she were in another world. Helena kept telling her, "Christina's death was an accident. You tripped. Don't blame yourself."

"I'm being punished. My body aches and my teeth are loose," Rose said.

"You have rheumatism. Cutting your hair will lessen your headaches. Having your teeth out will get rid of a lot of your aching." Helena advised.

After Helena went home, Rose asked Beth, "Do you think I should cut my hair?"

"It could make your headaches go away," Beth said.

"You can cut it right now. Get the scissors." Rose said. Beth saved the shorn locks in an envelope. Her mother's hair was short, but still lovely.

Dr. Malvec examined Rose's mouth, "You have bleeding, swollen gums and your teeth are mobile, a sure sign of Pyorrhea. You'll feel better after I pull all your teeth out."

They agreed to do the procedure when Josip and Beth were home from school so they could assist. On the appointed day, when Dr. Malvec came into the house, he asked Rose, "I heard a beautiful voice when I was on your door step. Was that you?"

"Ja, it was me," Rose admitted.

"You have a lovely, pure sound and can develop your talent by having voice lessons. And, I'll pay for the lessons," Dr. Mavec offered.

"No, no. I can't do that," Rose said.

Dr. Malvec did not pursue the matter further and began his dental procedure. He spread his steel instruments, including a small syringe with a needle, a tiny mirror on a long handle, a small chisel, and pliers, on the towels. The children stared at the fearsome arsenal, frightening them.

"Beth, take the children into the yard and play a game with them," Rose said.

All the children went outside, except for Josip. He watched Dr. Malvec inject the newest painkiller, Novocain, repeatedly into Rose's gums. "I can't feel my mouth." She said after a few minutes. Josip held his mother's head while she leaned back with her mouth open so Dr. Malvec could see her teeth with the aid of an overhead lamp.

The doctor poked Rose's gums with a probe, and she felt nothing so he pulled out the loose teeth before the numbness went away. Josip held a pan under Rose's chin to catch the exuding blood and the extracted teeth. When the operation was over, Dr. Malvec had Rose bite on rolled cotton to stop the bleeding. He rinsed the instruments in water, wrapped them in a towel, and put them back in his little black satchel. He thanked Josip for helping him and handed him a dime.

"I'll be back in a couple of weeks. The swelling in your gums has to abate before I can take impressions for your dentures."

Rose nodded, unable to talk. Her mouth was so sore she drank milk and sipped soup for sustenance. When Dr. Malvec returned, he took the impressions and offered a reduced fee, if Rose would sing for him at the next appointment. Wanting to save money, Rose gladly sang for him with her new false teeth in place. The dentures were more comfortable than her old aching teeth, but they loosened after a few months due to her shrinking gums. Dr. Malvec took new impressions and did not charge for the better-fitting dentures, in exchange for Rose's singing.

Rose's body aches subsided and used to her dentures, when she gave birth to a healthy baby girl. She resembled Christina, making the family feel the toddler was reborn and they named the baby Christy.

BROTHERS

Frank and Pavel mined bituminous coal, compressed organic matter from eons-old swamps, abundant in western Pennsylvania. This type of coal burned easily and created more soot than the harder anthracite coal that required deep-shaft mining. Bituminous coal was useful in homes, in steel mills and power plants, so it was always in need.

Bituminous coal was harvested by strip-mining the layers that lay on the surface of the earth, and by drift mining. Drift mines were tunnels dug into the earth to mine the deeper-lying coal deposits. The tunnels lacked safety standards and were dangerous due to avalanches, cave-ins, and methane gas.

In 1902, the anthracite coal miners asked for an increase in their hourly pay, and a decrease in working hours. The coal companies ignored the requests, so the miners formed the United Mine Workers Union. The owners of the companies stood firm in denying the demands of the union, causing the miners to go on strike. Violent confrontations occurred.

In the famous strike of 1902, President Theodore Roosevelt sent the National Guard to stop the violence between the strikers and the mine companies. The President feared that if the strike continued, there would not be enough fuel to keep the nation's houses warm in the approaching winter. He was able to negotiate a settlement, and the miners got a ten-cents-per-hour raise and a reduction in working hours to eight a day. However, the settlement did not affect the bituminous coal miners. Frank discussed the situation with Pavel.

"We ought to join the union to get the same pay as the anthracite miners," Frank said.

"I don't wanna pay dues. I'm doin' just fine," Pavel said.

"That's because you got a wife bringing in a paycheck and no kids," Frank said

"Ja, but I think joinin' the union would be a mistake," Pavel said.

"Why can't you understand that the coal companies are making a fortune. Their only interest is how much money they can make off our backs. They're not going to give us anything unless we fight for it. The union demands we get paid for laying track, shoring up shafts, and pumping water out of the tunnels, besides the coal we dig out," Frank said.

"The owners will never agree to that," Pavel said.

"It's not too much to ask. My knees ache from standing in water, my back hurts from stooping and I cough from breathing coal dust all day." Frank said

"Lots of miners have that trouble." Pavel said.

Just as Pavel said, the coal companies resisted the miner's demands and threatened the union members with layoffs. The striking miners were fired, and then evicted from the company-owned houses. The United Mine Workers Union provided tents and food for the strikers and their families, straining their treasury.

To replace their workforce, the mining companies began luring new immigrants by offering incentives such as paying moving costs and offering cheap housing. The strike organizers were hampered by only communicating in English. The language barrier made it difficult for new miners to understand the union's purpose. After a year of legal battles, the coal companies won, with no gains for the impoverished miners. Frank and Pavel never did join the union and were able to keep their jobs.

After another long day of digging out coal, the brothers walked home together, said goodbye at the crossroads, and went their separate ways. Frank's face and clothes were covered with coal dust, as he panted heavily while walking up the hill to his house. Frank picked up his pace and his blue eyes lit up his weary face when he saw his lively daughter waiting for him. Beth was jumping up and down.

"It's cold. Why aren't you wearing shoes?" Frank asked.

"I have to air out my feet," Beth said, as she wrapped her arms around her father.

Beth told a white lie. Taking her shoes off and walking barefoot made them last longer. She stuffed paper in the bottom of the shoes when worn spots appeared on the soles. And when her feet outgrew her shoes she wore Josip's old ones. Shoes were passed from one sibling to another. Beth did all she could to save money. She went to the train station and picked up the small coal lumps left on the ground after the railroad cars were loaded. The soft coal burning in the hearth kept the house warm and put a layer of soot on the walls.

Every morning, except Sunday, Frank rose at dawn when the rooster crowed, got dressed in his overalls, relieved himself in the outhouse, had breakfast, then put on his jacket and gumboots. After taking a last sip of coffee, he opened the front door and said, "What a beautiful day," no matter what the weather was like.

Rose handed him his lunch pail and lamp cap and kissed him goodbye. Frank followed a path beginning at his doorsteps that led down to an intersecting lane where Pavel met him.

"How're you doin this morning?" Pavel asked his brother.

"Not so good. My chest hurts. How's Helena?"

"She helped birth two babies yesterday."

Pavel toted the heavy pick and shovel while Frank carried the dynamite. They waited at the main mine entrance with other men to find out if the tunnels would be open that day. The miners worked about two hundred twenty days a year and were always elated when the whistle was blown, signaling a working day. The miners earned six to seven dollars a day and had to buy their own equipment. Demand for coal was seasonal, highest in fall and winter, lowest in spring and summer. Closing the mines periodically limited the supply of coal, keeping the price per ton constant.

Frank and Pavel toiled side by side as a team, sharing the workload with little disagreement. They alternated placing and igniting the dynamite to loosen the coal, picking out the black lumps, and shoveling them into the tramcar. The coal company paid by the pieces, so the faster and longer they worked, the more money they made.

"We are lucky, to be assigned a new tunnel. It's supposed to have rich veins. Let's hurry and find the biggest one before the other men do," Frank said.

They walked deep into the tunnel where the layers of coal became thicker. "Let's stop here; this is fine. I see a good spot to put the dynamite," Frank said.

"What is that crackling sound?" Pavel said. He was in the middle of the tunnel looking up at a crossbeam.

Frank yelled, "It's breaking! Get out of the way!" Pavel could not move in time to avoid the heavy piece of granite.

All Frank could see, when the dust cleared, was his brother's limbs and head protruding from the gigantic stone that lay on top of him. When Frank was certain no more rocks would fall, he kneeled beside his brother and called out his name, over, and over again. There was no response. Pavel did not speak, move or breathe and Frank wept.

Nearby miners came to help upon hearing Frank's cry. With mighty heaves, they pushed away the boulder and helped Frank carry Pavel out of the mine.

The news of the accident traveled quickly, and miners gathered around the shaft entrance, removing their caps as Pavel's body emerged from the tunnel. The infamous "Black Mariah," a special wagon to transport the dead and the injured arrived, pulled by two black horses. Pavel's body was lifted into the covered wagon by the sad miners. Frank cradled his brother's head as the driver started the slow journey to Pavel's house.

Frank took his kerchief and wiped the coal dust off his brother's face, and told him he loved him and that he had been a wonderful brother. He shuddered to think of Helena's reaction to her husband's death and telling his family their favorite uncle died. The jostling of the wagon made Frank start coughing. He thought of the terrible cost the mines exacted from its excavators. While holding his brother's cold hand, he vowed he would do everything in his power to prevent his sons from working in the mines.

The news of the accident spread quickly as the Black Mariah passed by silent women and children standing by the road, hoping the wagon would not stop in front of their houses. Helena stood with several neighbors and her face froze when the horses halted in front of her. Her screams echoed through the valley as Frank carried Pavel to his doorstep.

Helena was now a widow without death benefits or a penny of savings. Most of the Lodun widows moved to larger towns such as

Cleveland, Pittsburg, or Chicago, where work was available. Helena, educated in midwifery, was able to earn a wage in the small town. After Pavel's funeral, Frank asked her, "What are you going to do now?"

"I've decided to stay here and continue working for Dr. Malvec," Helena said.

Pavel's death was a devastating blow to Frank, who prayed daily for his brother's soul and an end to his own woes. He had periodic chest pains, coughed up blood, and had a decrease in energy, causing him to miss work often. Josip took on many of his exhausted father's duties, giving him less time to spend in the woods. Rose's burns affected the use of her leg and arm, which limited her usefulness. The ailing couple relied on their children to make the household function and had less money than ever. Josip went to the mines to find work, upsetting Frank. "I don't want you going there. It's dangerous."

"I won't go in the tunnels. Breaker boys don't have to go into the tunnels. I'll just be separating the coal from clay and slate," Josip said.

"I damn well know what breaker boys do. Promise me you won't go in the mines, no matter how much money you're offered. Those are death traps. Promise me," Frank pleaded.

"I promise," Josip said.

After much thought, Rose decided it was time to discuss their dire situation. "Frank, we can't go on like this. Our health is getting worse, and we are getting poorer by the day.

Our children are overworked. Josip has quit school, and Beth misses many school days because of us. We need a plan to change our situation."

"What have we done to deserve all this?" Frank said.

"Don't think like that. Be thankful for our blessings, our lovely children. Now, the good Lord gave us brains; let's use them and think of a solution."

Rose looked tenderly at her husband, took his hand and led him to their bedroom. She put her arms around him, kissed his calloused hands and his face and neck, arousing him. They had not made love for many weeks and coupled passionately. This took all of Frank's energy, and he fell asleep.

After a few days of thought and discussion, they decided that Josip should journey to Cleveland as soon as the snow melted. Frank wrote a letter to Anton Poncek, asking if Josip could stay with him and his family while looking for work. Anton wrote back saying he would be honored to have Josip live at his house and help his dear friend.

Their plan was to sell the house and move the entire family to Cleveland, where the children could have better opportunities. Earning a living in the big city would be easier and safer than toiling in the mines.

Josip was thrilled his parents were sending him to Cleveland by himself. After all, he had just turned sixteen, old enough to leave home and didn't like being a breaker boy. The job was boring and gave him backaches. He would miss fishing and hunting in the woods. Uncle Pavel taught him how to shoot a rifle, look for wildlife trails, and set traps for animals valuable for their fur. He also liked cutting trees for firewood and built a hut out of branches. He would also miss White Dove.

White Dove belonged to a local Indian tribe. Josip met the girl while fishing in the river near her camp. For several weeks, she sat on a nearby rock at the water's edge, watching him. One day, she got off the rock and walked toward him with a knife in her hand. He was nervous when she neared him and relieved when she lowered the knife toward the fish he caught. After cutting the fish's belly open, she emptied the innards and scaled it. He thanked her and asked her name while admiring her shiny dark hair and smooth skin. They became instant friends and thereafter were together as often as possible, hunting deer, rabbits, and badgers.

The day before he was to leave for Cleveland, he and White Dove met by the great tree he had injured. The Indian girl waited for him under the tree's canopy of limbs. She had her hand on the axe marks when Josip approached her.

"You almost killed this great tree, but it will survive." White Dove said.

"How do you know it was me?" Josip said.

"I saw you chop the trunk with your axe. You were angry and sad," the girl said.

"Yes. It happened when my beautiful baby sister died." Josip said.

"I'm sorry about your sister," White Dove said.

I came to tell you I'm leaving for Cleveland tomorrow."

"I will miss you. May no harm come to you," White Dove said.

"I will miss you too. I'll be back in a few months." Josip put his arms around her, startled at the warmth going through his body.

THE PONCEK FAMILY

It was late in the afternoon on the first day of May, when Josip knocked on Anton Poncek's door. A young man about his age answered and said, "Hi, who are you?"

"I'm Josip, Frank Koznar's son."

"Oh, yeah, yeah, Ma told me you'd be staying with us for a few months. We'll have to find you a place to sleep; there's no regular bed for you."

"Don't worry. I can sleep anywhere. What's your name?" Josip asked.

"I'm Ivan, Anton's son."

Josip was standing on a large fringed carpet covering a shiny wood floor. A grand piano stood in the corner in front of lace-curtained windows. The cozy room was spotless, and Josip felt good standing in it. This was a wealthy family, at least, wealthier than his family. Josip was puzzled by a piece of furniture that had a tenor singing from it.

"That's Enrico Caruso. His voice is playing on a phonograph record on a machine called a Victrola. Ma loves opera. The family bought the Victrola for her birthday. Ma, Josip's here!" Ivan called out.

A middle-aged woman wearing a print dress covered with an apron and slippers stepped into the living room. Her lilting voice greeted Josip in Slovenian. "Dobrodosli [Welcome].

"This is my mother," Ivan said.

In unclear English, Louiza said, "How are you?"

Josip laughed and answered, "Dobro [Fine]."

Caruso's voice was hitting a high note. Louiza asked, "Do you like opera? Hmm, maybe you haven't heard opera before."

"I think so. My mother has a wonderful soprano voice and sings a lot," Josip said.

"I'd like to hear her sometime. You must be hungry. Ivan will keep you company while I finish making dinner." Louiza said.

"C'mon, let me show you around," Ivan said.

Ivan took Josip into the dining room, and showed him the small room next to the stairs, saying it was his uncle's bedroom. It had an adjacent bathroom. Josip had never seen an indoor toilet before. Ivan said the house was very old and when the family moved in, his dad modernized the kitchen, put the toilet in the closet, and added the second floor. They climbed the stairs to the second floor where there were three bedrooms; one for the three sisters, one for Ivan and his brother, and one for his parents.

"Stefan and I sleep in this bed. I'll ask Ma for extra blankets so you can sleep on the floor next to us. Now I'll show you the gazebo Pa and I built." Ivan said.

They went down stairs, through the dining room, and into the kitchen, where Louiza was putting noodles in soup and an attractive dark-haired girl was cutting cabbage.

"This is my oldest sister, Theresa, named after my grandmother."

Theresa looked up from her slicing and said, "Hi."

Josip said, "Hello."

They exited out the back door of the kitchen and into the side yard, where a newly painted gazebo gleamed in the sunlight. The two-toned green structure had a swing inside.

"Pa wanted his gazebo to be the best in the neighborhood, so it has eight sides instead of six. We drew the plans last summer and finished constructing it just before the first snow fell." Ivan said with enthusiasm.

"It has two-by-four pieces of lumber supporting each side to give it strength. The wainscoting is two-and-a-half feet from the floor, and the lattice walls let the breezes flow through in the summer. We covered the raised brick floor with six-inch tongue and groove wood, and the sheeting on the roof makes it leak-proof. The thick chains attached to the swing make it quite sturdy. See the soldier at the top of the roof?" Ivan said.

A little wooden soldier was mounted on the roof peak and painted to look like a Turkish military man. He had a black fez cap, a red jacket with yellow buttons, blue pants, and black boots that reached to the knee. For his arms, he had propellers attached from shoulder to shoulder by a steel rod. When the wind moved the propellers, the little soldier whirled around, changed directions, stood still, and then spun again.

"The neighborhood kids like watching our soldier perform. Once, someone tried to steal him. We found gouge marks around the platform and an abandoned hammer next to the soldier. The thief had difficulty loosening him without damage and gave up trying. We securely anchored him so a strong wind wouldn't blow him away." Ivan said.

"Did you ever find out who did it?" Josip asked.

"Naw, Pa thought the culprit was one of my friends." Ivan said.

"Do you think I can sleep in the gazebo when the weather gets warmer?" Josip asked

"Sure, I think it's okay," Ivan said.

They returned to the house through the kitchen. Louiza was mixing a pot of soup.

"Can I do something to help you?" Josip asked

"Ne, ne, ne. Sit down and I'll get you some wine." Louiza said.

Josip sipped the red wine slowly as he watched Theresa move about the kitchen. The back door opened, and a middle-aged man entered.

. "Anton this is Josip, Frank's son," Louiza said.

"Zdravo [Hello]. Anton said.

Anton sat down at the kitchen table and poured himself a hefty jigger of schnapps. After swallowing all of it at once, he drank a glass of beer. He said, "How is your family?"

"Mom and Dad aren't well, but the kids are fine." Josip said.

"I'm sorry to hear that about your parents." Anton said.

At 6:00 PM, the family gathered in the dining room, and Ivan introduced Josip to his Uncle Boris, and his two youngest sisters. Anton sat down at the head of the table, Ivan sat on his right, and Josip was motioned to sit next to Ivan. Theresa and Louiza placed the food in front of Anton and sat at the other end of the table. The rest of the family filled the chairs at random.

Before anyone lifted a fork, Anton's deep voice thanked the Lord for all his blessings. His speech slurred by the boilermakers he drank. At the end of the prayer, Anton took the first scoop of soup and then helped himself to the meat, potatoes and slaw. Ivan, took his share and the food was passed around the table.

It was obvious Ivan was the oldest child by the respectful way siblings spoke to him. Anton's half brother, Boris, did not resemble Anton at all. He was shy, small of stature, and stuttered. Theresa was quiet compared to the younger two sisters, who laughed and chattered constantly. Halfway through the meal, Anton admonished them and they quieted. Josip thought the whole family was handsome, except for Boris.

The children spoke fluent English while Louiza and Anton struggled with their new language. By watching the parents listen to their children converse in English, Josip suspected they understood the language better than they could speak it. The family talked about work, politics, family, and neighbors. They did not hide their feelings, laughing at the slightest provocation or showing concern when they heard bad news. Dinner was over when Anton got up from his chair. The men meandered away while the women cleared the table.

Anton and Boris played cards, and Ivan, Stefan and Josip sat in the parlor while the women chatted, sang and washed the dishes.

"I need to find work, do you know anyone that would hire me?" asked Josip.

"Let me think. Hmm. We have a friend that owns a machine shop. He always needs workers. Get a pencil and paper and I'll give you his address." Ivan said.

"Thanks a lot. I'll go there first thing in the morning." Josip said.

"Tell me about your life in Pennsylvania." Stefan wanted to talk. There was a light knock on the front door.

Ivan opened it. "Look who's here. It's cousin Fritzy."

A rotund woman with a sweaty face came into the room. and greeted the three men. "Dober vecer [Good evening]."

Louiza came into the parlor to hug and greet her cousin-twice-removed. Everybody was somebody's relative or neighbor in the small ethnic community. She said to Fritzy, "This is Anton's dear friend's son, Josip. He's going to stay with us for a while."

Fritzy hugged Josip, her body odor repulsed him, and the shrillness of her laughter hurt his ears. He retreated from her, making sure he kept his distance.

Stefan whispered in Josip's ear, "She has some kind of disease."

Josip wasn't sure what that meant, but her odor must have something to do with her illness. Ivan wanted to read his book and retreated to the second floor. After chatting with Fritzy for an hour, Louisa yawned and said, "Lahko noc [Good night]," and went to bed.

"I'll come back tomorrow. Adijo," Fritzy said as she went out the door.

"Fritzy is really nice and gives us things she knits." Stefan said.

"Yeah, but I have to stand away from her. I have a sensitive nose." Josip said.

Stefan yawned, and said, "You'll get used to her. See ya upstairs."

Josip's attempt to sleep on the floor of the brothers' bedroom was futile, even though he had a soft pillow and a comforter. Stefan and Ivan kept pulling the blankets off each other, making a lot of noise. After an hour of frustration, Josip snuck downstairs with his bedding and slept on the parlor sofa. He woke before anyone else in the house, gulped down a breakfast of bread and butter and went to the address of the machine shop. He was nervous while answering the owner's questions and thrilled when hired as an apprentice.

As the weeks wore on, Josip learned to become a machinist and listened to the Ponceks' arguing. Coming from a quiet family, Josip was dismayed at the argumentative behavior of the siblings, for it always seemed one of them was mad at someone or something. He got used to Fritzy, who came to the house often. Everyone liked her, for she always brought gifts she knitted herself. She gave Josip a scarf and he held his breath when he hugged her in an appreciative gesture.

Josip told Ivan about his fondness for the Pennsylvania woods. On one humid day in July, Ivan asked him, "Do you want to come with me to a forest not far from here?"

"What a great idea," Josip said.

Josip loved being in the woods again. Ivan pointed out the different trees, insects and birds. The young men, both the oldest sons of immigrant parents, developed a kinship. Both were of opposite temperaments and got along well.

Ivan's brother Stefan wanted to do whatever Ivan did or have whatever he had. Always wanting his attention, he asked him questions or teased him, backing off when Ivan showed his irritation. Stefan had a pleasing personality and was the leader of a polka band, so different from the bookworm Ivan, who didn't try to please anyone, except his mother.

Stefan often played the accordion after supper. The family listened and sang songs with him. Josip enjoyed listening to the Poncek family blend their voices in harmony. He liked watching Theresa lose some of her reserve when singing and swaying gracefully to the sound of the accordion.

Josip talked to Theresa every time he had a chance, trying to cheer her and joke with her, to elicit a smile. At first, she looked at him with suspicion, and walked away. Not deterred, he succeeded in getting her mouth to turn up at the corners and smile. Then, after a few more days of jesting, she actually laughed.

One evening, Josip asked Stefan about the sizable scar on his arm, thinking he acquired it in a fight. Stefan answered ina joking way, "Ivan liked Pa's scar so much he decided to give me one arm too."

"What did Ivan do to you?" Josip asked.

"The accident happened when Ivan started first grade. I was waiting for him for hours to return from school so we could play together. When he came home, I hid behind the kitchen door and watched him eat a piece of bread while standing in front of the stove. He was looking out the window when I jumped on his back to surprise him. He twisted me off, causing my arm to fall into a pot of water boiling on the stove. I screamed. Ma heard my cry, rushed into the kitchen, and wrapped a wet cloth around my arm."

"We lived in an apartment then. Ma carried me downstairs, and asked a neighbor to call Pa at work. Pa took me to the local doctor, who said the burn was so severe he had to cut off my arm. 'No cut! No cut!' Pa protested. He rushed me to another doctor, who also said the arm had to come off. Again, Pa said, 'No cut! No cut!' This doctor told us about a young medic who just returned from the war in Europe. He saved many doughboy's arms and legs by using silver nitrate. We went to his office and the medic said he could save my arm."

Josip's eyes watered, remembering poor Christina and the pot of boiling water that killed her, and he thought of the horrible scars on his mother's arm and leg. Relating the story of his sister was on the tip of his tongue, but he didn't trust his emotions so instead he said, "Wow, how lucky you found him."

"That's for sure. Ma blamed Ivan for my burn, and was so furious that she chased him all over the house with a switch. He wedged himself under the stairs where she couldn't get to him and waited for her to cool off. When he emerged, he explained that my burn was an accident and was sorry it happened. You know, Ivan is Ma's favorite and he wasn't punished."

"The medic came every day to treat my arm with silver nitrate. On one visit, he brought a German helmet he got in the war and let me wear it while he treated my burn. It was a funny green color and had a leather strap. I asked about the war. He said it was terrible and didn't say any more about it. My arm gradually healed, and the medic was happy with the results of his treatment. The last time he came, he invited me to visit him at his office, but I never did."

"Now you and your father both have scars on your arms," Josip said.

"Pa doesn't like to talk about his scar. All he said was that he got it from an accident when he was in the Austrian Army."

"Did you ever see the young medic again?"

Stefan cleared his throat, "Our family went to his funeral about a year later. Ma always prays for his soul."

Ivan was munching on a piece of strudel when he stepped into the parlor and heard part of Josip and Stefan's conversation. Ivan interrupted, "He was a swell doctor. It's too bad he caught that deadly flu. In 1918, the last year of World War I, a flu epidemic spread throughout Europe and the United States, affecting large numbers of people, including the soldiers fighting in the war. In fact, more doughboys died from the flu than from fighting in the war. Some believe they brought the bug to the United States when they returned from Europe. This plague spread all over the world and one million people of the twenty million that were infected, died. Did the people in your town suffer with it?"

"I remember several of the villagers with the flu being isolated from the rest of us. The disease didn't spread to anyone else." Josip said.

Ivan continued, "When the flu hit Cleveland, many people got sick with fevers and sore throats, some even died. Our young medic caught the virus while treating infected people and died. I think our family avoided catching the flu by Ma hanging garlic around our necks. She made us stink so much, the virus wouldn't get near us."

FORGIVENESS

Anton became edgy talking about politics or religion or just about anything. Boris was the one who drank with him at the kitchen table and listened to his opinions. Boris rarely disagreed, but if he did, he struggled to say his sentences. However, when provoked enough, the stuttering stopped and his words came out clearly. If the children came into the kitchen and listened to their father, they were always quiet. Only Ivan was not intimidated, speaking up when he didn't agree with his father. Whenever Louiza heard the arguing while toiling in the kitchen, she offered food to Anton, hoping it would subdue his temper.

Nothing made Anton more upset than finding Louiza with shoes on, when he came home from work. He queried her endlessly about where she had been and with whom. One late afternoon, the girls were upstairs debating about who was wearing who's clothes. Josip, Ivan and Stefan were discussing politics in the parlor, when they heard Anton yelling at Louiza. Their father's voice became louder and more threatening by the second.

"Where have you been? What have you been doing?" Anton shouted.

Louiza defended herself, "I was shopping and didn't have time to change into my slippers before you came home."

"All the time you lie! Women lie!" Anton's face reddened.

Stefan and Ivan rushed to the kitchen and saw Anton slap Louiza across the face. "This is the last time." Ivan shouted.

As Anton started to strike again, Ivan stepped in front of his mother, raised his fist and said, "No more," then punched his father in the face.

Anton fell backwards, hit the wall, and slid to the floor with a thud. He was dazed.

"Don't you ever, ever hit Ma again! If you do, I'll hit you harder!" Ivan said.

Stefan stood watching the drama when suddenly Theresa was standing next to him and she asked, "What is going on?"

"There's been a scuffle." Stefan answered.

The two youngest sisters, Boris and Josip joined Theresa and Stefan at the kitchen doorway. They all saw Louiza holding onto Ivan and sobbing. Anton was sitting on the floor looking glassy-eyed and rubbing his jaw.

"W-w-what happened?" Boris asked.

"Ivan punched Pa because he hit Ma." Sefan said.

The daughters gathered around their mother. "Ma, your nose is bleeding. Ma, here's a towel. Ma, you ought to lie down."

"Stop, fussing. I'll be fine." Louiza told them.

For years, Louiza's children were afraid of their father and wanted to stop his abuse of their mother. It was inevitable that Ivan would be the one to defend her. As Ivan became physically stronger, he became less fearful of his father. He was the one to stop the attacks, and he did.

The son Anton was so proud of had turned against him. Anton was no longer the head of the family; the scepter had passed to a new generation. His oldest son had exchanged places with him in one angry punch to the jaw. Anton caused his own downfall by his dependence on alcohol, which weakened him mentally and physically. He did not listen to those who expressed concern about his drinking. Alcohol made him feel good and kept his demons at bay. He tanked up on whiskey in the morning and sipped it from a flask while working. After supper, he liked sitting in his basement tasting wine from his oak barrels to see if it was aging properly.

Anton adored his wife and was jealous of her smile, her cheerfulness and her friends. Driven by mixed feelings and his tainted childhood, he had a desire to punish her. When neighbors and friends came to visit Louiza, she was too congenial and too generous with food and drink. Her friends always overstayed his welcome. He made them uneasy by standing in front of them and scowling as they sat in the parlor. The ploy was successful and within minutes, they left the house.

Anton sat on the floor of the kitchen watching his children fussing over Louiza. He knew he had lost their respect. When they were very young they enjoyed helping him make wine by jumping up and down in the bathtub filled with grapes. During hot days, they wore only underpants while splashing each other with squished grapes. The fruit stained their skin and permeated the tub enamel, which never regained its white color, no matter how often it was scrubbed.

When the wine was aged to Anton's satisfaction, he consumed most of it. The barrels were empty by the time the grapes ripened again and ready to fill the bathtub again. His excessive drinking made food flavorless and a glass of wine or a boilermaker became more satisfying. Anton's ardor diminished as his intake of alcohol increased. He and Louiza still kissed before extinguishing the bed lamp, but turned away from each other, shifting around to find a comfortable position, to sleep. Anton often dreamed about Louiza becoming his mother or his mother becoming Louiza. The memory of the dream was vague when he awoke, but he knew the demons had visited him once more.

Hans had retired and Anton was the only blacksmith at the gas company. There was not much to do due to the change in the company's mode of transportation, from horses to cars and trucks. Horse-drawn vehicles were becoming a rarity, thus the need for fewer iron horseshoes and repairs. Anton often left the shop early, wanting to drink with his pals at Novak's speakeasy.

The passing of the Prohibition Act by the U.S. Congress made buying liquor illegal and selling contraband booze became very profitable. Novak's had a peephole door guarded by a brawny bouncer to make sure all who entered the bar were customers, not troublemakers. Tony Novak paid the local police free liquor and a small share of his profits, for protection.

Anton and his old friend Milan, who did not go back to Slovenia, stayed in the bar many afternoons drinking bootleg whiskey. Milan and Anton enjoyed conversing about their former home.

"I don't ever want to go back to my village. My mother is dead. I don't care what has happened to my stepfather." Anton said.

"My sister is still in Leskovo and is not happy being part of the new Yugoslavia. She says it's difficult getting used to the new government," Milan said.

"So much was destroyed during the war. I hope the ancient church in the middle of Lake Bled is still standing. It's one of the most beautiful places in Slovenia." Anton said.

"Say, I got news for you. I asked my sister about that girl that was your fiancée. She never married and became a nun."

Anton stared at Milan with amazement, his heart racing. "Are you sure?"

"Ja. She's lives in the Sisters of Charity Convent in Chicago. Anton was unable to speak He closed his eyes and envisioned Agnes standing at the train station. Why did he believe Jako's lies?

A week later, Anton watched a couple of men come into Novaks and sit at the other end of the bar. He could tell they were new immigrants by the way they were dressed and the way they talked. Something seemed familiar about the smaller man. Anton wanted a closer look at him, so he moved toward the men, trying to be unnoticed. The smaller man turned in Anton's direction, enabling him to see a full view of his face. He felt the blood rush to his head as he recognized Jako.

"Jako, it's me, you lying son of a bitch," Anton yelled.

Anton lunged toward his foe as fury overtook his senses. Jako was surprised and couldn't get out of the way before Anton pushed him to the floor and tightened his hands around his neck. The bartender had seen many brawls using fists or smashed bottles but he never saw anyone choked. He jumped over the bar and with Milan's help, pulled Anton's hands off Jako's neck. Jako gasped for air, holding on to the bar with one hand and clutching his throat with other. He recovered quickly and seeing Anton's arms restrained by his friends, punched him in the jaw.

Jako ran out of the bar. Enraged, Anton broke the grips of Milan and the bartender by shoving his elbows into their shoulders. Anton followed Jako out the door and onto the sidewalk. He took a small pistol from his pocket, aimed it at Jako and shot him. Anton saw Jako fall, then ran as fast as possible to his home, hoping no one would follow him. Anton flew into the kitchen, startling Louiza who was making strudel and took the stairs, two at a time to his bedroom. After a few minutes, he came into the kitchen carrying a valise.

"What's wrong with you, you look scared. What happened?" Louiza asked.

Anton answered, "I don't have time to tell you. I'm going away for a while. I did something terrible and must leave." He hurried to the train station, where he bought a ticket for the next train to Chicago.

The news of what happened in Novak's speakeasy spread throughout the inner city community. It was the gossip of the day, but quickly faded because Jako was hardly hurt, tripping on the sidewalk as the bullet from Anton's gun grazed his leg. However, Anton was not aware of this, thinking he had killed or seriously injured Jako. Another squabble erupted at Novak's the next afternoon, resulting in an unfortunate customer being killed by a drunk. The guy he was fighting with got wounded. The Jako–Anton incident lost interest, but not in the mind of a blacksmith sitting on a train to Chicago.

When Anton reached Chicago, he asked directions to the Charity Convent, which was within walking distance of the train station. He found the Charity Chapel and entered the sanctuary, where several people were praying. He dipped his fingers in holy water, crossed himself and after kneeling to the altar, sat at the end of the last pew. An elderly man walked past him and Anton asked, "Where is the Charity Convent?"

"Next door," the old man said.

Anton stared at the old brick building and hesitated, gathering his courage to face his former sweetheart. He entered the wide oak door and entered a foyer, where a young nun sat at a desk. She looked up from her reading and said, "Hello, may I help you?"

Anton did not know what name Agnes took when she became a nun.

"I'm looking for a nun …. used to go by Agnes."

"I know all the nuns. Please describe her to me."

"She has golden hair, blue eyes, sorta short. She's about thirty-five years old," Anton said.

"Yes, I think she is here. May I have your name?"

"Anton."

Anton watched the nun glide down the hallway, her black gown flowing behind her, and disappear through a hall door. He felt the sweat gathering on his forehead and under his arms, as he practiced his apology. After what seemed like an eternity, he watched two nuns come out of the door, one having a familiar walk.

Covered from head to toe in black, except for the white band on her forehead, Agnes looked genuinely pleased at the sight of him. She had developed a few lines around her lovely face.

"Anton, I'm so happy you've come to see me."

He was unable to speak. She took his hand and led him into a small private study. He knelt before her and kissed her hand. "Please, please forgive me."

"I forgave you long ago. I was so sad after you left, not knowing what made you angry with me. Through prayer and confiding in my Priest, I found peace and took my final vows five years ago," Agnes said.

Anton got up from his knees and sat on a chair facing Agnes. He told her about the lies Jako told him at the army camp. When Anton finished his story, Agnes said, "Jako often came to visit me and I thought he had something to do with your anger toward me."

Anton explained his confrontation with Jako. "I don't know if I killed him or wounded him."

Agnes frowned. "You need to forgive Jako, and yourself, so you can live your life in peace. I know you must forgive your Mother also.

Anton was surprised. But, of course, she must have known about his mother. Gossip blew like the wind from village to village. An uneasy silence came between them.

"Did you ever marry?" Agnes asked, breaking the stillness.

Anton told her about Louiza and his children. They reminisced about their villages, their childhood, and the friends they knew. When the silence descended again, Agnes took Anton by the hand and led him into the chapel, where she knelt in front of the altar, folded her hands, and bent her head in prayer. One of the holy statues seemed to be looking at him, expecting something from him. Anton glanced at Agnes as her fingers paused on each bead of her rosary. He knelt beside her and prayed for forgiveness. His knees began to hurt, so he sat in the pew while nun Agnes continued praying.

Agnes finished her devotions and they walked outside into the moonlight. It was time to say goodbye. Anton felt lighter, almost buoyant as Agnes looked steadily into his eyes and put her hand on his shoulder, saying, "You should pay for Jako's medical treatment, or give payment to his family, if he is dead, and ask for their forgiveness. I will pray for you."

Agnes went back into the convent and Anton walked back to the train station with thoughts of Jako and his mother swirling around in his head. He settled in his seat as the train pulled away from Chicago, quite pleased with the results of his mission. Yes, he was guilty of deeply hurting Agnes, but it was God's will that terminated their relationship, using Jako to help direct Agnes into a spiritual life. He still loved her, but not in a lustful way. He had vowed before the sacred altar, that he would pay restitution to Jako and his family. His mother's face came into his mind, and he wondered if she ever asked God to forgive her. He pulled out his flask of whiskey, hoping it would last until he got home.

Anton did not know that Milan followed him out of the bar and saw him shoot Jako and leave Jako lying on the cement walkway holding his bleeding leg. Milan helped Jako to his feet, and saw the hole in his pants near his calf, where the bullet entered. When he rolled up Jako's trouser leg, he saw that the bullet had missed his calf and tore away some of his flesh. Milan wrapped a towel around his leg to stop the bleeding.

"Boy, was I lucky! I could've been killed," Jako said.

"That's for sure," Milan said.

A police officer entered the bar. Someone had called the fuzz.

"Don't squeal," Milan whispered to Jako.

The officer fired questions at Jako. "What happened? Who shot you? Why did he shoot you? Did you know the gunman? What did he look like?"

Jako answered loudly so everyone in the bar could hear him and witness his testimony. "I dunno. Maybe he wanted my watch. I didn't see him. He was behind me."

"What's your name?" the cop asked Milan. "Were you a witness to the shooting?

"No, I didn't see what happened." Milan said.

The cop asked the bartender the same question and got the same answer. He looked at all three men and said, "I'm making a report and may need you for more questioning." Then the cop got into his police car and drove away.

Milan bought Jako a beer and helped the limping man get back to his home. He needed to tell Anton that Jako was alive and only nicked his leg.

When Louiza answered the door, she said, "It's good to see you Milan. How have you been?"

"I've been fine. I need to talk to Anton. Is he around?"

"He was here an hour ago. He said he was going to Chicago and wouldn't be home for a few days. He was very upset."

Louiza went into the kitchen and came out with two glasses of beer. They sipped the brews while sitting on the velvet chairs in the parlor. Milan told her about Agnes and Anton being engaged. How Jako betrayed them, how he showed up at Novaks and about Anton shooting him.

"I didn't know any of this," Louiza said.

"When you see Anton, tell him the cops aren't looking for him and that Jako is alive with just a flesh wound."

"I never heard Anton talk about Agnes. What happened to her?"

Milan looked uncomfortable when he said, "Agnes became a nun and is in a convent in Chicago."

Louiza apologized to Milan for all the trouble Anton had caused him and thanked him for telling her about the shooting and Agnes. The house was quiet after Milan left, for everyone was either at school or at work. Louiza sat in her favorite chair, musing about her many years of marriage. She had been happy until Anton became irrational and out of control. No matter how often she tried to discuss his unreasonable behavior, he ignored her and nothing changed. In fact, his attitude toward her worsened at the years went by.

Anton monitored her daily activities, making her feel imprisoned once again. Her body was tired from many pregnancies, but her children gave her the most pleasure. She had a miscarriage, a stillborn son, and a three-month old who died of convulsions. She was thankful that her six remaining children were smart and healthy. The sunny day beckoned through the screen door and Louiza felt the freedom she had sought since she was a girl. She now could do as she pleased, without her husband's permission. She took her slippers off, put on her shoes on, and walked out the door.

Anton stopped at Novak's Tavern on the way home from the train station, hoping to find out what happened after he fled. He spied Milan sitting at the bar.

"Hello," Anton said.

"Am I glad to see you," Milan said.

"How is Jako?" Anton asked.

"He's okay. You only nicked his leg," Milan said.

"That's good news, very good news," Anton said.

Milan told Anton what happened, how Jako responded to the questioning by police, and that no one was looking for him, not even Jako. Anton bought several rounds of drinks to celebrate his good fortune. A couple of hours went by before he staggered home, drunk. Not saying a word when he saw Louiza wearing shoes, Anton hugged her, climbed the stairs and flopped into bed. The demons didn't appear during the night, and he awoke refreshed.

The neighborhood had been abuzz with the recent shootings at Novak's bar and that is how the Poncek children heard about their father's involvement in one of them. The siblings agreed that Ivan was the one to question their father about the incident. After dinner, when the last forkful of food was eaten, Ivan asked his father, "We heard that you shot someone at Novaks Tavern. Is it true?"

The children stared at their father, waiting for his response. He told them. "I lost my temper settling an old dispute. The man is fine. I only scratched him on his leg. He's getting rich from the money I send him." Anton put his open hand in front of his face, a gesture indicating no more questions would be answered.

ONE SUMMER

The gazebo was a private place to escape from the busy house, gather thoughts, and talk about problems. Ivan just had his sixteenth birthday and was in his ninth year of school when his mother said, "Come to the gazebo with me."

This was going to be a serious conversation by the tone in her voice. After a minute of pushing the swing back and forth, a teary eyed Louiza said, "I have a lot of work taking care of the family. I need a washing machine and I don't have the money to buy one."

Ivan watched her intently as she talked, noticing the lines around her expressive eyes and the wisps of gray hair at her temples. Putting his arm around her, he said, "I want to make things better for you." His mother didn't ask him to work full-time, but the implication was there. He made a decision. "I'll quit school, get a full-time job, so you can buy that washer."

As the oldest son of a large immigrant family, Ivan was expected to help support the family or become a Priest. He added to the family income by doing various jobs since he was ten. One summer he had been a water boy for gas company crews, excelling at that job by keeping the dipper and pail clean and adding lemon and sugar to the water. The next couple of summers, he weeded, hoed and picked acres of vegetables. He helped truck them to the market every Friday. After going to school all week, he worked for a grocery store on weekends. He was used to working, but entering the Priesthood was another matter.

Becoming a Priest was unacceptable to Ivan, who read many history books and learned about the Popes' armies, the scourge of nonbelievers, and the Spanish Inquisition. In Sunday sermons, the Priests encouraged the congregation to give a portion of their income to the church, and the parishioners did, even though most of them lived just above the poverty line. Ivan's negativity toward the church was enforced when he served as an altar boy at his mother's insistence. A new Priest, transferred from another parish, made Ivan uncomfortable. When officiating on Sundays, this priest gave candy to the altar boys and touched them much too often. Ivan wanted to avoid him and the altar service, so he said to his mother, "I feel sick on Sunday mornings. I get up early during the week and don't want to get up early on Sundays. I need to catch up on my sleep." His mother relented as long as he promised to attend services every Sunday. Of course, he promised.

Ivan was bored with the repeated rituals of the Mass, including the strict doctrines of the religion. He wanted to feel free to explore other philosophies and belief systems. In contrast, his mother and sisters were deeply devout and loved the church and the sacraments, which gave them comfort. He never discussed his aversion with the family, not wanting to upset anyone, especially his mother.

Ivan had attended his first three grades at St. Peter's and thought the nuns were mean, punishing students for the slightest infraction. The exception was his second-grade teacher, beautiful Sister Angela, who had the sweetest smile and kindest eyes. He listened to her, obeyed her rules, and she answered his many questions with patience.

Sister Angela told him, "You have a curious mind, and I hope you continue with your education and graduate from high school."

It was rare that anyone in his peer group finished all twelve grades. His parents could no longer afford the cost of a parochial education due to their growing family, and Ivan was elated when they transferred him to the public school a few blocks from his house. He felt a wonderful sense of freedom, mixing with children of different religions and no longer having to attend daily Mass. However, his excitement dwindled when his new classmates teased him about his poor English. Determined to improve, he studied the language daily and soon the teasing stopped. His peers began to admire him for earning high grades and his ability to defend himself in a scuffle.

Ivan saw Sister Angela when he attended Mass with his family on Sundays. She sat in a pew with her rosary in hand and her attention on the altar. He made sure she had to pass him when leaving the sanctuary and delighted when she gave him a smile. On the last Sunday in June, he told her he had to quit school to help support his family. She looked at him with the bluest eyes he'd ever seen and said, "You're intelligent and will succeed at whatever you do. God bless you."

Hired as an apprentice at the Ford Motor Company, Ivan learned to rivet the linings on brake bands for the Model T. He mastered the technique quickly, and earned almost as much money as his father. Ivan gave most of his paycheck to his mother, keeping a few dollars for himself. Louiza bought a new ringer washing machine and a new icebox.

The Poncek family was having a pleasant summer. On weekends, Ivan, Josip, and Stefan went to the public beach on the edge of Lake Erie to swim and eye the girls. Anton took Louiza to a few dances and picnics. In the final week of August, Josip received a telegram. He never received a telegram before and knew something was wrong. It read: MOTHER ILL – STOP - COME HOME-.STOP - HELENA

In Pennsylvania, the situation at the Koznars was increasingly dismal. Rose was pregnant for the tenth time and was always sick. Unable to do necessary chores, she relied on Beth to make the meals and take charge of the children. Frank was becoming useless. His heart was skipping beats, making him weak. His clogged lungs make him cough, and he was unable to work. When he tended the animals, he had chest pains, so Eddi took over the job. Josip eased the money crisis by sending home most of his paycheck.

Taking on part of her ailing mother's workload made Beth exhausted at night, needing every minute of sleep she could get. One night she had a disturbing dream about two doves, each holding the end of a banner with the names of her parents written on it. The birds hovered over her bed for a few seconds and flew out the window with the banner. It was the middle of the night, and she awoke to the hooting of an owl sitting on the top of a tree outside her bedroom window. She tried to decipher the strange dream until she fell asleep again.

Rose felt better at the end of August, the time when wild berries were ripe for plucking. It was a hot and humid day when the children accompanied their mother to pick strawberries from plants growing in the fields. By the afternoon, their baskets overflowed. Frank had a basket of berries all to himself and enjoyed seeing his family look so happy.

Intending to make jam that evening, Rose felt light-headed while washing the berries and putting them in a pot on the stove. Feeling faint, she held onto the edge of the sink, afraid of collapsing on the floor. No longer able to stand without holding onto something, she leaned against the wall as she made her way through the parlor. Frank was sitting in his favorite chair reading a book, not looking up when he heard Rose say, "I need to lie down for a bit." She held on to the rail while inching up the stairs.

Rose managed not to fall before reaching her bedroom, where she vomited on the floor. Frank didn't pay much attention to Rose because she always was sick in her first months of pregnancy. However, after a moment of reflection, he put the book down, thinking Rose's voice sounded strange and decided to check up on her. As soon as he walked into the bedroom, he smelled vomit. Rose was in a fetal position, with jellied blood seeping from her vagina. He yelled, "Beth, Beth, get Dr. Malvec!"

Beth never heard that alarmed tone in her father's voice before and rushed to her parent's bedroom. She took one look at her mother, jumped down the stairs, and ran to Dr. Malvec's home. Mrs.Malvec said, "He's not here. He's at the Koch home."

Beth was out of breath when she pounded on the Koch's door. A boy answered and ushered her into the parlor, where a young man was lying on the floor with a pillow under his head. Dr. Malvec was tending to a gash in his leg.

"You've got to come. My mama is very sick. She's bleeding all over her bed."

"Calm down, child. I have to finish this before I can come to your house."

Beth flew out the door and ran to Helena's house, and told her that her mother was very sick and needed her right now. Helena walked as fast as she could, but was unable to keep up with Beth's pace.

Helena arrived huffing and puffing and smelled something burning when she entered the kitchen. She saw smoke coming from a pot on the stove, the contents burned to a crisp. She threw the pot outside. She ran up the stairs joining Frank while he sponged Rose's forehead with a damp cloth. Bloody sheets lay crumpled in the corner of the room, and the empty pan at the side of the bed had a foul odor. Helena placed her hand on Rose's pale face that felt too warm. She told Beth, who was watching her mother and father, to fill a pitcher with cold water and bring a blanket.

Beth was going by Dr. Malvec as he was rushing up the stairs. As soon as he saw Rose, he took her pulse and felt her forehead. "Rose has a blood infection which has weakened her. Keep watch over her and make sure she drinks lots of water. I've been seeing sick people since early this morning and need to go home to get some sleep. Helena, will you stay until I return tomorrow morning?"

"Of course," Helena answered.

Helena and Frank gave Rose sips of water and took turns massaging her body, trying to get her blood circulating to rid of the poison that was affecting her. As the hours wore on into the early morning, Rose slept while Frank dozed in a chair beside the bed.

Helena needed a break from her vigil and went outside to breathe fresh air as she watched the early rays of the sun rising over the mountains. She glanced at the burnt contents of the pan lying on the steps with half a berry stuck to the rim. The juice had boiled away, evaporating like the life in the upstairs room. Helena walked to the telegraph office and sent a telegram to Josip in Cleveland.

Beth slept for a few hours and awoke when the rooster crowed at dawn. She tiptoed into her mother's room and approached the bed. Her mother turned toward her and said, "Please comb my hair." Beth cradled her mother's head in her lap and ran the comb through her thick brown hair. Her mother said, "Promise me you'll take care of the children."

Beth took a deep breath before she answered, "Yes, Mama, I will."

Her mother closed her eyes and Beth went to her room. She knelt by her bed pleading to God for her mother's life. After an hour, she started to go into her mother's room again, when Helena stopped her at the bedroom door and said, "Your mother is dying."

"I can't help her," Beth said.

Helena embraced Beth and said, "No one can."

Frank held Rose's hand while Helena and the children stood around the bed as Father Rupnic gave Rose the final blessing and she faded away. Josip arrived at noon and only had to look at his father's face to confirm his greatest fear. He ran to his parent's bedroom, fell on his knees and put his cheek on his mother's cheek, and wept. When the undertaker came, he helped carry her body to the wagon. He sat in the parlor with his head clasped in his hands, trying to cope with his mother's death. His father cried with him, but nothing said or done could change his mother's death.

An embalmed Rose came home the next day in her coffin, dressed in her favorite clothes. The coffin was placed in the parlor for viewing and prayers. The strain from Rose's face was gone. She looked peaceful holding her rosary and wearing her blue blouse decorated with beads and her matching blue skirt. The tears flowed as her loved ones stared at her posed body lying on white satin padding.

The viewing lasted for two days, with friends and neighbors coming to pay final respects. Beth's best friend Maggie, the last of the visitors, was horrified to see a trickle of blood run down the corner of Rose's mouth. Maggie backed away, her hand muffling her scream as she ran down the stairs and out the door. Helena was the only other person in the parlor at the time. She calmly took a wet cloth and wiped the blood away, thankful none of the family saw it.

On the night before the burial, Frank was leaning on the back of his chair, looking at his wife, when Beth came into the room, wanting to be with her mother one last time. Her father said in a barely audible voice, "You're to blame for this."

Could a stab with a knife be sharper than this accusation? The words stuck in Beth's head as she crumpled to the floor and gaped at her father, feeling like he had hit her with a baseball bat. Frank sat staring at Rose and seemed unaware that his words had cut sharply into the heart of his daughter. Beth searched her mind to find the reason for his outburst. Even before Christina died, Beth had begged her mother not to have more children. She told her, "Don't have more babies, Mama. You're always so tired."

How did he know she said that? Then she understood as she looked at her father's glazed eyes fixated on her mother's body. He had said those cruel words to himself, guilty in making his ailing wife pregnant for the tenth time. Beth just happened to be there when he realized his guilt. Her father was unaware she had entered the room. Beth got up from the floor, put her hand on her father's shoulder, and kissed his forehead. He put his hand on hers, still focusing on Rose. Beth and her father were miserable and sleep eluded them that night.

Josip, Eddi, and several neighbors carried Rose's casket to the church and to the cemetery after the funeral Mass. Following the casket was Frank, limping with a cane, Beth by his side, then Helena walking with Katja. Behind them the town's children were carrying flowers followed by their parents. The children tossed their flowers on Rose's casket lying in the grave next to the small caskets of the premature baby and Christina.

After the graveside service, the mourners proceeded to the house for the customary reception. People talked while eating the donated food, glad to be together, but sad for the motherless family. The only time friends and neighbors gathered in the small mining town were at weddings and funerals.

The emotionally drained and exhausted family went to bed early. Beth woke first and made breakfast for the children. She let them eat even though their father hadn't come down the stairs yet. Josip thought it best to let his tired father sleep, but became worried when he did not come out of his room by midmorning. Josip entered his parent's bedroom and his father was lying very still under his covers. There was no response when he tapped him, so Josip turned Frank toward him and saw his open eyes. Frank had a fatal heart attack three days after Rose died.

Helena and Josip arranged Frank's funeral. Beth and the children were in a state of shock and couldn't function. Josip was the head of the family now and had to keep his wits about him. It seemed to the Koznar children that they were trapped in an endless nightmare. Beth thought of the bladed words her father uttered the night before Rose's funeral, wondering if he was punished for her mother's death. Now she knew what her dove dream meant.

The hushed, shocked villagers came to the house to pray and pay their last respects. The whole town came to a standstill, all the shops closing on the day of Frank's funeral. Again, the sad old Priest conducted the funeral Mass attended by all the people of the town. Once again, the children followed the funeral procession with flowers, placing them on Frank's coffin before burial in the rich soil of Pennsylvania. To the Koznar children, no day could ever be worse than this day.

The town's populace brought so much food it overflowed every table in the kitchen and the parlor. Beth appreciated the sympathy shown, but did not feel like socializing and went upstairs to cry on her bed. Josip had the duty of accepting condolences and thanking everyone for their kindness. As the throng of mourners started to leave in the early evening, a young Irish Priest came to the house to help the children cope with their huge loss. The senior Father Rupnic sent him in his stead, thinking the younger priest would connect with the children. Helena and the children gathered in the parlor to hear what the Irish cleric had to say.

The Priest began by asking all the children, aged two to seventeen, to fold their hands while he prayed. He said their parents were happy in heaven and would always love them. He preached that God didn't want their mother to be alone, so he called their father to join her. Beth watched the sad faces of her brothers and sisters as they listened to the Priest's brogue-accented words. She wasn't fooled. If God was supposed to be so loving and kind, why did he take their parents from them? No, God must hate her and she hated God.

Every day for a week, the young Priest came in the evening to say prayers and listen to the children's concerns. Helena stayed in the house to comfort them during the night hours. Josip was now the undisputed leader of the family and Beth and Helena shared the role of surrogate mother. With Helena's advice, Josip and Beth planned the family's future, keeping their parents' wishes in mind. They knew their parents did not want their children to be involved in coal mining and thought Cleveland was a better place for them to live.

It was too soon after the tragedy to move the youngest children and expect them to adjust to a new environment. They needed the tender care of Helena and Beth for a few years before moving to another city. In the meantime, Josip would keep working in Cleveland and send money home to pay the expenses of his family.

Christy and Jenny were much too young to understand the gravity of losing their parents. Christy kept asking for Mama, thinking she could come back from that place called heaven. Jenny was only two and started calling Beth, Mama and Josip, Papa. Eddi, age twelve, and Katja, age nine, understood death and were devastated, calling out to their parents during the night. Beth had all sorts of confusing dreams, but the foreboding doves never returned. Beth hated God, but still prayed to him to be merciful and let the remaining family live long lives. She believed in a powerful God in charge of heaven and earth.

The week Rose and Frank died was a blur, everything happening so fast. Josip had no time to deal with his emotions and needed some solitude. A day after his father's burial, he walked to the old pine tree he had mutilated when Christina died. This time, he did not take an axe with him and was glad to see the tree still healthy. He sat on the ground next to the tree, lost his composure and wept. He had been strong for his family, keeping his emotions under control, and needed to release his sorrow.

When he stopped crying, he saw White Dove come from behind a bush a few yards from the old pine. She walked toward him, crunching the leaves underfoot as she opened her arms toward him. She pressed herself against his chest. After they held onto each other for several minutes, he started to kiss her neck, cheeks, and mouth while stroking her breasts. A flood of emotions overwhelmed them as they walked to the hut. They lay on the soft bed of leaves, ascended into a world of desire, not being able or wanting to control their passion. Their union was as natural as breathing, expressing the love they had for each other. They cuddled watching the appearing stars dazzle the darkening sky. Josip was the first to speak.

"I love you. I want to marry you, but I can't right now," Josip said.

" I know," White Dove said.

"I must leave tomorrow and return to my job so I can send money home. I'll come back as soon as I can," Josip vowed. He walked back to his house, feeling better than he had in days. In the morning, he bid his family an emotional farewell and went back to Cleveland.

Josip aged considerably in the week he was gone, looking older than his seventeen years. He returned late in the day when all the Poncek family was home, and described the events that led to the loss of his parents. Everyone was solemn when Josip finished his story, not knowing what to say, except how sorry they were. Louiza bade Josip to go upstairs to rest before dinner.

"I want to sit in the gazebo." Josip said.

Tired from his emotions, tired of all the responsibility, Josip curled up in the swing and fell asleep as a warm September breeze brushed over him.

ADJUSTMENT

When new immigrants arrived in America, they settled into neighborhoods where their native language was spoken and their old world culture was practiced. Their American-born children bridged the gap between the two worlds, speaking at least two languages and adapted to two cultures. Old-world traditions, grudges, and conflicts were still evident in the gangs of boys from different ethnic neighborhoods. Altercations between them were frequent. This is how Ivan and Stefan learned to street fight. Ivan was one of the best brawlers justified, in throwing a punch if someone called him a name such as honky, or insulted him in another way. He was a hothead, not taking much to rile him.

The most popular sports in the blue-collar community were baseball and boxing. New York Yankee Babe Ruth was breaking home run records helping the Yankees' to win pennants, while the Cleveland Indians were struggling.

Ivan liked boxing the best since he defended himself with his fists most of his boyhood. He enjoyed listening to the boxing matches on the radio with his father, Stefan, and Boris. They admired the speed, graceful agility, and pure power of Jack Dempsey, who first learned his skill fighting in saloons. Dempsey was the reigning Heavyweight Boxing Champion. Another favorite was Lightweight Champion Benny Leonard called the Ghetto Wizard, thought to be the brainiest of all the boxers.

Ivan was born left-handed. His father said it was the sign of the devil and insisted he eat with his right hand. As he grew, this worked to Ivan's advantage, enabling him to use either hand to do almost anything, including fighting. At age sixteen, he joined the local gym and become an amateur boxer. The owner of the foul-smelling gym was a retired boxing pro with a split lip and a broken nose. He liked the watch Ivan hit the hell out of the gym's punching bag.

"Boy, you're a hitter. I can teach you the defense moves of bobbing, slipping, and blocking. Your punch is great, but you have to know how to jab, hook and use an uppercut. You need to get those feet moving too." The owner said.

Ivan paid for a series of lessons and was ready to practice his new skills with a gym member in his lightweight division. It wasn't an authentic contest; it was a boxing lesson. His opponent was experienced and could have knocked Ivan out of the ring several times but backed away when he had the advantage, paid not to hurt the newcomer. Ivan's opponent controlled the fight by maintaining a distance between them, using quick, long-range jabs and not letting Ivan get close enough to execute a punch.

Ivan needed to hone his skills before he could have a real match, so he bought a punching bag and hung it in the basement. Every evening, about an hour after dinner, he practiced defense moves, and footwork. Stefan asked Ivan to give him a few basic boxing lessons and Ivan obliged. He enjoyed them until Ivan said, "I think you're ready to spar with me."

"Nah, I've got to help Ma bat the carpets. She's counting on me." Stefan ran up the stairs and never asked for a lesson again.

One evening, a curious Theresa watched Ivan dance around the punching bag, practicing his jabs.

"Can you teach me to box?" Theresa asked.

"Nah, you're a girl," Ivan said.

"How can you say that? Haven't you heard we have equal rights now. We can vote!"

"Okay, okay," Ivan said.

Theresa admired the Suffragists and was elated when the nineteenth amendment, giving women the right to vote, became part of the constitution.

Theresa was a challenge for him because she was like him, independent, smart and well read. He thought she'd make a great schoolteacher. Until that happened, he wanted to cure her boxing ambition. "I'll start you out with some basics."

He demonstrated the various types of punches, how to protect the face, and the way to sidestep blows. Theresa concentrated and learned easily. She pestered Ivan to keep giving her lessons, and he did, grudgingly. To him, it was a waste of time.

After a couple of weeks, Theresa thought it was time to put her lessons to the test, and asked Ivan to spar with her.

"You're not ready yet," Ivan said.

"Yes, I am. I've had enough lessons. I'm ready," Theresa said.

There was no use arguing with her. They faced each other, pacing in a circle with Ivan making small jabs, and telling Theresa to keep her guard up. She lowered her right hand just enough to expose her face, and with little force, Ivan's gloved fist connected with her jaw. She dropped to the floor. He was surprised she fell so easily and bent down to see if she was hurt. As soon as he touched her, Theresa pushed his hand away, stood up and glared at him while rubbing her bruised chin.

"You're not going to see me cry." Theresa said.

"Gosh, I'm sorry. I tried not to hit hard," Ivan said.

Theresa gave him a scathing look and ran up the stairs. The next day, her swollen chin turned the color of light purple. Louiza scolded her daughter for being so brazen and had no sympathy for her. Theresa never went to the basement again when Ivan practiced his boxing moves and only spoke to him when necessary.

Ivan's first amateur bout was scheduled on the Saturday after Thanksgiving. His mother didn't like the rough sport, and forbade her daughters from attending any boxing matches, disappointing Theresa. Anton was confident in his son and generously bought tickets for himself, Josip, Stefan, and Boris.

Because Ivan was new and inexperienced, he was in the first bout. The men in his family were the first to cheer him as he emerged from the locker room. He and his opponent sauntered down the aisle, as the excited crowd hooted and hollered. Ivan's trainer reminded him of the strategy he must use to win, while Ivan sat in his corner waiting for the bell to ring.

The bell signaled the beginning of the first round, and Ivan advanced aggressively toward the slighter-built boxer. He jabbed a few times and punched twice, missing his opponent's chin. Nothing much happened in the first round and then, just before round two was over, Ivan executed a perfect one-two punch and knocked his opponent flat on the mat. The man lay on the canvas moaning and never got up during the ten-count.

The referee raised Ivan's arm and declared him the winner by a knockout. Hearing the clapping and cheering of the audience was an exhilarating experience and Ivan was thrilled to have won his first official match. The gym owner was elated too, for he had a winner who could lead him to a profitable future. "Well, Ivan you did very well. I'm going to line up more matches for you. By spring, you'll be ready to turn pro. What do ya think of that?"

"Sure, that sounds great," Ivan said.

The Christmas season started and St. Nicholas (the local barber decked out in a red costume) visited the neighborhood houses. He scared the children with his questions about whether they were good or bad during the year. He asked, "Do you help your parents? Do you clean your rooms? Do you do your homework," and so on. The children hid behind their mothers' skirts, fearing that old St. Nick would spank them or take them away. Of course, that never happened, and if a particular question wasn't answered to St. Nick's satisfaction, he did scold the offender and then gave all the children a piece of candy before he went on his way.

Josip hadn't been with his family since early September and intended to spend Christmas with them. He also wanted to see White Dove. He bought caps and scarves hand knitted by Fritzy for his sisters and a sled for Eddi. He wrapped the gifts in brightly colored paper and layed them under the Poncek's Christmas tree.

The decorated tree glistened with tinsel hung from every bough, giving a festive glow to the parlor. His thoughts turned to previous Christmases, reminding him of his own family tree decorated with handmade ornaments and candles. He murmured a little prayer for his siblings while looking at the angel perched on top of the blue-lighted tree.

The house was quiet except for Anton, Boris, and a couple of pals arguing over a competitive game of pinochle in the kitchen. Ivan, Stefan, and Theresa had gone to the movies and invited Josip, but he declined due to his early morning departure to Pennsylvania. The teenagers debated about which movie to see, the boys wanted *The Gold Rush* with Charlie Chaplin and Theresa wanted to see *The Phantom of the Opera* with Lon Chaney wearing scary makeup. *Phantom* was the newest movie in town, and *Gold Rush* had been around for weeks. Ivan made the decision in favor of the *Phantom*, wanting to please his sister and hoping to soften her resentment toward him for knocking her down.

They said goodbye to Josip and continued talking about the movies. Louiza came from the kitchen and watched Josip gaze at the tree. He nodded at her as she sat down in her favorite velvet chair and put her feet up on the matching hassock. They sat in silence, looking at the lights and sparkling ornaments on the holiday tree. It was the time of the year for reflection and Louiza's thoughts turned to her brother and sister, and best friend, Ljupa.

Ljupa, who came with Louiza to the United States, had died of the flu in 1918, leaving her husband Marko to take care of their five children. Every year Marko sent a card at Christmas signed with his name, but he never wrote anything in it. Andrew seemed happy in New York and visited every few months. Maria still lived in Gora with her family and kept in touch through weekly letters. Louiza's thoughts turned to Josip. Josip was beginning to recover from his trauma and this was the right time to have the discussion.

"I'm sure your brother and sisters will like your presents. Do you have a gift for your Aunt Helena?" Louiza asked.

"No, I don't. She deserves the best. I don't have money to buy the best." Josip said.

"I have something she would like that I have treasured for many years." Louiza unpinned the broach she had on her blouse. "This broach was given to me by my dear neighbor, Mimi. She never had children and was like a second mother to me. Your Aunt is a special lady and I want her to have this" Louiza handed the pin to Josip. In the center was the finely etched head of a woman surrounded by filigreed gold.

"It's very nice. Helena will love this pin. Hvala, [Thank you]."

"Prosim [You're welcome]. You know, Josip, I was only thirteen years old when my mother died. My friend, Ljupa, lost her mother a year earlier, and together, our sadness lessened as months went by.

Our mothers are loving memories and in time, the pain of losing them softens." Louiza yawned. She kissed Josip on the cheek and said, "I'm going to bed. I hope you have a blessed Christmas."

Heavy snow was falling when Josip awoke early after sleeping fitfully on the sofa. He pulled on a wool sweater and put gloves and a scarf in his overcoat pockets. He vowed that even if a blizzard developed, it would not keep him from going to Lodun. He took the family gifts from under the tree and a block of cheese out of the icebox, grabbed an apple, and stuffed them in his shoulder bag before taking the trolley to the train station.

Josip walked up the snow-covered steps to his old home and when he opened the door, pandemonium ensued. Christy and Jenny squealed, hugged his legs and would not let go, making him laugh. Beth and Katja kissed him many times while Eddi gave him a big hug that almost knocked him down. He saw Helena sitting at the kitchen table, watching and smiling at the homecoming greeting. When the children let go of him, Josip hugged the frail Helena.

A special dinner of roast beef, mashed potatoes, and gravy was devoured. Jenny was old enough to eat finely chopped pieces of meat. Christy ate the potatoes with her tiny hand, getting it all over her face, bib, and her high chair. This was the first meal the family had together in three months, and it was noisy, however quieting whenever Helena spoke, for her voice was soft. Her friendship and support for the family, through all their misfortunes, made her dearly loved and highly respected. The stress of the past few months was taking its toll on the thin Helena; her head and hands constantly shaking.

Beth had lost all traces of girlishness and had become a mature sixteen-year-old. She worked as a cook in one of the company-owned boarding houses while Katja helped Helena take care of Jenny and Christy. When Beth came home in the late afternoon, Helena left to help Dr. Malvec in exchange for free medical care for the children and, of course, herself. Eddi was only twelve and insisted on working at the mines to help support the family. He separated coal from rock when the trams came out of the tunnels. Ever mindful of their father's wishes, Eddi never went into the tunnels, and Josip was determined to get him away from them soon.

After putting the children to bed, Helena, Josip, and Beth sat staring at the tiny Christmas tree with a few decorations hanging on its small branches. Helena brought out small glasses of brandy from the kitchen, and they sipped slowly, warming their bodies on a cold night. The fireplace was dancing with flames as they talked about memories of past Chistmases when they sang carols, laughed and told stories.

"Let's not talk about this any more, it's too painful." Beth said to Josip.

"I think so too," Josip said.

"God has turned his back on us," Beth blurted out.

Josip frowned. "Don't say that. Things will be better with time. I've been thinking of our future. When you turn eighteen, Beth, I want you to come to Cleveland and we'll rent a large apartment for all of us. Then in a few months, Eddi, Katja, Jenny, and Christy will join us. Don't you think that's a good idea, Aunt Helena?"

"Yes I do. Soon Christy will be out of diapers and Jenny will be in school. I think my energy will hold til then. Eddi needs to keep his job until he goes to Cleveland."

Josip and Beth agreed on the plan. At last, they were looking to the future instead of dwelling on the past. They went to bed satisfied with their decisions.

On Christmas Eve day, Beth went to work at the boarding house, and Eddi went back to work at the mines as a breaker boy. During the day, Josip took care of Katja, Jenny and Christy, giving Helena a day of rest. He let the children play in the fresh layer of snow that had fallen during the night. The girls had fun throwing snowballs and making a snowman decorated with an old hat and scarf. By the late afternoon, everyone was becoming wet and cold and needed the warmth of the house. Holiday kindness infected the mine owners and they released their employees an hour early on Christmas Eve. Eddi was grateful to get paid for an hour he didn't work.

The sun was getting low in the sky, and Josip longed to be in the woods.

"You take care of the kids. I want to take a short walk before the sun sets."

"Supper will be ready when you get back," Beth said.

Just a few steps down a path behind the house and Josip came into a world of trees, brooks, and streams. He breathed deeply, inhaling the fragrance only the woods could give him, making him feel more alive than ever. He walked to the old pine tree and saw the axe marks he made by his abusive anger. He studied the sturdy tree, wondering if he could stand the test of time like the tree, for he was scarred too. Determined to survive, he would never give up on life. He heard a delicate voice coming from behind the pine.

"You can sit on my blanket and we can look at the tree together."

There, peeking from behind the pine was White Dove. She walked to him carrying a blanket, and they embraced. How good it felt to have his arms around this wonderful girl. Josip led her to the summer shack he built a few years before, examining it before opening the ill-fitting door. The roof had not leaked, and the straw floor was dry, a cozy place to snuggle. They wrapped the large blanket around them, kissing and fondling, pledging their love for each other no matter what their future would be. Josip wanted to stay with White Dove all through the night, but he needed to get back to his family to celebrate Christmas. "I won't be seeing you for a while. I have to go back to my job in Cleveland."

"I understand. Please write to me." White Dove said.

Josip kissed her goodbye and said, "You have my heart."

After dinner the children opened their gifts from Josip. Beth and Katja giggled with delight when they saw the scarves and hat. Jenny squealed when she put the hat on her head and said, "Tankku."

Christy sat in her highchair, fascinated with the bright colors of the yarn. Helena took the hat and scarf away from her afraid she would pull the knitting apart. Eddi was thrilled with his new sled and sat on it the rest of the evening.

Josip put a small box in Helena's hand, and she held it like she was holding gold. "Oh Josip, you didn't have to buy a present for me."

"Please open it! We want to see what's in it," Katja said.

Helena removed the box lid and lifted out the delicately carved broach. With tears in her eyes, she said, "Thank you. It's lovely. You shouldn't have spent so much money on me."

"I didn't. It's an heirloom from my family in Cleveland. My stepmother Louiza, wanted you to have it." The expression on Helena's face soured the minute he mentioned the word stepmother. Josip realized that Helena thought she filled that role. He tried to make amends by saying, "Now I have two stepmothers, you and Louiza."

On Christmas Day, the whole family went to church because Helena insisted on it. Beth complied to please Helena, even though she was still mad at God and wrestled with this feeling during Mass. On the other hand, Josip gave thanks for his family and his adopted family in Cleveland. A pleasant surprise greeted them at home. On their doorstep was a large basket containing oranges, roasted chestnuts, and a turkey with a note saying, "Merry Christmas!"

"The basket is probably from our neighbors; they have been so kind to us," Beth said.

The day sped by, with the children taking turns sliding on the snowy slopes with Eddi's new sled. They stopped playing, when a shiny new car parked in front of their house.

"Merry Christmas!" Dr. Malvec exclaimed as he got out of his car.

"Same to you," Josip said as he shook his hand.

"Thought I'd come to see you on this wonderful day," Dr. Malvec said.

"How are you and your wife?" Josip asked.

"Just fine. I surprised her by buying this car. Isn't she a beauty?"

It dawned on Beth that Dr. Malvec was the one who had left the food on the doorstep. "Thank you for the basket of food."

"How did you know?" Dr. Malvec asked.

"I had a hunch," Beth said smiling.

Eddi and the girls started tossing snow at the doctor, and he threw a snowball back, missing them. Josip stopped the the fun, brushed the white flakes off Dr. Malvec, and invited him in for a cup of coffee. He accepted and talked about his new car.

"It's a Packard. I had a choice of color, so I picked light gray. My neighbor took me to Johnstown to pick it up and I drove it home. It was a bumpy ride. The roads aren't good around here. Of course, I keep my horse and buggy for those days when the roads are muddy or clogged with snow. This summer, my wife and I are going to drive to New York and break the car in. It can go up to seventy miles an hour on a smooth road."

Helena, Beth and Josip listened to the doctor talk about his future road trip. Josip was jealous of the fancy car and the luxurious vacation plans. When could he buy a car or and take a vacation to New York or anywhere. Beth hid her envy by looking at the floor. Dr. Malvec said goodbye after an hour visit, and they watched him get into his expensive car and drive off.

The envy dissipated by the time Beth and Helena had dinner on the table. Josip said grace over their Christmas meal, including being thankful for Dr. Malvec's generosity. The next morning Helena borrowed Dr. Malvec's buggy to take Josip to Johnstown to catch the train to Cleveland.

CRIMINAL ACTIVITY

In l920, the Federal Prohibition Act (the eighteenth amendment) was passed by congress and it forbade the selling of liquor in the U.S. The amendment did not forbid making liquor at home, so Anton continued making his wine. However, to some people, drinking at home wasn't as much fun as drinking with friends at local speakeasies, where everyone had a great time defying the law. Gang members hung out at these bars, looking for young men to help smuggle booze into the United States from Canada, where the sale of alcohol was legal after a two-year attempt at prohibition failed.

One evening, as Ivan and Josip were coming home from a movie they passed Novak's and two familiar-looking men came out of the speakeasy. They were clean-shaven, their hair neatly trimmed, and dressed in expensive suits. Josip recognized Joe's round face with the droopy eye and Moe's hawk-like face.

Josip poked Ivan in the arm and exclaimed, "Look! It's Joe and Moe, our old boarders from Pennsylvania." "Hey, remember me?" Josip yelled at them.

"Yeah," Joe said.

"You guys look like you're in the chips," Josip said.

"Yeah," Moe said.

They didn't seem to be in a friendly mood, so Josip started to walk away and called out, "See you around."

"Hey, kid, want to make some dough?" asked Joe. His English had improved.

Josip and Ivan stopped in their tracks, wanting to hear more. Joe explained that he and Moe were working for a big dealer in Chicago and needed some drivers to pick up a load of whiskey in Canada. A truck would be provided, and the job paid one hundred dollars.

"Wow, I gotta talk to my friend about this," Josip said, as he motioned Ivan to walk a few steps away from the men so they wouldn't be heard.

They whispered to each other;

"I wonder which mob these guys are working for. The Al Capone and Bugsy Moran gangs control the Chicago bootlegging industry and they hate each other."

"Does it matter? Fifty bucks for each of us is a whole lot of money."

"Yeah…. It does sound easy. All we have to do is pick up the liquor and drive it back home. Let's do it,"

The job needed to be done the following weekend, and Ivan was glad he didn't have a boxing match scheduled. How was he going to explain to Ma why he and Josip would be gone for a couple days? Josip came up with a plan; he was taking Ivan with him to visit his family in Pennsylvania. Louiza did not detect the lie when Josip informed her of the trip. The boys were relieved when the fake story passed Louiza's scrutiny. The night before their adventure, they tossed and turned, getting little sleep.

In the morning, a black truck was waiting for them in the back parking lot of Novak's bar just as Moe said it would be. Joe stood next to the Ford with the keys, a map, instructions, and one hundred dollars in cash (to pay for the contraband whiskey,) plus twenty-five dollars for gas and meals. What they didn't spend they could keep, plus one hundred dollars more when the booze arrived in Novak's parking lot. The truck was only a year old and dented, looking like it had been beaten with a baseball bat. Joe instructed them to go west to Toledo, north toward Detroit, and cross into Ontario. They were to pick up the load of liquor from a boathouse on the edge of St. Clair Lake, adjacent to a small hamlet called Tilson.

Ivan had never driven a car such a long way, had never had so much money in his pocket, and began to doubt the decision to take on this job. The commandment, "Thou shalt not steal," kept repeating itself in his head.

"We shouldn't be doing this. I think we're in over our heads," Ivan said as they reached the outskirts of Cleveland and drove through miles of farmland.

"We can't stop. The mob might beat us up or, worse yet, kill us if we back out," Josip answered.

"We could keep going west to California; they wouldn't find us there," Ivan said.

"C'mon, they could hurt your family. No, we have to go through with it," Josip said.

"You're right. No turning back." Ivan was driving forty miles an hour at full speed, too fast for the bumpy country road. He reluctantly slowed the car to a safer speed. "Why don't you read me the instructions Joe gave us?" Ivan asked.

"Not now, I'm hungry. Let's stop at the next café for some steaks." Josip said.

They never ate steak at home, for Ma only bought inexpensive meats such as heart, liver, kidneys, and stew meat, cooked for hours to tenderize it. They sat down at a corner table and a pretty waitress approached them.

"Are all the waitresses as pretty as you?" Ivan said.

"Yeah! What are ya goin eat?" The waitress retorted in a shrill voice as she cracked her chewing gum.

Ivan stopped flirting and he and Josip ordered their steaks.

"She looks at us like we were thugs." Josip said.

"Aw, that's your imagination." Ivan said

As soon as they wolfed down their chewy steaks, they left a small tip on the table and high tailed it out of the café. They drove along the road for a while, stopping under a street lamp to read the instructions.

Two hours after sunset, they were to meet a man named Huey at the entrance of the boathouse. Huey was to signal them by blinking his lights three times. The first two flashes would be quick and the third one was to come fifteen seconds after the first two. Huey was to walk toward them with a flashlight, shine it in their eyes, and say "Hudson Bay." They were to answer him by saying "Novaks." After the proper identification, the liquor and money were to exchange owners.

They found the boathouse easily, for it was the only one located at the edge of the tiny town. As they got out of the car, the full moon shimmering on the smooth surface of the lake caught their attention, until car lights flashed twice a few feet away. After fifteen seconds, the third light flashed.

A man's voice said loudly, "Hudson Bay."

They responded, "Novaks."

A flashlight shining in their eyes prevented them from seeing the man's face or any of the men with him, if there were any. A deep voice, sounding like it came from a big man, said, "I'm Huey. The stuff is in front of the boathouse. Give me the money."

From behind the glaring light came an outstretched arm with an open hand. After placing seventy-five dollars in Huey's palm, the flashlight turned off and a dim light appeared on a building in front of them. They could see stacks of wooden crates with the word peaches stamped in large letters on each one of them. While they were scrutinizing the boxes, they heard a car drive away. Ivan pulled the top off a crate, and inside were four one gallen cans.

"How do we know whiskey is in those cans?" asked Ivan

"Well, if they've cheated us, it's too late to do anything about it," Josip answered.

"Let's open one of them and give it the taste test."

They each had a sip, and yes, it was the real stuff. Satisfied they had successfully completed their assignment; they loaded the truck bed with the boxes labeled peaches and covered them with a large tarp tied down with rope to the sides of the truck. They breathed a sigh of relief when they pulled onto the main road.

Off the main street just before the Canadian–U.S. border, there was supposed to be an obscure road that led past three farms and crossed the border into Michigan. Moe told them to cut the lights and drive slowly when going by the farms. They found two unmarked roads, one leading west and the other leading east. This confused them because they wanted to go south to the border. They flipped a coin, heads to the west and tails to the east. West won, but the road turned north after about a mile, and there were no farms.

"Let's not panic," Ivan said in a panicky voice.

"We've got to turn back," Josip said, trying to sound calm.

Ivan headed back to the main highway and turned onto the road going east, which did indeed curve to the south after half a mile with a farmhouse appearing in the distance. They drove at a snail's pace past the house with the truck lights off and did the same as they passed a second farmhouse. They were about to turn on the headlights back on, when bright lights suddenly appeared from the left side of the road.

"Holy cow!" Ivan said.

"My God," Josip said.

Ivan saw a gravel path off to the right and pulled the truck onto it, driving until it ended at the edge of a narrow river. They hid behind a clump of trees and waited several hours, wondering why those bright lights came on and, if they were being pursued.

"I don't think we were followed." Josip said.

I heard gangs steal liquor from other gangs by hijacking smuggled supplies. It could be another gang or the Klan," Ivan said.

"The Ku Klux Klan?" Josip asked.

"This is probably too far north for them," Ivan said.

"That's good news," Josip said.

"You know, the Klan was started in the south when two southern soldiers saw the destruction of their property after returning home at the end of the Civil War." Ivan stated.

"I can't believe it. We're in a tight spot and you're giving a history lesson. I don't want to hear about it. We gotta think of what to do next," Josip said.

"We have to wait here til morning," Ivan said.

They fell asleep and awoke at dawn. The truck was stuck in mud, and they had to push it to get it moving again. The sun was above the tree line when they got on the road, the third largest farmhouse was ahead of them, just as Moe described. The gas gage was on empty, and they had no choice but to stop at the farmhouse and ask for gasoline. They were taking a big chance, but abandoning the truck with it's elicit cargo was out of the question. They knocked on the farmhouse door. A big man opened the door, about forty-five years old with white hair and pale blue eyes. His face showed no surprise at seeing them.

"Good morning, sir. I'm Ivan and this is my friend, Josip. Our truck is very low on gas. Do you think you could spare a gallon?"

Without hesitation, the man answered, "Ya, for sure, but you gotta pay for it. My name is Sven. You guys vant some coffee and somethin' to eat?" His speech had an accent they had never heard before.

"Gosh, we're starving!" they answered in unison.

Sven invited them to sit at the kitchen table and gave them each a cup of very strong coffee and a piece of coffee cake. The cake was delicious, but the coffee was bitter.

The sun-tanned farmer talked about his wheat crop and all about the weather. Ivan was nervous and more interested in the shotgun sitting in the corner near the door. Ivan interrupted Sven by asking, "I noticed your shotgun over there by the door. Do you hunt?"

"Yah, geese and deer; bagged a stag a month ago. There's other game around here too. They walk on two feet."

A shiver went down Ivan's back, as he and Josip got up from their chairs.

"Sit down fellas, I'm just havin' some fun with ya," Sven said.

Sven explained that his farm was in the state of Michigan and only one mile from the Canadian border. He and his neighbors had seen many trucks carrying crates past their houses since the United States government passed the Prohibition Act.

"You're doin' somethin' illegal or you woulda taken the highway last night. We scared the livin' daylights outta you guys." The farmer laughed and slapped his thigh. "You guys are still wet behind the ears. Whad-ar ya doin' smugglin'? You could go to jail. We saw you comin'. Farmers can spot a bootleggin' truck a mile away and you are first timers."

Ivan and Josip were thankful it was the farmer's lights that discovered them instead of the cops or, worse yet, gangsters.

The farmer continued, "You look like good fellers, and I'm not goin' to turn you in, but I hope you've learnt your lesson and never do dis kinda ting again."

"No, no, never again," they vowed. It was an easy promise to make.

"Tell you vat; I'm goin' help ya avoid bein' arrested."

Sven had them park the truck by the barn, remove the tarp, and cover the crates with straw. "You guys gotta look like farmers." He had Ivan put on worn overalls, gave Josip a faded jacket and had them replace their caps with wide brimmed hats. Sven laughed. "Here's five gallons of gas. I vant two cans of whiskey to pay for the gas."

Ivan and Josip filled the tank, gave the farmer two cans from the opened crate and thanked him for his hospitality. They drove slowly down the dirt road toward the main highway and did not attract attention for the rest of the trip home. They delivered the truck with the crates to Moe and Joe waiting at Novak's parking lot at the appointed time.

Joe was checking the crates when he said. "Two cans are missing. Did you take them?

"No, we had to trade them for a gallon of gas."

"Well, you gotta pay five dollars for each of those cans. So, here's the ninety dollars you're owed." Joe handed Josip the money. "How about doing another job next week?"

"We're not good at smuggling," Josip said.

"Yeah, we thought we got caught and were scared out of our wits. Our scare turned out to be a sympathetic farmer," Ivan said.

Joe frowned and said, "You know what happens to squealers."

"Don't worry; don't worry. We ain't squealers," Josip said.

"We're not stupid, you know," Ivan added.

Josip and Ivan walked home from Novak's bar, relieved the whole thing was over and vowed never to do anything for the mob again. However, the money sure felt good in their pockets. When Ivan and Josip walked into the kitchen, Louiza hugged both of them. "Did you boys have a good trip?"

"We're hungry, Ma," Ivan said.

Louiza fried pieces of liver and potatoes for them and asked questions about their trip while they ate. They knew it would be difficult to answer her questions, so lies were rehearsed while driving home. "We never got to Pennsylvania We stopped to see Niagara Falls and spent so many hours sightseeing, we didn't have time to go to Lodun," Josip said.

"You shouldn't have done that," Louiza said, scolding them.

"My family didn't know we were coming, so they couldn't be disappointed. We stayed in Niagara overnight." Josip was good at lying

"Did you have enough money?" Louiza asked.

"Sure," Ivan nodded.

"What do the falls look like?" Louiza asked.

"They are spectacular, very hard to describe. You must go there," Josip said.

"We're tired, Ma. We want to rest upstairs," Ivan said as he yawned.

"Tell me more about your trip after you get a nap," Louiza said.

Ivan and Josip vowed to keep the smuggling trip a secret, but some day they might tell their grandchildren. To keep the ill-gotten money safe, Josip hid his forty-five dollars in a small metal box under the floor of the gazebo while Ivan hid his money in a sock in his bottom dresser drawer in his bedroom. His thoughts turned to boxing.

Joe and Moe started betting on Ivan's fights and they gave him part of the winnings, to secure his loyalty when he turned pro. Ivan's dedication to perfecting his boxing skills was making him a first-rate amateur contender. He took the betting money the mobsters gave him, because he felt he deserved it. It occurred to him that Joe and Moe might want something in return for the money in the future.

Ivan was winning all his matches in the first few rounds, knocking most of his opponents out with a right-hand punch to the jaw. In one of his fights, his opponent let down his guard and he punched him square in the face. Ivan was sorry he caused his opponent's broken nose, rationalizing that it was part of the game. The matches were getting tougher and lasting longer than Ivan's first fights. The weakest were eliminated in the early bouts, and the strongest fighters remained in the sport, hoping to turn professional and earn loads of money.

Young women were smitten with Ivan, who looked muscular and toned in his boxing shorts and they flocked to his fights. They cheered him from the back seats, daring not to sit too close to the ring for fear of male disapproval. They waited for him outside his dressing room, each one hoping he would ask for a date. Ivan liked the attention but was careful, seeing his friends marry because they got their girlfriends pregnant. He avoided entrapment by double dating and going to dances and picnics with a group, feeling there was safety in numbers.

Ivan was serious about improving his boxing skills. As the year wore on, the weaker boxers dropped out of competition and Ivan fought the better boxers. Labeled a boxer-puncher, he used hooks and uppercuts to beat his rivals. Because he was ambidextrous, he could use either hand to deliver a good punch to the jaw, surprising his opponents. He had a winning record, except for one, caused by late night drinking with friends the night before the match.

One year passed and Ivan needed only a few more fights to turn pro. It was exciting to be in the main bout of the evening. His opponent was a big, brawling Irishman who had a winning record equal to Ivan. The club hall filled to capacity, including Joe and Moe, who made bets all week on Ivan to win. The crowd went wild as the two fighters wearing bright-colored robes swaggered down the aisle.

"Ivan! Ivan!" half the audience shouted.

"Sean! Sean!" yelled the other half.

Ivan sat in his corner, sizing up Sean while he waited for the bell to start the first round. Sean looked bigger than when he saw him fight a few weeks ago. The man was formidable, a southpaw, light on his feet, and Ivan's toughest opponent. Most amateur boxing matches did not go more than four or five rounds, but it was agreed to go eight rounds in preparation for the fifteen possible rounds of a professional match. During the first and second rounds, all they did was spar, keep their distance, and look for an opening, a weakness. In the third and fourth rounds, they danced in a circle and threw a few punches that missed their mark.

In the fifth round, the combatants clinched often, keeping the referee busy pulling them apart. By the end of the sixth round, Ivan's legs were tiring and the Irishman surprised him by punching with his left fist instead of the right, grazing his jaw and dropping him onto the canvas. Ivan could have gotten up right away but decided to wait until he heard the referee count to nine. The bell rang to signal the end of the round just as the ref was going to say ten. He got up and both fighters went to their corners. During the break, Ivan's trainer encouraged him to switch, by using his right fist to guard and his left fist to jab. This strategy was intended to confuse the Irishman and keep him off guard.

Sean was ambidextrous too, switching from his left to his right. The seventh round ended when Sean delivered a solid punch to Ivan's jaw, putting him on the canvas for the ten-count. Ivan lay with his eyes unfocused, feeling dizzy. He heard the crowd roar when the referee declared Sean the winner. Ivan's head and eyes cleared after a few moments. His fans were quiet as they watched him walk with downcast eyes to his dressing room.

Ivan sat in his dressing room, trying to cope with his first loss and wounded pride. Anton, Josip, and Boris stormed in the room, glad to see him sitting up and unhurt, except for the large red bump on his chin. Boris put his hand on Ivan's shoulder, "G-g-gosh, I-I-I'm sure glad you're o-o-okay."

"Maybe boxing isn't for you, son. We bet two bucks on you to win," Anton said.

"Sorry you lost money, Pa," Ivan said.

Josip said. "Boxing is a brutal sport Maybe you should give it up."

The men were quiet as they rode home in an old flivver Anton had recently bought from a Ford dealer.

The next day was Sunday, and the family attended Mass as usual. Ivan knelt, stood, sat, murmured his prayers, and genuflected mechanically, all the while thinking about his future as a boxer. His mother was concentrating on her prayers and watching the Priest perform the rituals. Ivan stared at the altar, rubbed his sore jaw, and reviewed last night's fight in his mind, trying to figure out what he could have done to win the match. He was strong and had a good, hard punch, but his main problem was the slowness in his legs. He had a mild headache and wondered what would have happened if he had his nose broken or his eye mangled or, worse yet, had his brain damaged. Was boxing worth the possible physical disabilities he could incur? By the time Mass was over, Ivan had made his decision.

Joe and Moe were stunned their boy had lost and now owed big bucks to guys who could get nasty. "We ought to beat up Ivan," Moe said.

Joe liked Ivan and didn't want him hurt. "Aw, what would that do? The kid doesn't know we had all that dough riding on him."

"How are we goin' to pay the money we owe?" Moe asked.

"Let's go see Sean. Bet you he's turning pro after his big win. He might make us a pile of money," Joe said.

CHANGES

Beth was excited to reach the legal age of eighteen and anxious to leave her house of sadness. She had been preparing for the move by selling the farm equipment, packing dishes and the children's clothes. Each piece of her parent's clothing was kissed in remembrance before giving them away. Her fathers working clothes (overalls, jacket and gumboots) were given to a grateful neighbor. Helena passed on Rose's modest clothing to needy friends.

Beth quit her job to take care of the children, relying on Josip's salary and Eddi's meager earnings to support the family. Two years had past since her parents died, and Christy and Jenny had dim memories of them. Katja, Eddi, Beth, and Josip would never forget the tragedy, haunting them for the rest of their lives.

Helena could no longer help care for the children. Her muscles were weakening, and she was barely able to care for herself. It was heartbreaking for the children to see her health deteriorating. Dr. Malvec kept an eye on her and gave her free treatment for her debilitating disease.

Josip rented an old truck to transport the family belongings and found two families to rent the house until someone wanted it and had the money to buy it. Because Beth had prepared in advance, it didn't take long to load the bundles, trunks, packages, and the children into the truck. The hardest thing was saying goodbye to Helena.

"We'll write. We'll come back to see you as soon as we can."

Teary-eyed Helena, steadied herself with her cane while each child embraced her. When the family got in the truck, she called out, "Goodbye, goodbye. I'll miss you." The truck rattled up the road and disappeared over the hill.

The only affordable place large enough for the family was in the center of Cleveland, on the second floor of an old apartment building. The living conditions were quite different from the Koznars' former two-story house. After the euphoria over the convenience of an indoor toilet and bathtub wore off, the children started to feel claustrophobic, causing them to squabble.

To keep the utility bill to a minimum, baths were taken once a week, and the water was not changed between bathers. The last child got the dirtiest water. The children fought to take the first bath, and Eddi usually won, being the strongest competitor. If Katja managed to be first, Eddi would push open the unlockable bathroom door, and call out, "I see your R.A.H"

"You can't spell," Katja yelled from the tub.

If Katja won the battle to be first in the tub, Eddi had to be second, by pushing Christy and Jenny behind him. The girls began hitting and biting him. He defended himself by teasing, tickling them and slapping them on their behinds. Only threats of punishment by Josip or Beth ended the ruckus. Josip solved the problem by changing the first bather on a weekly basis. Discipline was in effect when Josip and Beth were home; however, chaos returned when the four youngsters were by themselves in the apartment.

The rambunctious children bothered the occupants living on the first floor below them, and they complained to the apartment manager. The manager was sympathetic to the children but he did not want to lose his other tenants. He warned Josip to keep the noise down or they would have to move. Discipline was impossible to enforce, because Josip had to go to work and Beth had to look for a job.

Beth had no special skills, so finding something that paid a decent wage was difficult. She answered an ad in the Cleveland Plain Dealer seeking someone to wash hair in a beauty salon. The shop was in a rough part of town, where stores had bars on the windows. The salon was neat and clean, and the owner liked her, offering her twenty-five cents per hour plus tips.

The owner examined her from head to toe and said, "Good Lord, child, you're too skinny. Don't you get fed? You look like a country bumpkin. I'm going to cut your hair for free only if you start working for me today."

Beth felt stylish with her new bob and began washing customers' hair that afternoon. The job was easy compared to working in the boarding house. She was able to be home when her brother and sisters returned from school. Most of the customers were kind and generous, and the owner praised Beth, except for the smell of her lunch. Beth ate Klabase, and the spicy odor from the sausage permeated the shop. She ignored the request not to bring the pungent-smelling lunch, and after paying her week's salary, the owner told Beth not to come back.

Josip was perplexed as to why Beth disobeyed the owner's request. "You really didn't want to keep that job, did you?"

"No, I didn't," Beth answered, "It was in the poorest part of town. Tomorrow, I'm going where people have money and find a job cleaning their fancy homes."

Beth took the streetcar to the area of the city where large, neatly painted houses stood behind manicured lawns. She knocked on many doors and was successful in getting two families to hire her. One of the owners gave Beth something to eat and asked if she would clean the kitchen before returning home. Fifty cents was jingling in Beth's pocket when she walked into the family apartment and saw Josip in the kitchen. "See, Josip, I'm already making more money than I did in that beauty shop."

The next day Beth started her new jobs and enjoyed cleaning the expensive homes where luxury abounded. The furniture was intricately carved, the wood floors had a rich sheen and the carpeting was luxurious. Even though Beth liked keeping the posh home clean, she avoided her employers' children. She thought they were spoiled, had too many clothes, too many toys and too much candy.

Beth stretched her meager earnings by searching the newspapers for special buys and getting needed items on sale. She bought a secondhand sewing machine and made the children's clothing, including her own.

Warned by the apartment manager that the children were too noisy, Josip changed to the night shift, increasing his salary and enabling him to watch Jenny and Christy during the day. He was home when Eddi and Katja returned from school and waited for Beth to step in the door before going to work.

Eddi and Katja often watched the activity on the street below their apartment windows and the orphanage opposite their building that housed about thirty children of all ages. The orphans marched in formation when entering and exiting the building. They wore warm coats, colorful hats, and polished boots and carried umbrellas if it rained. The large backyard was visible from their windows and they could see the orphans playing all sorts of games.

Katja asked Beth, "Why do they have better clothes than us? We're orphans too."

"People donate money to them," Beth answered.

"I want to go and play with them in their yard," Katja said.

"You can't do that unless you live in that building," Beth said.

"You're so mean," Katja said.

"Don't you talk to me that way! I'm in charge here," Katja began to cry.

"Some day we'll have enough money for better clothes." Beth took her in her arms and held her until she stopped crying. She gave her a penny, delighting the girl. Katja continued to watch the orphanage when Beth wasn't around.

When Josip moved out of the Poncek house, Andrew, Louiza's brother, moved in. Andrew never married and traveled all over the states doing odd jobs until he hurt his leg junping off a moving train. He could not hop on and off trains any longer, so he asked Louiza if he could live with her. Anton was not enthusiastic, but how could he refuse. After all, his half brother Boris had been living with them for many years, and it would be unfair not to agree. Besides, the boarding fee would more than cover Andrew's food, giving them some extra money.

Josip was like an adapted so to the Ponceks and they wanted to meet his brother and sisters. It had been a month since Josip moved out and Louiza sent Ivan to the Koznars' apartment to invite them to Sunday supper. Ivan had a box of candy in his hand when Josip opened the apartment door. Four children almost knocked him down trying to grab it from him. Beth scolded them, making them sit on the couch and apologize for their behavior.

"This is my sister, Beth," Josip said.

"Glad to meet ya. Kids sure like candy." Ivan gave the box to Beth.

Beth was weak in the knees when she looked at Ivan's handsome face and dark, slicked-back hair, a close resemblance to her movie star idol.

"You look like Ramon Navarro," Beth said.

"Yeah? I've seen Ramon in several movies." Ivan said.

Embarrassed by her outburst, Beth focused her attention on opening the box, giving each child a chocolate.

"My mother wants all of you to come to dinner on Sunday evening at about five."

"Yes, we'd love to come," Beth said. No one had ever invited them to dinner before.

"Great!" Josip said.

"Good. See you Sunday." Ivan said.

After making sure Ivan was out the door and down the stairs, Beth said, "You never told me he was so handsome."

"I don't see men like girls do." Josip replied.

Beth was busy getting everyone ready for Louiza's dinner, wanting the children to look as perfect as possible. She started by washing and ironing the children's best clothes, the ones that weren't patched. She made sure they bathed early Sunday afternoon and lectured them on how to behave, wanting to make a good impression on Ivan and his family. The attentive children listened as Beth instructed them to be quiet during dinner, to eat carefully, and to say thank you often.

The children lined up in front of Beth an hour before the dinner, and she inspected each one, making sure they looked neat and clean. Eddi was the only one with messed hair. "Eddi, go comb your hair."

"Yeah, yeah. I'm hungry."

Eddi grew taller by the minute and was always hungry. He wasn't adapting well to his new environment, fighting often with classmates and neighbor kids. He was the authority in the family when Beth and Josip weren't home. His sisters loved to be alone with him, for he was lenient compared to Beth and Josip. He paid scant attention to them and let them mess up the house while playing their games.

The children waited in the living room while Beth readied herself. It was easy to decide what to wear, having only one good dress. Beth put on her homemade flapper dress and took out the bobby pins that formed finger curls in her naturally straight hair. Looking in the mirror reminded her of how styles had changed since she was a girl.

Skirts were shorter, pinched waists were out, and rolled stockings were in. Women were smoking cigarettes, getting divorces, and allowed in speakeasies. Large busts were not in fashion, so Beth wrapped her generous breasts tight against her chest to flatten them. This made her uncomfortable, the price she paid for being stylish. She smoothed her eyebrows with a wet finger and roughed her cheeks and lips. When she emerged from the bedroom, the children were turning summersaults in the middle of the living room, wrinkling their clothes..

"What took you so long?" Josip asked.

Ignoring the question, Beth shooed the children out the door. The family walked the few blocks to Ivan's house. Beth was excited to meet the family that Josip liked so much. He told her how sweet Louiza was, that Stefan was charming and the sisters were pretty. He said Anton had a bad temper, Boris stuttered and Andrew was pleasant.

Josip knocked on the door instead of walking right in, thinking this time, it would be rude with the children in tow. Stefan welcomed the family into the parlor.

"Hi, I'm Stefan and this is my mother." Three girls were standing next to Louiza.

"I'm sorry we're late." Beth said.

"Not much. No need to apologize." Louiza said as she opened her arms to welcome each of them with a hug. Beth started to relax as she embraced the kind woman. Stefan continued with his introductions, "These are my sisters." The two youngest giggled.

The tallest sister introduced herself by name, "I'm Theresa."

Theresa and Beth started chatting, for they were the same age and were eager to know each other. Beth avoided talking about her parents, wanting this to be a happy occasion. She just began to feel comfortable when Ivan came into the parlor with two older men.

"These are my Uncles, Boris and Andrew," Ivan said.

Boris's face turned red as he stuttered, "H-h-hello" He looked at Beth and whispered in Andrew's ear, "b-b-big b-b-breasts."

Andrew ignored Boris's comment and said, "It's a pleasure to meet all of you."

Louiza ushered everyone into the dining room, where a huge pot of steaming goulash and a plate of homemade bread sat in the middle of the table. They all sat down and were quiet, while Anton, full of whiskey, slurred through the blessing. Beth ate and chatted with the sisters while glancing at Ivan as he talked to Josip. Minding their table manners drilled into them by Beth, the children behaved. Only Jenny dripped food all over the front of her dress.

After dinner, they all went into the parlor and sang Slovenian songs accompanied by the accordion played by Anton. Beth felt wonderful to be part of a family that had parents and sing in harmony as she did before her own parents died. It felt wonderful to blend her soprano voice with Louiza's alto voice. Stefan and Josip had baritone voices, Ivan was a base and Andrew was a tenor. Theresa was a soprano, and her sisters were altos. Boris tried to sing but couldn't get his words out fast enough to keep up with the rhythm of the music.

Louiza declared an intermission and served Flancate (cookies) with cups of ice cream. The children's eyes were as big as saucers when they saw the ice cream, and they put it in their mouths as fast as they could. Josip looked at his pocket watch and declared it was time to go home. The children needed no prompting in thanking the Ponceks for their hospitality.

Beth smiled more after that evening, and the children smiled more too. The whole family was happier. The following Sunday, the elation continued when the teenagers went to the local carnival and Louiza and Andrew took care of Eddi, Katja, Christy and Jenny. Anton and Boris avoided the noise of the children by going to Novaks for the afternoon.

At the carnival, the group was fascinated watching barnstormers soar their airplanes high into the sky and then dive dangerously close to the ground. The pilots steadied their planes when carrying daredevils who performed stunts like wing walking and parachute jumping. After the aerial performance, an airplane ride was available for five bucks a person.

This type of aerial entertainment began in the early nineteen twenties, after Charles Lindberg successfully flew his plane, "The Spirit of St. Louis," from New York to Paris, in thirty-six hours. Lindberg was a new world hero and his accomplishment made airplane stunts popular.

The teenagers watched the airplane antics with trepidation. No one in the group was brave enough to take a plane ride except for Ivan. He seated himself in the cockpit behind the pilot and the plane lifted off the runway, rising higher and higher. Beth was tense watching Ivan's flight and relieved when the two-seater landed. The spectators clapped as a grinning Ivan climbed down from the plane.

"Weren't you scared?" Beth asked.

"No. It was swell. I could see all of the carnival and beyond. The ten-minute ride seemed like a few seconds." Ivan said.

Three days after the carnival excursion, Josip answered a soft knock on the apartment door. Who should be standing there, but Maggie, Beth's best friend from Lodun. Beth was sitting on the couch reading about Ramon Navarro in a movie magazine. She jumped up and squealed when she saw Maggie. "I'm so surprised. What are you doing here?"

"I'm living here with my aunt. Helena gave me your address."

"How is Helena?" Josip asked.

"She is weak. Dr. Malvec told me she has Multiple Sclerosis. The neighbors do her laundry, clean the house and bring her meals." Maggie said.

"She really must be in a bad way. We get letters from her, but she doesn't say much."

Maggie explained she was in Cleveland because her uncle was a manager in a men's clothing factory and he had offered her a good-paying job. She could never get paid that well in Lodun. Beth told her about her job cleaning houses, the wealthy folk who lived in them and all about the Poncek family. Beth smiled when she talked about how fearlessly Ivan flew in an airplane at the carnival.

"Is Ivan your boyfriend?" Maggie asked

"No, he's a friend, that's all," Beth said.

"Not the way you talk about him," Maggie said.

Beth changed the subject. "Wanna go to a movie with me on Saturday night? Everyone's excited about the new talking picture, 'The Jazz Singer.'"

"I want to see that movie too." Maggie said.

Going to the movies was the one thing Beth did for herself, a place where she lived vicariously through the characters, where she could leave her responsibilities and poverty behind. She read every movie magazine and knew the plots of all the films and the biographies of all the movie stars.

Ivan came to the Koznar's apartment unexpectedly one afternoon. Beth was surprised to see him standing in the doorway, holding another box of candy.

"Hi," Ivan said.

"Hi." Beth did not know what else to say.

"Can I come in?" Ivan asked.

"Of course, I'm forgetting my manners. Can I get you some coffee, a beer, or water?"

"Beer sounds good," Ivan said.

The children were eyeing the candy box. Ivan opened it and gave each one of them a chocolate while Beth poured two glasses of beer for Ivan and herself. While Beth and Ivan sipped beer and chatted, Katja and Eddi played checkers, and Christy and Jenny played house with tin pots and pans.

Ivan told Beth why he quit boxing and Beth told him about her life in Pennsylvania. An hour had flown by when Ivan looked at his watch and said, "I must go. Ma is expecting me home for dinner. Want to take a spin in my car?"

Beth felt her pulse quicken, and all she could say was, "Uh huh."

"I'll pick you up after work on Friday."

On Tuesdays and Fridays, Beth cleaned house for the family of a department store owner. Mr. Cappo was very successful and about to open another store in Euclid. His wife was a sweet, dowdy woman always ready to do her husband's bidding. Mr. Cappo was a flirt, winking and smiling at Beth and telling her she was pretty. She was embarrassed when he did this and stared at the floor. She finished her work early on Friday, and waited for Ivan by the front door when Mr. Cappo came into the parlor.

"I'm waiting for my friend to take me home in his car." Beth said.

"You have a boyfriend, eh?" Mr. Cappo said.

"No, he's just a friend," Beth answered.

There was a knock on the Cappos' ornate door.

"Your friend is here," Mr. Cappo said as he winked at her for the hundredth time.

"Ivan this is Mr. Cappo." Beth said after opening the door. The men shook hands.

"I bet you have a good time together," Mr. Cappo said with a wink.

The inference was obvious to Ivan and he did not respond to the remark, instead he grabbed Beth's hand and said, "Bye" to Mr. Cappo. He led Beth to his car. The Model T was a few years old, but in good condition. Ivan opened the door for Beth and jumped into the driver's seat. He said, "Wow, that's a nice house. Don't trust Mr.Cappo, he's a jerk. You should find another job."

"I don't want to. They pay me well," Beth said.

"Mr. Cappo may expect some affection for that money. Let's talk about something else. It's a sunny day; let's go for a walk on the beach."

It was a warm September afternoon, and they drove to the public beach on the edge of Lake Erie. They took off their shoes, dug their toes into the sand and dipped their feet in the cool lapping waves of the lake. A slight wind blew their hair into their faces. They strolled without talking, watching the sun shimmer on the lake as it descended. There were numerous colorful pebbles in the sand, and Ivan picked a few and tossed them into the waves.

Beth spied a crescent-shaped stone with a streak of orange-red color running through it. Ivan was about to take it out of her hand when Beth closed her fingers around the stone and clutched it to her heart. "I want it for a keepsake ----- Do you like poetry?" Beth asked.

"I haven't thought about it much," Ivan said.

"The lake makes me think of this poem." Beth said. She began reciting.

"The tide recedes, but leaves behind bright seashells on the sand.
The sun goes down, but gentle warmth still lingers on the land.
The music stops, and yet echoes on in sweet refrains---
For every joy that passes, something beautiful remains."

"Isn't that a nice poem!" Beth said

"Yeah! Who wrote it?" Ivan asked.

"The author is unknown," Beth said.

Their hands touched and they locked their fingers together as they walked back to the parking lot.

"Your car is swell," Beth remarked as she got into the passenger seat.

"Thanks. I bought it with my savings. I never know what's coming my way, so I put away as much money as I can. I was fired from my job yesterday," Ivan said.

"Oh, I'm so sorry," Beth said.

"It's okay. I got a better-paying job today at a lamp factory. They needed someone like me who knows how to sharpen a drill. I make forty cents an hour."

"That's swell," Beth said as she patted his hand.

"At my old job, I made spindle bodies for Model T cars. I worked for the Ford shop for over a year. I didn't like my supervisor and he didn't like me. I knew more about spindle bodies then he did and he was telling me what to do. I ignored him. He irritated me by always asking why the drill broke so often. I said it was made from poor steel. He didn't accept my answer and kept hounding me. He annoyed me once too often so I said, 'Why don't you find out yourself,' and shoved the drill at him. Then he fired me."

"Wow." Beth said.

"I should have shoved that drill up his ass." Ivan said.

Ivan pulled up in front of Beth's apartment building, and leaned toward her, expecting a kiss. Beth moved away from him, not wanting him to think she was easy.

"How about going to Euclid Beach Park with me on a Sunday afternoon?" Ivan asked.

"That sounds like fun. I've always wanted to go there. Would you mind if my friend Maggie came along?"

"Of course not," Ivan lied. An idea popped into his head. "I'll bring Stefan along too. Maggie will like him."

"That would be swell." Beth waved goodbye.

Ivan needed to convince Stefan to come along and be Maggie's date. As usual, Stefan was in the parlor, practicing a tune on his accordion.

"Hi," Ivan shouted over the sound of the button box.

Stefan stopped playing "Hey, what's up?"

"Boy, have I got a deal for you."

Stefan knitted his eyebrows. "Sounds fishy."

"I've asked Beth to go to Euclid Beach Park with me this Sunday. She wants to bring her girlfriend. How about being her date?"

"How old is she?"

"About Beth's age. They've been friends since childhood."

"Is she good-looking?"

"I don't know. I've never seen her. Look, I don't think Beth will go without her friend, so do me a favor just this once. I'll even pay for your ticket to the park."

"Wow, you really must be smitten. That's very generous coming from a skinflint like you. Yeah, I'll go."

"Don't call me a skinflint. Everyone saves pennies, except for you. You've never saved a dime." Ivan retorted.

"Come on Ivan, enjoy life and spend a little." Stefan said.

"I am. I'm paying for you, Maggie, Beth and myself to get into the park. That's a lot of bucks. Don't tell me I'm not spending money. Anyway, thanks for being a good sport. I'll tell Beth we'll be by at three on Sunday."

"Never in my wildest dreams did I ever think I would have a date with Stefan Poncek. I've seen him with his polka band at weddings and parties. He is so good-looking. All the girls are crazy about him." Maggie said.

"Come over early on Sunday so I can fix your hair and put makeup on you. You want to look your best for Stefan." Beth liked seeing her friend so happy.

Beth would have to use a lot of make-up, for Maggie lacked physical beauty. However, if she were confident and amusing, this might outweigh her plainness. She was loyal, compassionate, and honest, but most men valued beauty upon first sight.

Sunday arrived and Ivan rapped on Beth's apartment door. His face showed disappointment when Beth introduced Maggie to him. Stefan opened the car door for his date. and smiled when Beth said, "Stefan this is Maggie." They said hi to each other and Maggie began talking endlessly. She chattered about her church, the priests and nuns she knew. Stefan had a glazed look on his face when they reached their destination.

The group wandered through the park watching people play in the sand, swim in the lake, eat hot dogs and cotton candy. They viewed the rides and walked past the music hall. Ivan and Beth got on the roller coaster called the "Flying Turns," and Stefan and Maggie went on the Ferris wheel. Ivan noticed that some women were sitting on their boyfriend's lap on the coaster, so he asked Beth to ride it again. This time, with some coaxing, Beth sat on Ivan's lap. After jostled by the jerky, fast ride, they sat on a bench for a few minutes to regain their sense of balance.

"It's getting late and we all have to work tomorrow. We better find Stefan and Maggie." Beth said. They found them in the dance hall listening to Frank Yankavic's band.

Stefan drove the car home, and Beth and Ivan sat in the rumble seat with a blanket over them. Beth was becoming very warm with Ivan's arm around her and his hand caressing her shoulder. He kissed her lightly on the lips and then again with more pressure, transmitting his desire. Beth gently pushed him away. Stefan saw the kiss in the rear view mirror and started whistling a tune. When Stefan stopped the car in front of Beth's apartment, he thanked Maggie for spending the afternoon with him.

Inside the apartment, Maggie said to Beth, "You and Ivan really like each other."

Beth giggled, "Isn't Ivan wonderful! He's irresistible. What did you think of Stefan? Don't you think he's nice?"

"Yes, Stefan is nice, but I felt awkward even though he tried to make me feel comfortable. He's everything a girl would want, but I have to confess, I was afraid he would try to kiss me. That sounds unnatural, doesn't it? I'm not like you. I don't really know if I want marriage and children. I'm happiest when I'm praying and worshipping in church."

Beth didn't know what to say. She put her hand on Maggie's hand and told her they would be friends no matter what path she chose in life. Maggie thanked Beth for her friendship and walked home to her Aunt Bea's house.

DECEPTION

After working a week at the lamp factory, Ivan went to Novaks to celebrate his new job. The speakeasy was noisier than usual, a sign that something exciting had happened. He spotted Milan, his father's old friend, sitting at the bar. Ivan took the empty stool next to him and ordered a beer. Milan didn't notice him, for he was in an intense conversation with a man sitting next to him. Ivan listened as he sipped his beer.

"It's hard to believe. I just saw the two of 'em here a couple of nights ago, sippin' whiskies. They was havin' a good ole time. They're kissin' the golden gates now."

"Only one was killed. The other guy's in the hospital. They say he's gonna live. You know, I got to the scene just as the ambulance took him away. The police were examinin' the truck full of bullet holes. Blood was drippin' from the front seat down to the runnin' board."

Ivan tapped Milan's shoulder. "What are you talking about? What happened?"

"Where've you been? Everybody knows about it," Milan said.

"Not me. I've been working. C'mon, c'mon, tell me," Ivan said.

"You know, Joe and Moe! They was always drinkin in here. They were workin' for Al Capone's gang. They was bringin' in booze from Canada when the two of 'em were trapped in an alley a couple of blocks from here. Moe and Joe got plugged good. The killers took the booze. Moe was drivin'--- died sittin' behind the wheel. Joe was still breathin' when the cops and ambulance showed up," Milan said

"I like Joe. Hope he's gonna be okay. I wonder if the hijackers were part of Bugsy Malone's gang. Ya know Malone and Capone battle for control and kill each other's men. Remember, about a month ago, just a few blocks from here, a mobster was shot while sitting in Sam's barbershop. They say he was a lieutenant in Capone's gang. I saw a picture of him lying in a pool of blood next to the barber chair in the Cleveland Plain Dealer," Ivan said.

"Sure, I remember that picture. Can I buy you a beer? Milan said.

Ivan watched two cops come in the door and belly up to the bar for their free liquor. The customers bombarded them with questions. The cops said Joe had several bullets removed from his legs and would survive, but probably be crippled.

"Those gangsters got what they deserved. How's your Pa?" asked Milan.

"He drinks too much," Ivan answered.

"Your pa has a problem with liquor and women, something to do with his mother."

"He never talks about her. Do you know anything about my grandmother?" Ivan asked.

"Not much, except your Pa is bitter about his childhood." Milan answered.

Ivan's grandmother was a mystery and Ivan suspected she did something awful to cause his father to resent her. Ivan asked Milan about his rheumatism.

"It never goes away. I try to ignore it. Let's play some pool."

The owner of Novak's bar, was doing so well financially that he added a poolroom for his customers. Ivan and Milan entered the smoke-filled room and watched a pool game in progress.

Two players circled the table, positioning themselves with their cues to make the best possible shot. The red-haired competitor looked shabby, except for a large diamond ring on his left hand. He played poorly, missing several easy shots. When his opponent missed a shot, it was the red-haired man's turn again and he ran the table, finishing the game by acing the black ball. The observers hooted and clapped as the winner of the game chose a chair next to Milan and ordered a sandwich and a beer.

"Hi. My name is Red." The red-haired winner said.

"I'm Milan, and this is Ivan. At first I didn't think you were so hot, but you sure revved up your game. You made some fancy shots at the end.."

"When I'm done eatin', would ya like to play some eight ball?" Red asked.

"Gosh, I used to play years ago. I'm sorta rusty." Milan said.

"I'll play you," Ivan said.

"Okay. I'll give you a two-shot lead. Fair enough?" Red said.

"Fair enough," Ivan said.

They racked the balls, and Red let Ivan have the opening shot. Ivan dropped two solids and missed the third ball. Red kept his word by putting two of Ivan's solid balls into a side pocket, which gave Ivan a four-ball lead. It was Red's turn now, and after rubbing chalk on his cue tip, pocketed two stripers. He changed his stance several times, clearing all the striped balls off the green felt. He paused, smiled at Ivan, and shot the black eight ball into a corner pocket. The spectators clapped for Red's expert shooting.

"Ha, he sure suckered you in," Milan said to Ivan.

"You owe me that beer now," Red said.

"I don't owe you a beer," Ivan said.

"Yeah, you do. I won the bet," Red said.

"We never bet, and I'm not buying you a beer," Ivan said.

Red stood up, grabbed a cue, and smashed the end into Ivan's face, knocking him off his chair. Surprised by the attack, Ivan was stunned for a few seconds. Milan grabbed the cue out of Red's hand, and was unable to stop the conman from running out the back door. Red disappeared into the darkness of the night.

Milan brought Ivan a towel to dab his bleeding nostril and split lip.

"Damn, I think he broke my nose." Ivan said.

Milan took Ivan to the nearest hospital, where his nose was taped, stuffed with cotton, and his lip stitched, then he took him home.

"What happened to you?" Louiza asked when she saw Ivan's face.

"A pool shark hit me with his stick." Ivan sounded like he had a cold.

Louiza scolded her son for playing pool with a stranger and said, "You'll be alright. It could have been worse. Was your nose broken?"

"Yeah. I can't stand this cotton." Ivan took the cotton out of his nostrils.

Louiza put ice on Ivan's bruised face and gave him chicken soup pungent with garlic. He slept til noon the next day and then went to Novaks to learn more about Red. Everyone he asked, knew nothing about him. If they did, they weren't talking.

The following day, Ivan visited Joe in the hospital. Joe's face was so swollen he couldn't tell if his eyes were open or closed. Joe's legs were wrapped in bandages, and a tube connected to a liquid filled bag was inserted into his arm. Ivan sat next to the bed and tapped his hand. Joe turned his head toward Ivan and tried to smile with swollen lips. He was barely audible and Ivan had to lean closer to hear him.

"My favorite boxer must've been clobbered in a fight." Joe whispered.

"Remember, I gave it up." Ivan said.

"I forgot. Why is your face bandaged?" Joe asked.

"Some pool shark hit me with a cue. I'm not as messed up as you are. I'm glad you're going to be okay." Ivan said.

"Bein' crippled is not okay." Joe's voice was getting stronger. "Have you seen Moe? Is he here in the hospital?"

"He's dead," Ivan said in a solemn tone.

Joe looked away, tears welling in his eyes. "Moe was my cousin and best friend. We grew up together."

"Sorry to give you the bad news. He was killed when you were ambushed." Ivan said.

"We shoulda known and gone another way. They trapped us by stacking barrels at the end of the alley. We shoulda plowed through em' without stoppin'" We shoulda known. We was stupid. I bet the guys who shot us were Moran's men."

Ivan told Joe about the pool incident and described the man with the red hair.

"He's one of Bugsy Moran's top men. Betcha he's one o'the guys who gunned us."

"I've got to go. I'll come back in a few days, after Moe's funeral." Ivan said.

Moe was better looking as a corpse than he looked when he was alive. Never had Ivan seen so many flowers around a casket. At the end of the funeral ceremony, Josip and Ivan watched the crowd with a few familiar faces file past them. The black suited men sitting in the front pews exited out the side door. Josip and Ivan watched the casket loaded into a hearse and then drive slowly away, followed by a motorcade of pricy black cars. Rumors circulated that Al Capone was in the first car behind the hearse.

"We need to visit Joe and tell him about Moe's funeral." Ivan said.

"Sure. We need to do that." Josip said.

Joe had been in the hospital for a week and he was improving. His face was less puffy and he was sitting up sipping a glass of water.

"Hi, guys, wish I could offer you something stronger than water." Joe said.

"Those pretty nurses make you feel better?" Josip teased.

"They help me forget my troubles. Love lookin' at 'em. How's the family, Josip?" "We're having trouble with Eddi; he's been caught stealing. I'm thinking of taking him back to Lodun, where he can live with Aunt Helena."

"Good idea. You don't want 'em gettin' in more serious stuff." Joe said.

"You mean like the Mafia?" Josip asked.

Joe avoided answering and asked, "Did ya go to Moe's funeral?"

"Yeah, it was nice. Moe looked good. There were tons of flowers and many people paid their last respects." He omitted the fact that most of them were just curious, not mourners. "It was rumored Al Capone was there."

"Nah, he wouldn't be there. Capone only goes to upper-level Mafia funerals. Moe and I wasn't with the top guys. Ya know, I have nothin to do but lay here and think. We always got to Novaks by drivin' through the alley. Moe stopped the truck when he saw the exit blocked by huge wooden barrels. I was gettin' out of the truck to push the barrels away when the bullets hit us. I'm tryin' to figure out how Bugsy's boys knew we was gonna go through that alley."

"Maybe you've taken that alley once too often." Ivan said.

"Nah, I think someone snitched. Moe and me had plenty to drink at Novaks a couple of days before doin' the job and our tongue's got loose. We was off in a corner with no one sittin' near us. Only the bartender coulda heard us. Come to think of it, I never saw the guy before."

"Huh. That's interesting. I'll ask Tony Novak about him." Ivan said.

"We was stuck in that alley and goin' no place. Those sons of bitches coulda taken the booze without shootin' us. Moe and me never killed nobody. We got money from Capone by beatin' up a few guys. I let Moe do the beatin.' He liked it. Poor Moe! I was lucky." Joe frowned and yawned.

"Glad to see you're getting better," Ivan said as he and Stefan exited the hospital room.

PROGRESS

A chill was in the air as Josip and Ivan walked from the hospital to the car. Dark clouds were gathering, a sign that a storm was approaching.

"Boy, I'm hungry," Josip said after they got in the car.

"Me, too. Why don't you have dinner at my house," Ivan said.

"Sure. I love your ma's cooking," Josip said.

Stefan was playing the piano when they entered the house, his music mingling with the aroma of goulash permeating the house. Anton and Andrew were in the kitchen, involved in a heated debate, disagreeing with each other on who was the best boxer in the world.

Louiza looked up from stirring a pot on the stove, and smiled, "Josip! It's so good to see you. We have lots of food, so you'll stay for dinner."

Josip kissed Louiza on her cheek and said, "I was hoping you'd say that."

Ivan and Josip grabbed beers and waited for dinner in the gazebo. The first snowflakes of winter were falling, settling wherever they touched.

"When are you going to Lodun?" Ivan asked as he pushed the swing back and forth.

"I was thinking of taking Eddi with me between Christmas and New Year's. I'm afraid he'll wind up in jail if we don't do something to change his stealing. He stole a bike last week and we restricted him to the house. We've punished him before when we found out he was stealing. It didn't do any good.

"Did you ever think that you might harm him further if you leave him in Lodun?"

"I can count on several families that will watch over him," Josip said

"No. I mean he'll feel abandoned by you," Ivan said

"I hadn't thought of that," Josip said.

They sat in silence, pushing the swing and watching the snow put a thin white coat on everything in the yard. Josip's mind wandered to the woods, where he imagined White Dove waiting for him at the tree. He hadn't told anyone about White Dove, not even Ivan. He had mixed emotions, for he was attracted to Theresa too.

"Let's get out of the cold and go inside," Ivan said

"Dinner is almost ready," Louiza said while taking lettuce out of the icebox. The huge ice block had melted into the size of a brick. Soon her new Philco refrigerator would arrive and the iceman would not be needed.

Just then, the old clock above the kitchen table struck the hour, and the tiny wooden boy and girl began their circular journey. "That old clock was in my house when I was born," Louiza explained to Josip. She looked out the kitchen window above her sink. "When it starts snowing, I see the mountains surrounding my old village. They were so beautiful." She picked up the large pot of stew and put it in the middle of the dining room table.

After Josip had sated his hunger he said, "Beth will be wondering where I am. I've got to go." He ran home.

Beth shouted at Josip, "Where have you been?"

"I had dinner with Ivan and his family." He answered

We've been evicted! Our neighbors have been complaining about the noise we make. The manager came here and said we have two weeks to move!"

"Darn." Josip wanted to use another word, but he never swore in front of the children.

"What are we going to do? Where will we go?" Beth asked

"Don't worry, we'll find another place," Josip said.

"I hope so. When I get off work tomorrow, I'll go looking." Beth said.

They found an apartment on the first floor of an old brown stone building, a few blocks from the Poncek house. Even though it was shabby compared to the previous one, the rent was the same. They moved their sparse belongings on Thanksgiving morning, with the help of Ivan and Stefan. By Christmas, the family had adjusted to their new home. The children were happy to be on street level and not scolded every day for making noise. The siblings had undergone one change after another in their short lives and learned a valuable lesson; change is constant and adaptability is the key to survival.

After Christmas, Josip prepared to take Eddi to Pennsylvania to visit Helena and check on the renters of his old house. He also wanted to see White Dove.

Beth could not afford to take time off, for fear of losing her job. She baked potica and wrapped them as gifts for Helena and Dr. Malvec. "Be careful with these packages, they crush easily. Give my love to them." Beth said to Josip, as he and Eddi left for Lodun.

Helena let out a little shriek of joy when she saw Josip, but she didn't recognize Eddi. He had grown taller, had peach fuzz on his face and his voice had deepened. Josip was stunned seeing Helena so aged and frail. Her paralysis had spread to her neck and only her face moved. Josip saw how upsetting this was to Eddi and sent him to see a childhood friend. Josip realized Eddi would be depressed living with the ailing Helena.

Resigned to her progressing illness, Helena told Josip not to grieve. "I look forward to being reunited with Pavel, Rose, and Frank and holding Christina in my arms again."

Josip thanked Helena for her years of friendship and help.

"I wish I could have done more. Your parents were wonderful people and such a comfort to me when Pavel died. I don't know why Pavel was hit by that boulder, or why baby Christina died, or why your parents died so young. This is God's world, and the mystery of it will hopefully be solved after I leave this life," Helena said.

"I admire your faith," Josip said.

After having breakfast with Helena the next morning, Josip and Eddi went to their old house to see the renters. A wave of sadness overtook them as they walked up the familiar front steps and knocked on the door. Mrs. Zesko, a woman in her forties, recognized them and invited them in. As Eddi entered the house, he started to hyperventilate and ran out the door. He crumpled on the front lawn and started sobbing. Josip realized he made a huge mistake bringing Eddi back to Lodun.

Mrs. Zesko came out of the house with a mug of tea laced with schnapps to help calm the distraught boy. As soon as Eddi stopped trembling, Josip took him back inside the house telling him there was nothing to fear. Mrs. Zesko gave Eddi another mug of tea without the scnapps. She said, "I feel fortunate that I live in this nice house instead of a coal company shack. You both must be hungry. Eating some lunch will make you feel better." As she prepared the sandwiches she asked, "Can my family and I stay here another year?"

"You can stay until I find a buyer for the house." Josip said.

"What price will you be asking?" Mrs. Zesko asked.

"I'm not sure; I'll let you know," Josip said.

The three of them ate the ham sandwiches and the color in Eddi's face returned. While Mrs. Zesko and Josip were talking, Eddi looked all around the bottom floor of the house. It looked different with the Zesko furniture and curtains. He would not go up the stairs to the second floor even though Mrs. Zesko gave him permission.

"Thank you so much for the lunch. We must be going." Josip said.

"Goodbye. It was good seeing you again. Glad you're feeling better, Eddi."

Josip took Eddi to his boyhood friend's house to stay for the afternoon, while he went to the edge of town, where the woods began.

"At least someone is happy in that house," Josip muttered to himself as he walked toward his favorite tree. The oak stood tall and healthy, the axe marks faint, for the tree had grown bark around its wound. From behind the tree trunk emerged a lovely head of dark hair.

"Hello, Josip."

White Dove came out from behind the tree with a blanket wrapped around her. Josip ran to her and embraced her. They walked arm and arm to the small hut Josip had built so long ago and cleared the snow from the entrance. They lay on the blanket, covering leaf-covered earth.. Josip removed White Dove's clothes, kissing every part of her body until she moaned and they could no longer contain their passion. After their exploding union, they dozed, awakening with their bodies still entangled.

"We should get married. I love you," Josip said.

"I love you too," White Dove said.

"I'll be twenty-one soon, and you'll be nineteen next month. When I sell the house, the money will be shared with my brother and sisters. Even so, our share will be enough for the two of us for a while. I'll come back for you in the spring."

After kissing each other goodbye, Josip picked up Eddi from his friend's house. Eddi was cheerful. Maybe that's what he needs, more friends, Josip thought. Both he and Eddi returned to Cleveland, happier than they had been in a long time.

Heavy snow fell in January and February was just as snowy and just as cold. On Valentine's Day, Ivan marched over to Beth's house with another box of candy with his gift hidden inside. The children got excited when they saw the candy box, but Ivan told them only their big sister could open it. Beth carefully took the cover of the candy and found a small box wrapped in red paper in the middle of the chocolates.

"Oh, my!" Beth exclaimed when she took out the gold pendant shaped like a heart, pressing it to her bosom. She gave Ivan a peck on the cheek. He responded by putting his hands on her waist, drawing her closer to him and kissing her with intensity. She wriggled out of his grasp and sat on the couch.

"How sweet of you! Help me put it on." Beth said.

Ivan fastened the chain around Beth's neck and nestled her in his arms. They sat like that for a long time while Jenny and Christy played with dolls, Katja was reading a magazine and Eddi was in the kitchen, trying to understand his homework.

When Ivan returned home, the radio was announcing news of a gangland style execution of several mobsters in a downtown garage in Chicago. The garage was a favorite gathering place for Moran's gang. Since it was public knowledge that Al Capone and Bugs Moran were bitter enemies, Al's men were the suspects in the killings.

The next afternoon, he visited Joe in his new lodgings, a board and care facility in the middle of the city. Ivan found the former Capone gangster sitting in his wheelchair, staring out his bedroom window. He wheeled his chair around when he heard Ivan say, "Hello."

"Did you ever find anything out about that bartender?" Joe asked.

"He was a stand-in for the regular guy that was sick. He must have been the snitch. No one knows where he is. Did you hear about the massacre in Chicago?"

"Yeah! That Moran gang deserved what they got. They're the ones that killed Moe and put me in this wheel chair.

Ivan shifted his feet, "How do you like it here?"

"Cut the crap. You wanna know more about the gang, don't ya?" Joe snapped.

Ivan, surprised by Joe's outburst, nodded.

"I'll tell you. I came to the U.S. with Moe after the Bolsheviks took over Russia. We didn't like the way we was livin' and heard there was lots of money in America. So, we sneaked out of Russia and came here. Coal mining was the best payin' job we could get, but we didn't like the work and the dangerous tunnels. Transportin' liquor and roughin' up a few guys for Al Capone's operations was easy money. We paid a high price for that dough; Moe is dead, and I'm a cripple."

"What did you do with all the money you made?" Ivan asked.

"I stashed it in a secret place." Joe changed the conversation. "It's nice to see you. You're the only one who comes to visit."

"Yeah? I like hearing your stories. I'll come next week." Ivan left.

The week before Easter, Helena died and in her will she bequeathed her house to Josip. Dr. Malvec notified the Koznar children by phoning the Poncek home. No one was shocked by Helena's death and Josip was glad her suffering was over. Josip traveled alone to Lodun to claim the house and sign the necessary papers. Once again, he met White Dove by the giant tree and noticed her stomach had enlarged.

"I'm going to have your baby," she said.

Josip felt weak in the knees. He was stunned, filled joy and pride. "We are getting married, now."

The next morning in the Johnstown courthouse, they exchanged vows witnessed by old Dr. Malvec. White Dove and Josip were legally married, although in their hearts and minds they had wed four months ago. They spent their one night honeymoon in Helena's house and Josip was a happy man. He left for Cleveland in the morning, promising to return as soon as possible. The train clicked and clacked along the tracks as he pondered whether to tell his family he was married. When he arrived home, Beth kept staring at him. "You must have enjoyed your trip, I've never seen you smile so much."

"Yes, it was nice. I rented Helena's house to a friend." The half-truth seemed to satisfy Beth's curiosity.

THE POOR

Beth continued cleaning house for the Cappos, avoiding Mr. Cappo whenever he was working at home. Whenever they met in a hallway or a room, Beth kept her distance and he kept his. Meeting Ivan cooled his ardor. Beth had a suspicion that Mrs. Cappo was aware her husband philandered. Many evenings he made many excuses to stay late at the office. She never confronted him about his evenings out, because he could limit her supply of money, or even worse, divorce her. Then she would have to give up her lavish life style. Tolerating her husband's suspected disloyalty kept her ability to buy what she wanted.

While Beth helped serve food at several home parties, she learned that the Cappo's were one of the wealthiest families in Cleveland. They were generous to politicians and charities and had many influential friends. She circulated appetizers among the guests and overheard many conversations. The women chatted about their children and the latest fashions while the men talked about business and the stock market.

"I'm worried. My stocks are decreasing in value and I've been counting on them to help finance my second store." Mr. Cappo was talking in a low voice to two men smoking stogies in the corner of the spacious living room.

"Yes, I'm worried too. We should all put money back in the market, to bolster it," one of the men suggested. Another said, "That's a good idea."

Their plan did not work. It was like trying to stop bleeding from a large gash with a small bandage. The price of stocks kept dropping, sputtering for a few days, then spiraling downward until their worth was almost nothing. The two worst days in the year of 1929 were Black Thursday, October 24 and Black Tuesday, October 29. A group of leading bankers tried to calm the market by buying up stocks, but it was futile. President Herbert Hoover initiated many programs to curb the devastating effect the failed market had on the economy. The programs could not prevent the inevitable.

Mr. Cappo invested heavily in the stock market and was one of the first victims of the crash. Like most investors, he paid only ten percent of the price of his shares. The brokerage houses owned the other ninety percent. Stocks were a good investment since the end of World War I. When the market became unstable in the fall of 1929, the brokerage houses called in the money owed them on stocks bought on margin. It was similar to buying a house for ten percent down and owing the rest to the bank, hoping the property would increase in value, and sell for a profit.

The cause of the depression was the lack of laws preventing investors from buying stocks at highly inflated prices on margin Prices plunged as investors and brokerages sold at any price to minimize their losses. Mr. Cappo's wealth evaporated and he closed his second store before it was opened to the public. He tried to save money by lowering his expenses, resulting in the dismissal of most of his employees, including Beth.

The stock market crash had a domino effect, causing one fourth of Americans to become jobless due to business closures. The excess of the twenties disappeared. No longer did people buy on the installment plan or buy the latest gadget, a new car, or anything else for that matter. Fewer customers led to fewer employees, which lowered income and consumerism. The poor, the hungry, and the homeless multiplied astronomically. Saving everything and not wasting anything, was the prevalent mindset. The nation's citizens shared food with neighbors and the increasing number of beggars that came to their doors

Josip and Ivan had no families to support and were the newest employees at their jobs, therefore the first to be laid off. Fortunately, Josip still had the money from smuggling booze hidden underneath the gazebo in the Poncek's yard. A portion of this ill-gotten money saved the Koznar children from eviction. Other apartment dwellers who could not pay their rent, found their possessions sitting on the street when they came home from a day of job hunting. These people sold what they could and left most of their furniture behind.

President Herbert Hoover tried to pump up the economy, but his policies failed. The homeless joined other destitute families to form shantytowns called Hoovervills, blaming President Hoover for their poverty. They constructed dwellings out of scrap such as wood crates, corrugated metal, and abandoned cars. These shantytowns lacked electricity and basic sanitation services, leading to the spread of disease. The squatters scavenged and begged for food. It was common to see them hunting through trashcans for anything edible. Farmers had food and the hungry traded all sorts of goods for it, as they did for medical care.

The Poncek family was fortunate, because Anton was able to keep his job. Instead of firing part of their work force, the gas company limited working days to nine days a month per employee. This substantially reduced Anton's paycheck, but it was better than no job at all. In order to feed the family, Louiza and the children raised chickens and kept the unsightly coops hidden behind the gazebo.

The neighborhood came together on Saturday nights to share food, stories, and gossip. Every family suffered from the economic crisis, and it was important to stick together and help each other. Potlucks alternated from home to home, where people shared all sorts of foods, and discussed the weak economy. The immigrants, however, didn't understand anything about the stock market; it was only for the wealthy.

One of the biggest stories circulating at the weekly community supper was the one about the local jeweler, Mr. Velko. No one was buying jewelry any more, so he closed his store. He boarded up the display windows and put his inventory in a vault, blaming capitalism for his woes. He decided communism was the best form of government and joined the American Communist Party. Believing Russians shared all wealth and were treated equally, he sold his store for less than its value and moved to Russia with his wife, daughter and inventory

"Mr. Velko was smart to go to Russia. People don't starve there. I'd go too, but I'm too old. I don't have the money to get there," Fritzy said.

"I say good riddance to Mr. Velko. My son bought a pair of pearl earrings from him for my birthday. The pearls dissolved when they became wet. They were made of clay, painted to look like pearls. He's a cheat and Russia deserves him," a neighbor said.

Louiza chimed in, "Mr. Velko did seem a bit sneaky, never looking straight at me when I talked with him. But, he should have waited until we have our new President before going to Russia."

Ivan arrived late to the community supper and scraped up the last of food on his plate. He listened to the crowd debating the merits of communism versus democracy while he ate. After finishing his meal, he said loudly so all could hear. "I feel sorry for Mr. Velko. Joseph Stalin rules Russia with an iron fist. Stalin is cruel and kills anyone who disagrees with him. He's murdered thousands of Russians and others. Don't believe the Communist propaganda that all their citizens are treated equally. There's no freedom or wealth in that country, unless a person is on Stalin's staff or belongs to the KGB. Those are Stalin's henchmen, similar to Mafia gangsters. They get extra food, a nice apartment, and vacations on the Black Sea for spying, torturing and killing."

Ivan continued. "The USSR government controls everything, including its publications and news agency, TASS. Here in the United States, we have representation, freedom of the press and a fair judicial system. We, the people are the government."

Fritzy and the neighbors listened with respect to Ivan, who was informed about such matters. Most of them were immigrants and could not read English, limiting their information. The young ones read English, but no one read as much as Ivan. The crowd stopped talking about Communism and commented on the excellent apple strudel Fritzy had baked. Every crumb was gone by the time the potluck participants dispersed.

Beth was again experiencing the poverty she had known most of her life. She walked from store to store and house to house, looking for work, but to no avail. The bottoms of her feet were sore due to the thinning soles of her shoes. She found some cardboard pushed up against a fence and tore it in half to line the inside of her shoes. Beth walked past neglected luxury homes, where lawns were overgrown and weeds flourished in the flowerbeds. The sun dipped below the horizon as she viewed the once brightly lit Cappo house. The house was dark except for a flicker of light in an upstairs window.

Nearby was the small business district where she once shopped for the Cappos. In the dim light of a lone street light, she could see that most of the store windows were boarded up. The street was deserted, except for one man digging through a garbage can. Beth gasped. It was Mr. Cappo, looking scrawny and unkempt. She hid behind a wall and watched him. He pulled something out of the can that looked like a piece of meat, or was it something else. Mr. Cappo examined it, tucked it inside his jacket, and walked toward his house. Observing Mr. Cappo digging in a garbage can, seeing homeless families living in cardboard lean-tos, and witnessing long lines at the soup kitchens, saddened Beth. The old levels of class distinction were blurred; everyone was poor, except those who were lucky enough to have a job.

It was time to go home and make the same bean dinner she had fixed three nights in a row. She was tired of eating beans that bloated her stomach and tired from weeks of searching for work. Instead of looking for work the next morning, Beth went to the Office of Public Assistance and asked for help.

A prim, grim woman sitting behind a large desk asked her, "How can I help you?"

"My brother and I take care of four siblings and we never have enough to eat. I want to apply for food stamps." Beth said.

"Where are your parents?" The woman asked

"We are orphans," Beth said.

The woman's demeanor softened. "You are too young for all that responsibility. We'll place you all on farms where you can work and have plenty to eat."

"Will we be together?" Beth asked.

"No, that is not possible." The woman said.

"I can't let you do that! As long as I can lift one finger, no one will separate us." Beth stomped out of the office.

A dejected Beth returned home. Josip was sitting on the couch, watching the children play jacks. "You are looking glum. No luck at job hunting, huh." Josip said.

"Let's talk in the kitchen, and I'll fix some tea," Beth did not want the children to hear what she had to say. She heated water on the stove and poured it in a cup over an old soggy teabag. She poured half of the beige water in another cup for Josip.

"For God's sake, throw that teabag away," Josip said.

"This is our last teabag. What are we going to do? We don't have money to pay the rent next month."

"Beth, I should have told you this a few months ago." Josip took a deep breath. "I'm married to White Dove, and we have a baby son. They are living in Helena's house."

Beth eyes widened and her mouth was agape.

"Don't be mad at me. I've loved White Dove ever since Mom and Dad died. You should know what it's like to be in love. I see the way you act when you're with Ivan and the affection in your voice when you talk about him. Look, I have a plan that will save us from living in a shantytown. I'll move back to Lodun with Christy and Jenny. White Dove and I will take care of the girls. You and Katja can move in with Maggie and her aunt. Eddi can board at the Poncek house where Louiza will look after him and he'll be well fed."

"I knew it would come to this. You're splitting us up," Beth said.

"These are harsh times, and tough decisions have to be made. I want to be with my wife and child, and you don't need me anymore, Beth. You have Ivan.. Katja and Eddi are teenagers and only need a bit of supervision. This move will benefit you; you won't have to worry so much, or work so hard taking care of all of us."

"How will I pay Maggie's aunt?" Beth asked.

"I'm sure she'll let you stay rent free until you find work. She is a kind soul."

That evening Beth walked to Aunt Bea's house and asked if she and Katja could stay with her for a few months. Without hesitation, Aunt Bea said that was a splendid idea and suggested Beth seek work at her brother's suit factory. Nothing could have made Maggie, an only child, happier than to have Beth as a roommate.

The plan was in motion and Josip gave notice to the apartment owner, who said, "I'm sorry to see you leave. Yours is the third apartment vacated this year and I have another family moving out at the end of the month. Would you stay if I lowered the rent?"

Josip was polite, "No, thank you. We have to move."

Ivan and Stefan helped Josip load the rented truck with furniture and trunks of clothes. When Christy and Jenny realized they were going to Pennsylvania without Beth, they cried.. Beth calmed them by saying she would visit soon and gave them lollipops. The children all hugged and assured each other it wouldn't be long before they were together again. It seemed to Beth that she was always saying goodbye to a part of her family. Ivan and Stefan put Beth, Katja and Eddi's suitcases in their car and drove to their house. Beth had mixed feelings, sad that her family was separating, yet happy to be staying in Cleveland where Ivan lived.

Eddi was to share Boris's room, for there was no other place for him to sleep. The other bedrooms were full, and Louiza's brother Andrew slept on the sofa in the parlor. After staying a couple of hours at the Poncek house, Beth and Katja said goodnight to Eddi and reminded him they lived only a few blocks apart and would see each other in a day or two.

Louiza said to Beth, "Don't worry child, you'll all be together again. Eddi will like living here. He'll never go hungry."

The next morning, Maggie took Beth to the warehouse and introduced her to Uncle Ted. He was a large, affable man with a keen business mind and a good judge of character, resulting in an efficient, honest staff.

"Have you ever sewn?" Uncle Ted asked Beth.

"Yes. My mother taught me. I make clothes for my sisters and myself."

"Okay. I need someone to sew sleeves on men's jackets two days a week. I'll pay you the same rate I pay Maggie; 20 cents an hour." His business had dwindled since the depression began and he survived by reducing his employee's hours and lowering his suit prices.

The first person Beth phoned, to tell of her good luck, was Josip.

"I'm happy for you, my dear sister. Splitting up the family was difficult, but it was the right decision. Life will keep getting better for all of us," Josip said.

"How are Christy and Jenny?" Beth asked.

"They are fine. They like White Dove and enjoy playing with baby Frank. We named him after Dad. I think he looks like him. I'll call you next week. .Bye now."

The second person Beth notified was Ivan.

"That's great. I sure hope I can get a job soon," Ivan said.

"Can I talk to Eddi?" Beth asked.

"He's not here. He was gone when we awoke this morning. We

177

found a note on the kitchen table, saying he was going to California to pick oranges. He said not to worry about him and he will write you." Ivan said.

Beth should have known. Eddi was restless and wanted adventure. She wished he had told her he was going to California.

Eddi developed a tough skin going through the agony of losing his parents and experiencing the struggles that followed. Overcoming his sense of abandonment, he felt old enough to take care of himself. He hoped Beth and Josip would respect his decision.

At the train station he figured out which trains ran west, in the direction of California. The freight trains had guards posted around them when they stopped to load and unload goods. He watched to see where he could hop on a boxcar unnoticed. His chance came when a freight train spewing blinding smoke, adjacent to a passenger train, was about to leave. Being quick, he was able to dart behind the last car of the passenger train. Running as fast as he could, he jumped into the last boxcar as the train chugged out of the station. The boxcar was empty with only a bunch of straw on the floor. He enjoyed watching the scenery whiz by, until the train slowed down in a small town and two hobos climbed into his car.

"Got any food?" one of them asked him.

"No. I'm hungry too. I've got to get off this train before it gains speed."

Eddi jumped off the boxcar and hit soft dirt, getting his clothes dirty. He hunted through garbage cans next to a café near the train station and found some half-rotten cabbage leaves. He ate the musty-tasting leaves, assuaging his hunger. At the opposite end of the town was a residential area where he stopped at the nicest home on the block. He knocked on the door and a young mother holding a crying baby answered the door. "What do you want?" she said.

"I'll work in exchange for some food," he said loudly, to be heard above the noisy baby.

"I don't have any work for you now, but I can give you some soup and bread."

"Thank you. God bless you, ma'am," Eddi said.

After Eddi waited on the steps a few minutes, the woman came out with a bowl of soup and a piece of bread. There were a few small pieces of meat in it. She also gave him a wet rag to wipe his face and hands. He felt better after filling his stomach and walked back to the station where he hopped on another train going west. All types of people joined him in the boxcar, mostly young men who had the agility to jump on or off a boxcar. He jumped off the train in Des Moines, Iowa, and stayed for a few days, earning food by helping a farmer plant his crop. The masses of people traveling west, relied on the rumor that there were jobs aplenty in California. Crops needed picking, but not in great quantities due to the lack of consumer money from the lack of employment. One affected the other, going round and round, like a dog chasing its tail.

Eddi often sunned himself on the top of his boxcar on warm days, enjoying the varied landscapes as he moved through each state. When the land became barren and the sun became too hot to stay on top of the boxcar, he knew he was nearing California.

Eddi was never arrested for riding the trains illegally due to his craftiness in avoiding the law. He often went to city jails asking to sleep in one of the bunk beds, if available. If there was an empty bed, he was welcomed. He managed to mail a few brief letters to Beth, saying he was fine and hoped all was well with the family. He reached Los Angeles on a hot October day, and hitchhiked to the corner of Hollywood and Vine looking for movie stars.

There weren't any famous movie stars on that infamous corner and Eddi ambled west on Hollywood Boulevard. He walked several blocks to the Egyptian Theater and became awed by its ornate facade. After viewing the entrance from all angles, he went into a soda fountain next to the theater called the Pig 'n' Whistle. He bought an ice cream cone and stared at the pretty girls sitting at the counter whom he thought might be starlets. One of them looked at him and he was embarrassed. Aware of looking disheveled and needing a bath, Eddi ate his ice cream cone outside the café. He continued walking west and came upon another architectural beauty, Grauman's Chinese Theater.

"Holy cow! Beth would love to see this!" he said aloud to no one in particular, unable to stop his enthusiasm. A bystander near him was startled at his outburst and backed away. He was anxious to tell Beth, an avid moviegoer, about the theaters. She read movie magazines and talked about movie stars, fascinated with their glamour and romances.

Another person who yearned to go to California was Andrew. He had lived with his sister's family for several years and was getting restless. He once enjoyed wandering all over the country after working a year in New York. He liked the freedom of going where he pleased, meeting all kinds of people, and seeing the different areas of his adopted country. The limited use of his leg caused him to settle down in his sister's house. With time, the leg gained strength and he was ready to hit the road again.

There were other reasons Andrew wanted to leave. He disliked living with Boris, a thorn in his side, and tired of the arguments in the crowded house. The spring and fall weather was lovely in Cleveland. However, the humidity and mosquitoes in the summer bothered him and the cold winter made his body ache. Warm dry air is what he needed. Eddi's adventure trip to California intrigued Andrew, for in all his travels, he had never been west of the Mississippi. Southern California is where he wanted to go.

Andrew told Louiza, "My dear sister, I need to leave and go west for my health. Don't worry about me. I'll be fine and will keep in touch."

"I understand why you're leaving and I'll miss you. If you don't like it out west, you are always welcome here," Louiza said.

Andrew bought a train ticket that took him all the way to Los Angeles. He got off in the ornate train station of Los Angeles. A newspaper stand had several newspapers with headlines stating Franklin Delano Roosevelt had won the presidential election and would take office in March. An article titled, "Dust Storms in the Midwest Abating" was also featured. He emerged from the station into a warm sunny day and everything seemed brighter. He hailed a cab and went to Eddi's apartment.

Beth liked her new job of fitting sleeves on men's jackets. Learning the sewing technique was a cinch and she hummed while working. Not Maggie, for she was bored and much too slow.

Uncle Ted was not happy. "Maggie, you've got to work faster. It takes you too much time to sew on those collars."

"I know I'm not good at this. Can't I work in the business department? I like math and can help you with accounting," Maggie responded.

"Okay, I'll give you a try. Sewing is not for you." Uncle Ted said.

The girls were fortunate to have jobs when approximately a fourth of the U.S. population was out of work. The resulting poverty caused many serious situations: Groups of men stormed into stores demanding food and only stopped from looting by armed intervention. Three thousand people assembled in Detroit for a Communist-initiated protest march to the Ford factory in Dearborn, believing the auto mogul, Henry Ford, was partly to blame for the depression. The peaceful demonstrators did not obey the order by police to turn back, and four people were killed in the melee that ensued. World War I veterans gathered in Washington DC, insisting on immediate payment of bonuses that Congress voted to pay them in 1925. Police dispersed the angry vets.

Hey, Taxi.

The national mood became optimistic even though people were still living in shantytowns, looking for jobs and waiting in soup lines. The populace was hoping the newly elected President and his cabinet would initiate programs to boost the economy once they came into power. Some of the jobless did find work, like Ivan. He was talking with friends on a street corner late in the afternoon, when Fritzy's cousin, Artie, stopped his car near the corner and called out,

"Hey, Ivan, wanna job?"

"Sure." Ivan said.

"The Cityside Cab Company needs a driver, and you're the first one I've told."

"Gosh, how did I get so lucky?" Ivan said.

"I like you, kid. When you apply for the job, tell 'em Artie sent you."

"Will the office be open now?" Ivan asked.

"Yeah, the office manager will be there til five. You have an hour to get over there."

There were two taxicab companies in the city, one was The Dependable Cab and the other was Cityside Cab Company. Ivan never used either one of them because a taxi ride cost more than a streetcar ticket. He walked the few blocks to the Cityside office. An open garage next to the office had one yellow-and-black colored cab parked in it. He assumed the other taxis were out on the road. The manager hired Ivan after he said Artie sent him and assigned him to the taxi in the garage painted with three sixes painted on it. Ivan did not want to drive a cab that had the sign of the devil on it. "Those numbers are unlucky and I want another cab."

"Sorry," the manager said, "You either take that car, or I'll hire someone else."

Ivan dismissed his superstitious feeling, for he needed the job. He drove the taxi that evening for his first customer. The calls for a taxi were few and the tips were small, if any. Most people in his area were too poor to hire a taxi and walked or rode the trolley to their destinations. At least he was working and earning a few dollars a week. He had been on the job for a month and was eating dinner when he got a phone call from his manager, asking him to pick up a woman at fifty-five Mill Avenue.

"Where am I taking her?" Ivan said.

"The woman said it's not far, about halfway to the airport. She'll direct you."

Ivan inspected the car to make sure it was clean and full of gas, then drove to fifty-five Mill Avenue. A pretty woman about thirty years old, wearing an expensive fur, was waiting on the curb in front of the house. This was a wealthy dame.

"Hello, handsome," the perfumed woman said as she got into the cab.

She must have seen too many Mae West movies. Ivan said, "Well, lady, where do you want to go?"

"Here's the address." She handed him a piece of paper."

"I know this street, there's nothing but empty fields on it."

"My friend built a house on one of the lots recently," she said with a nervous laugh.

"Okay, we're on our way" Ivan said as he stepped on the gas peddle.

Ivan drove to the outskirts of the city, found the street and slowed his speed while looking for the house. All he saw were fields and he stopped the car and said, "I think you have the wrong address, lady."

Instead of responding, his passenger opened the car door and ran. Ivan got out of the taxi to call her back when two men jumped and felled him to the ground. They punched him, cut his head and then his arm with something very sharp. He was in pain and screamed and he could not see.

"Enough! Enough!" Ivan cried.

One of the men whispered in his ear, "Join the union."

The attack stopped and Ivan heard the men retreating. He wiped his eyes with his hand so he could see and blood dripped from his fingers. Thankful he wasn't blinded, he tried to lift himself off the ground, but couldn't. Two boys on bicycles were staring at him.

There was blood all over the pavement. He heard a siren and it stopped in front of him. A man in a white uniform asked. "Can you talk?"

"Yeah, I can talk." Ivan said.

The medics checked Ivan's vital signs, stopped the bleeding and put him on a stretcher. The ambulance started and the siren came on. "We're taking you to the hospital," the medic said.

"You came just in time. I was being killed," Ivan said.

"If someone wanted you killed, you would be dead already. Some female called emergency saying you were injured and named the street where we could find you."

At the hospital, a doctor examined him. "No major blood vessels are severed or internal organs damaged. The cut on your head is deep, and needs stitches, but the slice on your arm is slight, and just needs a bandage. You're a healthy young fella and will heal quickly. I'm injecting an anesthetic around the cut in your head, so you won't feel the stitching. I'm putting some iodine on your arm."

While the doctor stitched his head wound, Ivan reviewed the events of the evening and looked at the hospital clock. Three hours had elapsed since he picked up the sleazy woman and it seemed like an eternity. The possibility of his death on the dead-end street was sobering. His life could have been over in a second.

"You'll have some scarring when your wounds heal. Hair will hide the scar on your scalp and the one on your arm will fade with time. Come back in two weeks and I'll remove the stitches," the doctor said.

Ivan changed from his hospital gown to his blood-spattered uniform and went to the receptionist desk to check out. Two police officers were waiting for him, their badges gleaming with authority. He recognized the cops, for they often stopped in Novak's bar.

"I'm Officer O'Malley, and this is Officer Flannigan. We have to ask you some questions about your attack." They guided Ivan into a small office near the reception desk. The portly O'Mally asked, "Tell us what happened to you?"

Ivan described his passenger, gave the house number where he picked her up and the false address the woman gave him. "Two men attacked me from behind after the woman got out of the car. They forced me to the ground and cut me up."

"They were trying to scare you," Flannigan said.

"Your watch and money weren't stolen. Ya know what they wanted?" O'Malley asked.

"They wanted me to join a union," Ivan said.

"Why'd they pick on you?" Flanagan asked.

"I don't know. Maybe 'cause I'm a greenhorn," Ivan said.

O'Malley wrote down the Mill street address along with Ivan's address and phone number and said, "We'll keep in touch."

Ivan walked into the hospital lobby and saw his brother waiting for him.

"Boy, am I glad to see you. You really had your ass kicked," Stefan said.

"Yeah, I was set up by a dame and attacked by two hoods," Ivan said.

Stefan led Ivan into the parking lot where taxicab number 666 sat.

"How did you get my cab?" Ivan asked.

"Boris drove me to the spot the ambulance found you, and your keys were in the gutter, next to the cab. Lucky it wasn't stolen." Stefan said.

"No one would steal a car with those numbers painted on it. That cab is a jinx." Ivan said.

That night, with Stefan driving, the taxi was returned and the keys were given to the manager who expressed anger over the attack. "I bet those thugs were hired by the union. They want to force my drivers to join the union and go on strike with the Dependable Cab drivers. I'm going to hire my own thugs to ride in my taxis. Fight fire with fire I always say."

"By the way, I quit." Ivan said.

"Boris is waiting in the car for us. Let's get out of here." Stefan said.

Everyone made a big fuss over Ivan when he got home. While he recuperated, Beth brought him crossword puzzles, magazines, and books from the library. Friends dropped by to hear his story and wish him a speedy recovery.

Fritzy also brought him gifts. "I knitted this pair of socks for you and this bottle of whiskey is from Artie. He said to tell you he's sorry you were beaten up."

"I bet he is. That's expensive whiskey. Why didn't he come himself?"

"He said he was too busy getting ready to move to Detroit."

"Was Artie ever involved with a union?" Ivan asked.

"I don't know. I never heard him say nothin about a union." Fritzy said.

"I sure would like to talk to him." Ivan said.

"How're you feelin'?" Fritzy asked.

"My head hurts."

Louiza came into the room, and Fritzy started gossiping about a mutual friend. Ivan was not interested in the conversation, annoyed he couldn't read his book in peace. He said, "Thanks for the socks and coming to see me Fritzy" and went to his bedroom. He put the socks in a drawer and hid the whiskey bottle under the socks.

Officer O'Malley phoned Ivan, "We went to the house on Mill Avenue and a young family lives there. They know nothing about the woman you described. Is there something you haven't told us?"

"I've told you everything." Ivan didn't have anything more to say.

"Until we find more clues, the investigation is in a holding pattern." O'Malley ended the call.

"I wonder if O'Malley was involved in the set up. He drinks at Novaks and you know he's a dishonest cop." Ivan told Stefan.

"You can't prove anything. Forget it. Just be glad you weren't killed," Stefan said.

Vows

One of Ivan's favorite activities besides reading was going to Novak's Tavern, discussing sports, politics and cars. His pals nicknamed him "The Professor," and they often questioned him about history. Ivan became irritated if asked to repeat the answer or when his siblings questioned him too often. The only sister that Ivan never shooed away was Theresa, his intellectual equal. She read as much as he did and treated him with respectful distain. However, he had the upper hand, for he was the oldest in the family and a male.

Women discussed babies, clothing and shopping, subjects of no interest to Ivan. Beth didn't talk about those things when she was with him. She was no shrinking violet and offered her opinion even if it disagreed with his. He liked her spunk. Having debates was the way his family functioned and he was used to altercations.

Ivan's wounds healed rapidly and he only spent a day in bed. The taxicab attack put Ivan in a reflective mood, making him think about his future. Beth visited him daily, showing her care and concern, which touched him. It was five days since the attack, and he was sitting alone with Beth on the sofa in the parlor. He felt comfortable talking with her, they had so much in common. She was fun to be with, except when she talked about her parents. Ivan put his arm around Beth, her fragrance intoxicating. He watched her stroke Macek, the family's new kitten.

I love this cat's blue eyes." Beth said.

Ivan took the purring cat out of Beth's lap and put it on the floor. It scurried away.

"Why did you do that?" Beth asked.

"I want your full attention." Ivan said.

Her eyes widened. "Is something the matter?" Beth asked

That depends on your answer," Ivan took a deep breath and said,

"Let's go downtown tomorrow and get a marriage license." as he looked into Beth's eyes.

"That's a great idea." Beth said and they kissed.

The wedding was set for May 30, a holiday when friends and family could attend the ceremony. Beth asked for wedding advice from her future mother-in-law.

"We don't have enough money to afford renting a hall." Beth said

"We can use our yard for the reception," Louiza offered.

"That's wonderful. I should ask Katja to be Maid of Honor. She has been sick every day with her pregnancy and I don't know if she would make it down the aisle.

"Why not have Theresa as your Maid of Honor. I'll pay for her bridesmaid dress. Your sisters in Pennsylvania won't care." Louiza said.

"Yes. Theresa is a good choice," Beth said.

The loss of Ivan's job reduced the amount of money the couple could spend on the wedding. Because Beth had a steady income from her sewing job, she paid for her wedding gown, bouquet, Ivan's tuxedo and the wedding rings.

Eddi and Andrew sent a telegram from California congratulating Beth and Ivan on their forthcoming marriage. Josip arrived the day before the wedding with White Dove, their son Frankie, Jenny, and Christy. The young girls were thrilled to be in such a big city and excited to see their older sisters again.

Louiza fed and housed the family, borrowing quilts and blankets from the neighbors. Josip, White Dove and Frankie slept in the gazebo decorated with garlands of ivy, ready for the reception the next afternoon. The next day everyone awoke early, and the men donned their best suits. Stefan drove the dashing groom, dressed in a black tuxedo with a white tie, to the church. Josip borrowed a neighbor's car and drove to Aunt Bea's house to pick up Beth

When Josip arrived, Aunt Bea was putting Beth's veil on her head, while Maggie fussed with the myriad of buttons on the back of the white satin gown. Katja, looking rather pale, sat in the corner of the parlor observing the activity. Beth's headpiece had tiny flowers at the sides that fastened the gauzy veil.

"Beth, you look beautiful," Josip said.

"Thank you. You look great too. I'm nervous," Beth said.

"Well, this is a big day. I'd like to be alone with you for a few minutes," Josip said. The women left the room. "Here you are, all grown up and ready to marry. You and I have had a tough time, but we've managed to survive. Mom and Dad are here in spirit. I know they are proud of you."

Beth kept her emotions in check, determined not to cry. "Josip, you've been a pillar of strength to me. You're my hero!"

They hugged, and Josip said in a cheerful voice, "It's time for you to get married."

A radiant Beth walked down the aisle holding Josip's arm with Theresa leading the way as the organ played, "Here Comes the Bride." Ivan was waiting for her in front of the altar with Stefan next to him. Her heart beat quickened.

Beth pretended her parents were with her and she was happy. She saw her family sitting in the front pews. Pale Katja looked miserable as she leaned on her husband, holding her hands on her expanded stomach. Jenny and Christy's eyes were as big as saucers gazing at her dressed like a princess.

When the entourage stopped at the foot of the altar, Josip placed Beth's hand in Ivan's outstretched hand. The couple held hands during the incantations until they bowed in prayer. They opened their mouths with their tongues slightly protruding to accept the communion wafer, careful not to let it touch their teeth. Ever since she was a girl, Beth wanted to chew the thin wafer instead of letting it dissolve, but this was not the time to do the forbidden.

At the conclusion of the Mass, it was time to say the traditional vows. Theresa handed Ivan's plain gold ring to Beth. In the midst of Stefan handing the bride's ring to Ivan, he dropped the platinum band set with six tiny diamonds, on the marble floor. The sound of the ring bouncing down the stone steps made an echoing ping in the vaulted sanctuary. Stefan quickly retrieved the ring and transferred it to Ivan. The accident broke the seriousness of the nuptials, and the amused couple giggled as they placed the bands on each other's fingers and each said, "I do" to the age-old question

The Priest pronounced the couple man and wife as Ivan lifted Beth's veil and kissed her. They turned toward the pews with wide smiles and the audience clapped. After photos were taken, the newlyweds emerged from the church, were pelted with rice as the crowd cheered. They hurried to the sedan decorated with white crepe paper and the words "JUST MARRIED" chalked on the rear window.

After the hungry wedding party ate a festive breakfast at Aunt Bea's house, Beth napped, needing energy for the rest of the day. Ivan went to his mother's house to help ready the back yard for the reception. No one had money, so the neighbors contributed food as their gifts. Anton gave a barrel of wine and several people brought beer to the party.

In the late afternoon Beth joined Ivan at the house and they entered the Poncek's backyard filled with their guests. Stefan announced, "Mr. and Mrs. Ivan Poncek." Everyone clapped and the band played a waltz as the newlyweds danced alone on a rented wooden platform. After a few minutes, the platform became crowded with dancers and the band played a polka. When the hot afternoon turned into a warm night and the mosquitoes began to bite, the party moved into the house.

It was time for Josip and his family to catch a train back to Lodun. He thanked Louiza and Anton, for their hospitality and invited Beth and Ivan to visit him in Pennsylvania. The party became livelier in the evening hours as the band played on. Soon the noise level increased to a high pitch with singing, laughing, and talking. Louiza was glad everyone was having a good time, but she was tired and ached from all the activity, and went to bed.

After spending half the night sitting in the kitchen debating politics and drinking too much liquor, Anton, Milan and Boris stumbled into the dining room at midnight. The boisterous crowd quieted and joined Stefan as he sang and played the old wedding song on his accordion. Theresa took off Beth's veil and pinned a red rose in her hair.

It was two A.M. when the exhausted newlyweds entered their apartment on the second floor of an old brownstone building. Ivan lay on the bed while Beth changed her wedding gown to a nightgown in the bathroom. The man she loved with all her heart was waiting for her, wanting her, and she was nervous. She had not told him of her accident jumping over the fence. When she came into the bedroom, Ivan got up from the bed and handed her a small box tied with a white bow and said, "I bought this for you."

Inside the box was a wristwatch with their names and date of marriage engraved on the back of it. "I will cherish it always." Ivan pulled her to the bed and took her gown off. There was no resistance and they consummated their marriage easily. Ivan had a puzzled expression on his face.

"Don't look that way. I should have told you this long ago. I was the best at jumping in my neighborhood when I was young. One day, I was showing off and jumped the fence in our backyard. I landed on a pointed slat spread-eagle and it tore into me. You believe me, don't you?" Beth pleaded.

"Of course I do," Ivan answered.

"I was afraid to tell you."

"Uh, huh." Ivan's eyes closed. He was falling asleep.

Beth had started her marriage with a huge mistake; not telling Ivan about her accident.

Several months before Beth and Ivan's wedding, Katja became enamored with a fair-haired man named Benny while waiting on tables in a local café. He had breakfast at the café every morning and said he was in sales, but Katja never knew what he sold. Benny was a smooth, fast-talking guy and persuaded her to date him. At seventeen, Katja was shy, had an attractive figure, and her facial scar was less noticeable than it was in childhood.

Katja never had a boyfriend before, and Benny made her laugh and feel important.

He kept telling her how pretty she was, giving the attention-starved teenager what she needed. After going to the movies, Benny would park his old car in a deserted area and they petted. On each date, he became more aggressive, pushed his tongue into Katja's mouth, and then moved his hand up her thigh. She shoved him away, "We have to be married before you can do that."

"Okay, then let's get married." Benny said.

The next day, after Katja finished work, she collected her pay for the week and told the manager "I'm quitting, 'cause I'm getting married tomorrow."

"Can't you stay until I train someone to take your place!" The manager said.

"I can't. It's been great working here." Off went Katja with Benny in his jalopy to his hometown in Oklahoma. Before going to work, Katja had packed a suitcase and wrote a hasty note to Beth. It said she was eloping with Benny and would call in a few days.

A surprised Beth discovered the note that evening lying on Beth's bed. She showed it to Aunt Bea. "Do you know who Benny is?"

"Katja talked about a cute salesman she met at the café. Maybe that man is Benny. She's too young to get married." Aunt Bea said.

"I've been so involved with Ivan that I haven't paid attention to Katja. I had no idea she had a boyfriend. I'm worried."

"I am too." Aunt Bea said.

Katja called two days later, "Hi Beth, don't be mad at me. I married the most wonderful guy in the world."

"I'm not mad, I'm upset. Why didn't you tell me about him?" Beth said.

"Well, I suppose I shoulda. Gotta go, running out of dimes. I'll write." Katja clicked off. No letter came and Beth fretted. It had been two weeks since the phone call when the doorbell chimed. There stood Katja with a blond-haired man by her side.

"Hi, this is Benny, my husband," Katja said.

Beth hugged Katja, "Boy, am I glad to see you!"

"Sorry I never wrote you. We drove all night to get here. We're so hungry."

"Come, come in the kitchen. I have plenty of food." Aunt Bea said. After the newlyweds were fed, they dozed on the sofa, the only place for them to sleep.

In the morning, Beth pulled Katja aside to have a private conversation and said, "What is the matter with you? I was scared half to death worrying about you. What do you know about Benny? He could be a criminal. Why didn't you tell me about him before you ran off with him?"

"You woulda tried to talk me out of it. I love him. I don't care what ya think" Katja said.

"Why did you go to Oklahoma to get married?" Beth asked.

"Ya don't have to wait to get hitched and that's where Benny was born. Thought we'd stay there, but the state has a drought and there's no work."

"Benny doesn't have money, does he," Beth said.

"No. It doesn't matter." Katja said.

"What are you going to do for money?"

"I'm going back to the café to ask for my old job back. Benny can sell something. He's a good talker."

"He sure is." Beth said.

"Do ya think we can live here for a week or two?" Katja said.

"There isn't much room for you. Ask Aunt Bea." Beth said.

"Can Benny and I stay here for a couple of weeks? Soon, I hope, we'll have enough money to get a place of our own."

"Of course, child. We'll be crowded. But, you can stay until you get on your feet," Aunt Bea said.

Benny said he could not find work, so the only income they had was Katja's earnings from the café. Every morning Katja ate breakfast in the café kitchen. However the smell of food began to nauseate her. As time went by, she could not hide her pregnancy. The café manager was fond of Katja and let her work a few hours every afternoon until she became too cumbersome to maneuver around the tables.

CHANCES

Beth and Ivan spent their brief honeymoon in the apartment and Beth's fence accident was never mentioned. Beth returned to her sewing job on Monday and Ivan hunted for work. After beating the pavement all day with no results, Ivan stopped at Novak's bar for a beer. The Roosevelt administration had legalized beer and a few months later voted out the Volstead Act, eliminating prohibition. The atmosphere in the bar was tame, compared to the days of elicit drinking. There was no need for a guard at the entry door and the cops paid for their booze, just like everyone else. The thrill of drinking in spite of the law was gone.

Still, the men and women liked to gather at Novaks to drink, talk and have fun. Ivan was a handsome man and there were always women in the bar who flirted with him, but he was not interested. He liked talking and playing pool with his pals. One afternoon the bartender called in sick and the owner was overwhelmed waiting on thirsty customers.

"Want some help?" Ivan asked

"Sure," Tony Novak said.

Ivan tended bar until the early hours of morning and Beth became concerned when he didn't contact her or come home. She did not know what to do, so she called the Poncek house. After the phone rang many times, Borris picked up the receiver and said, "Who-o is it?"

"It's Beth. I'm worried. Ivan isn't home yet. Is he there?"

"No-o., he's pro-ably having a go-od time at some bar."

Ivan came home at two in the morning. "Where have you been? I couldn't sleep worrying about you, and I have to go to work tomorrow." Beth scolded.

"Calm down. I was bartending at Novaks. I took the place of his regular man, who was sick. I got paid for the hours I worked and besides that, I got plenty of tips." Ivan said.

"Why didn't you call me? Didn't you think of me?" Beth said.

"I was busy. Look, get this straight. I'm not letting you henpeck me."

This was their first fight. There was a lot of restlessness and no lovemaking that night. Ivan returned to Novak's the next afternoon and the regular bartender was back. Ivan was drinking a beer at the bar when the bartender made a funny sound, doubled over and fell to the floor.

Tony said, "Ivan, can you take over?"

"Sure!"

I'll call an ambulance," Tony said

Ivan wasn't going to repeat last night's mistake and phoned Beth after the bartender was taken to the hospital. "Hi, I'm going to be home very late. The bartender is sick again and Tony has asked me to take his place."

Beth sounded pleased. "Thank you, sweetheart. I'm so glad you called."

Ivan became very good at bartending. Tony taught him how to mix fancy cocktails and operate the cash register. Ivan knew most of the customers and enjoyed his new job.

One afternoon, a stranger sat at the bar and ordered a beer and a meatloaf sandwich. The cook was out on an errand, so Ivan made the sandwich. A fresh meatloaf was cooling on the counter, and he cut a nice-sized piece in the middle of the loaf, thinking it was the best part. He noticed part of a baked cockroach sticking out of the slab of meat. He dug out most of it, put the meat on toasted bread, and covered it in thick gravy. He served the sandwich to the customer and watched him eat it while wiping the bar.

"Hey, bartender, this is the best meatloaf sandwich I've ever had." The customer said.

The man left a generous tip when he paid the bill, making Ivan think cooked cockroaches must be tasty. Only starvation would make him want to find out. At night, whenever lights were switched on in the kitchen, dozens of the bugs scattered across the floor looking for cover. The saloon staff tried to get rid of the ugly creatures, but to no avail. Ivan told the cook about the cockroach in the meatloaf and the customer, and they laughed and laughed.

Beth was making five dollars a day and enjoyed her sewing job at the suit factory, except for the lint permeating the shop air that made her cough. A few weeks before her promotion to a management position by Uncle Ted, she began feeling strange in the mornings and her breasts were sore.

Ivan smiled and hugged Beth when she told him she was pregnant. "Wow! That's terrific! You'll have to quit your job. Give at least two week's notice to Uncle Ted."

"I don't want to quit my job. I can still work. I'll take three months off and get a babysitter for the little one when I go back to work. We need the money," Beth said.

"No, you're going to quit. That place is a health hazard with all that lint floating in the air. You're going to stay home and take care of yourself and our baby," Ivan said.

Beth knew she was in a losing battle. She relinquished her job

"I'm sad to see you go, but I understand. You're one of the best employees I've ever had. Here is something for you and the baby." Uncle Ted was a generous man and gave her a gift of ten dollars for the baby.

Beth kept herself busy during her pregnancy by knitting baby sweaters, and booties. She kept the little apartment very clean, almost sterile. She vacuumed and dusted daily, cooked, canned, baked, hunted for bargains, and cut out coupons. Beth was an early bird, awakening at dawn. Not Ivan, for he slept and worked late, which suited his night owl habits. Beth missed her job and the money she made. "I think I'll go back to work when the baby is a year old." Beth said to Ivan at dinner.

"A one year old needs its mother, not some babysitter," Ivan said.

His answer was no surprise to Beth. She had to think of a way to change her husband's old-fashioned ideas.

Many events happened during Beth's pregnancy. Katja and Benny became parents of Benjamin Junior and honored Beth and Ivan by asking them to be godparents to their first-born. The infant's name was the same name as his father's, and Katja avoided confusion by calling the baby, Ben. Katja and Benny still lived with Aunt Bea, sleeping in the small bedroom Beth and Maggie once occupied.

Maggie moved out of her Aunt's house soon after Beth married and entered the convent as a novice, with the intention of taking her final vows Maggie was happy. She had gone to Mass every morning since she was a girl and prayed several times a day. Maggie found her true vocation.

Aunt Bea liked having Katja, Benny, and the baby living with her. She only charged them the cost of the utilities, which was all the young couple could afford. To anyone's knowledge, Benny never sold anything, never had a job. Katja worked as many hours as the café owner would allow her, as much as forty-eight hours a week. Aunt Bea took care of baby Ben while Katja worked. Benny was gone all day and came home late at night. Several months went by and Aunt Bea was becoming suspicious of Benny.

One late evening, when Katja was sound asleep, and Aunt Bea was still awake reading a book, Benny came home. "Hi. My, you come home late. I'm curious, what do you do when you leave here?"

"I look for work. I can't find anything." Benny answered.

"What do you do when you're gone all day and half the night?" Aunt Bea asked.

"I sit on a bench or lean against a wall and watch people. I used to sell medicinal products." Benny stretched the truth. He used to tout elixirs, to cure all ailments, from the back of a truck. His supplier got in trouble with the law, which halted his supply of the elixer bottles containing sweetened water with ten percent alcohol. With that livelihood gone, he started playing in high stake poker games. Being a shark at cards and card tricks enabled him to win often. He hid the fact he went to the racetrack and played poker on a regular basis. Gambling was his way of life, in his blood, and he loved it. He didn't tell Katja his true occupation.

Little Ben was a cute, lovable baby, and Beth enjoyed giving Aunt Bea a break by babysitting. One day while Aunt Bea was shopping, Beth had just put Ben in his crib for a nap, when the doorbell rang.

A policeman was at the door." May I speak to Mrs. Benjamin Smith?" he said.

"She's at work. I'm her sister. Can I help you?"

"Well, ma'am, her husband Benny Smith has been hurt and is in the hospital. Don't worry; he'll be okay. We found him unconscious in an ally. He's at Euclid Hospital. Can you relay this message to Mrs. Smith?"

"Yes, I'll tell her," Beth said, shocked by the message.

Aunt Bea came home a few minutes later.

After Beth related the Benny's problem, Aunt Bea said, "I'll take care of the baby. You go on and tell Katja."

Beth ran to the café, where Katja was busy serving a large group of customers. Katja spied Beth after she put a plate of food in front of a customer. She rushed over to Beth and said, "Something is wrong. I can tell it on your face. Is Ben alright?"

"The baby Ben is fine. Aunt Bea is with him. Benny is injured and in the hospital."

Katja's face paled. She found the café manager in the kitchen and told her, "My husband is in the hospital. I need to leave."

"Go, I'll take over for you," the manager said.

Beth and Katja took the streetcar to Euclid hospital and found Benny lying in bed with a bruised face, his right leg and left arm in casts.

Katja kissed his cheek. "Benny, it's me. What happened?"

"I can't remember. I think I was hit by a car," Benny said.

"I feel so bad for you. Are you in a lot of pain?" Katja's voice was full of sympathy. Beth remembered the cop saying they found Benny beaten up in an ally. A man wearing a white lab coat entered and said, "Is one of you Mr. Smith's wife?"

"Yes, I'm Mrs. Smith," Katja said.

"I'm the doctor in charge of taking care of your husband. He'll have to be here for at least a week. Don't worry; he'll recover. His leg was quite battered and he might have a limp the rest of his life."

Katja thanked the doctor. While holding Benny's hand, he fell asleep and she started to weep. "I don't want him to see me cry."

"Don't be sad. Be happy that he's going to be okay."

Beth went to the police station to talk to the officer who came to the house. "My name is Beth Poncek. May I see this officer?" She gave the receptionist the police officer's badge number.

The receptionist went into the next room for a few seconds and when she came back she said. "He's in that room. You may go in."

The cop was at one of the desks using a typewriter.

"Excuse me. Remember coming to my sister's house to tell me about Benny Smith?"

The officer looked up, "Yeah, I remember. What can I do for you?"

"Benny says he thinks a car hit him."

"The evidence indicates he was beaten. I think Benny knows the perpetrators but doesn't want to snitch. He is a gambler and hangs out with men who have mob connections. Whoever robbed him was vicious. Benny had no money or jewelry on him when we found him unconscious in that alley. Until he talks, the case won't be solved. What else I can do for you?"

"Nothing, thanks for talking to me," Beth said. While walking home she went over the words of the officer. Benny has been telling us he's a salesman. I always thought he was a liar.

Katja visited Benny in the hospital every day. One afternoon after seeing her husband, she went to Beth's house.

"How is Benny," Beth asked.

"He's changing. He confessed he likes to gamble and when he cheats at cards, he cheats himself of his self-respect. I suspected he gambled, but never said anything about it. A hospital minister has been persuading him to change his ways. Benny is talking about getting a job and saving money to buy a house. This is the first time he's said anything like that."

Ivan was sitting reading the newspaper nearby and heard the sisters' conversation. He interrupted, "A brush with death changes people. Katja, did you know Beth and I will be married one year next month! We're going to celebrate by going out to dinner."

"I'm too big to go out to dinner. I feel like I'm carrying a bowling ball around. Besides, it's too expensive to eat out," Beth said

"C'mon, Beth, we won't be going anywhere after the baby is born. Let's go to Nardini's and have Italian food," Ivan said.

"Don't be so frugal, you need to splurge once in a while," Katja said.

Beth and Ivan picked Saturday night to celebrate at Nardinis. The restaurant wasn't too far away and they walked to it. Ivan recognized two men, he and his brother fought back in their youth, standing in front of the eatery. They were staring at Beth.

The big one called Gorilla said, "Boy, is she knocked up," and snickered. The little man called Mouse, laughed. Beth ignored them, but not Ivan; his temper flared.

As soon as he and Beth were seated at a table, Ivan said, "I'll be right back. Why don't you look at the menu?"

The two men were still talking, when Ivan snuck up behind them and grabbed Gorilla by his shirt collar. He gave him the one-two punch he had learned in the boxing ring and before Mouse could respond, Ivan punched him in the nose.

"Don't you ever make fun of my wife," Ivan said as the men struggled to get on their feet, but just managing to sit up.

Gorilla and Mouse were sitting on the curb and Ivan was leaning against the lamp post, when a police car pulled up next to them. The cop yelled, "What's going on here?"

"Nothin'" Gorilla said.

The cop turned his engine off and sat in his car, watching the three men.

Gorilla and Mouse walked away, and Ivan joined Beth in the restaurant.

"Where have you been?" Beth asked.

"Just talking with some guys I know."

"The food here is expensive."

Ivan groaned. They should have stayed home.

Walking home from the restaurant, Beth said, "That is some of the best Italian food I ever had. I'm glad we came here even though it cost way too much."

Beth was very uncomfortable in the last week of her ninth month of pregnancy. She could not sleep in her bed and slept on the couch instead. Her mother bore nine children at home and Beth felt she would do that too. When her water broke, rolling contractions started, increased, then stopped and then continued again.

Ivan became worried and phoned Dr. Parme. "Please come, I think something is wrong with my wife. She's been in labor a long time and exhausted. The baby seems stuck." It only took Dr. Parme a few minutes to get to the apartment and only a few seconds to determine the problem. He said, "The baby has to be turned inside the womb with forceps, so it can be born face up.

Even in Beth's pain wracked state, she cried out "no, no" during the procedure, remembering what happened to Katja when forceps were used. Beth regretted not listening to Ivan, who wanted her to give birth in a hospital.

A lovely baby girl emerged in a healthy condition. Beth had seen a film in which the heroine's name was Jacqueline, and with Ivan's approval, she gave the baby that name. Jacqueline Rose was a hungry baby and nursed often. Grandma Louiza, thought Jacqueline was to long of a name for a baby and called her first grandchild, Jacky. All the new Aunts and Uncles adored Jacky and fought to hold her in their arms.

A week went by and Beth had recovered enough from the birth to visit to Aunt Bea's house. Benny answered the door and seemed genuinely interested in Jacky. He was recovering from his wounds and was always home, except for medical appointments.. Katja came out of the back bedroom, happy to see her sister and Jacky.

Beth said," Hi, sis. You're getting skinny. You must be working too hard."

"I know. I don't feel good," Katja said and started coughing.

"She coughs up blood. I keep telling her, she's got to see a doctor," Aunt Bea said.

"You better take Aunt Bea's advice." Beth said.

"You're right. I'm feelin' worse every day. I'm makin' the appointment today." Katja said.

After examining Katja from head to toe and taking X rays, Dr. Parme was direct. "You have tuberculosis, which is very contagious. You must be isolated in a sanitarium for at least six months to recover. I have to report your disease to the health department and I will monitor your progress."

Katja was stunned. She had heard of people dying of T.B. and panicked, thinking she might have infected her baby. Her thoughts raced in all directions. Was Aunt Bea strong enough to care for Ben and

Benny while she recuperated in the sanitarium? Maybe Beth could help take care of Ben. She was young and strong, loved baby Ben, and had to stay home with Jacky, anyway. Yes, that's it; Beth was the answer. Katja was tired, and she welcomed the prescribed rest. She started coughing and put a handkerchief to her mouth.

Dr.Parme continued, "My secretary has made the arrangements for you to stay at the sanitarium. It's in the mountains, about an hour from here where the air is fresh and clean. I'm giving you this pamphlet on the facility. Please fill out these papers for permitting treatment and for financial aid. I understand your husband cannot work and neither can you. We can place your baby in a foster home until you are well."

"No, that's not necessary. My Aunt and sister will take care of Ben."

"Please make your arrangements. I'll have a cab waiting for you in the morning. I don't want you on a streetcar, coughing and spreading the bacteria to other people. This is going to be a difficult transition for you. Keep in mind, you're very sick and need months of care to recover. If your family needs me to explain the situation, I will talk with them. In a few days I'll check on you in the sanitarium and see how you're doing."

Katja gathered Benny and Aunt Bea in the kitchen and told them her problem. Aunt Bea said, "I knew something was wrong with you."

After Benny cleared his throat several times, he put his arms around Katja and said, "Honey, you'll get better, I know you will."

"I'm goin' to ask Beth to help care for Ben while I'm in the sanitarium.

"That's a good idea. We will all take care of the baby," Aunt Bea said

"Hello Beth, this is Katja,"

"Hi Katja, I was just changing Jacky's diaper. She can really kick those pudgy little legs. How are you?" Katja told her the bad news.

"How awful! Of course, I'll help take care of Ben."

"You're a lifesaver. You're always there for me," Katja said.

"Getting you healthy is the important thing. Jacky will love having Ben as a playmate," Beth said.

That evening, Katja tied a rag over her mouth while cuddling Ben. It would be a long time before she would hold her baby again. That night, she and Benny wrapped themselves around each other, dozing fitfully, before the alarm went off. As promised, the cab pulled up in front of Aunt Bea's home at nine a.m. Beth got into the sedan and joined two people who were coughing into bloodstained cloths.

INVESTMENT

Ivan had a variety of jobs since childhood, and the one he liked best was working on the lathe in a machine shop. To expand his knowledge of machining, he registered for a night school class that met twice a week. Stefan took his place bartending at Novaks those two nights. Tony Novak agreed on the arrangement since he knew Stefan, whose band played occasionally in the bar on Saturday nights.

Ivan was at the top of his class, and felt confident enough to open his own machine shop. To do that, he needed money to rent a space, buy equipment, and fire insurance. He and Beth had saved money, but it was not enough to start a business. He needed investors and discussed his plans with Beth.

"Opening a machine shop is a fine idea, but aren't you taking a big risk?" Beth said.

"It's a calculated risk. Germany owes huge amounts of money to the countries that defeated them in World War I. Their depressed economy makes paying the debt difficult. Adolf Hitler, the head of the Nazi Party, has written a book called *Mein Kampf.* If he implements what he's written, Europe is in trouble. I believe the U.S. will be involved in some kind of protection from this crazy, dangerous man."

"Where are we going to get the money to start a shop?" Beth asked.

"I think I can get a couple of investors to help us." Ivan said.

"Who would that be?" Beth asked.

"I know two people with money: Milan, my father's old friend, and Joe."

"Joe? You can't trust him! He's a gangster." Beth said.

"He's changed since he's become a crippled man." Ivan said.

"Well, there's no harm in trying. Boy, did I get a good buy on liver today," Beth said

"You are frugal, even more than me." Ivan said.

Milan always went to Novak's bar Thursday nights. Ivan made sure he was there on Thursday night and spotted him laughing with the bartender. "Hey, Milan, let me buy you a beer." Ivan called to him.

"Sure, you've never treated me to a beer before. You must want something."

"Why don't we sit at the corner table where it's quiet. I have a proposition for you."

As soon as they sat down, Milan asked, "What's up?"

"I have an idea that I think you'll like." Ivan explained his plan and the reason why it would be a good investment.

"So, you think there's going to be another war in Europe, eh? My dough don't earn a dime sittin' under my mattress and I don't trust banks. This country will be on England's side if war starts in Europe. "Okay, I'll take a chance. I'll give ya money for your shop," Milan said.

"I want to make this partnership legal with notarized signatures. Read this paper carefully before signing it in front of a notary." Ivan handed him the document.

"We don't need to do that, let's just shake hands." Milan said.

"Those were the old days. Think of the document as insurance."

"I only read a few words in English. Why don't you read it to me," Milan said

"It would be better to get someone like a banker or insurance agent to read it to you. They could explain it to you." Ivan said.

When Ivan got home, he told Beth, "Milan said yes. Now I have to talk to Joe." The next day Ivan went to the convalescent home. Joe was looking frail sitting in his wheelchair.

"Hi, Joe!" Ivan said.

"Well, look who's here! If it ain't the boxer." Joe said.

"I'm done fighting. I'm a married now and have a baby girl." Ivan fished in his wallet, took out a picture of Jacky, and showed it to Joe.

"Yeah, she's a cute one. Wish I had a kid. I got the feeling this is more than a social call. You want something from me. I bet its money." Joe said

"Yeah, you've got my number. I hope you'll invest in my business venture." Ivan told him what was going on in Germany and why it was the right time to open a machine shop.

"I got nothin' to do but sit in this damn wheelchair. Moe is gone. I have no wife, no children. No one comes to see me except you. I spend my hours looking out the window or reading. I read Hitler's book, and what you say is true. You're an honest fellow, so I'm givin' you this key to locker 251 in the central train station. It contains a box. Bring it to me."

Ivan went to the station the next day and found the locker. The key worked perfectly and inside was a black metal box secured with a combination lock. It crossed his mind that if he had the right tools, he could open it, but he didn't. He brought the box to the convalescent home and handed it over to Joe.

Joe smiled, "Boy, it's good to touch this box again. I think I remember the combination." After fiddling for a few minutes, he hit the right numbers and the box opened. Inside was a bulky, brown envelope with many one hundred dollar bills in it. He took one bill out, stroked it and said," I'll loan you two thousand dollars. This will be the first legitimate business I've ever been in."

"I'm glad you trust me, but to seal the deal, you need to read this document and sign it in front of a notary." Ivan said.

"We agreed. I don't need to do that." Joe said.

"I want to make this legal, so please do it for me," Ivan said.

"Okay, okay." Joe said.

With his investor's money, Ivan leased the first floor of an old downtown building. He bought a secondhand lathe machine in good condition, organized his small shop and all he needed was business. He asked Stefan to be his sales representative and he agreed to be the front man if he got a percentage of the contracts he brought in. Stefan had to learn about the production end of the business before he could call on potential customers.

Ivan explained the process of machining in general terms and gave Stefan a booklet to read called "Machining Operations." He coached his brother, "Tell the customer our machine shop specializes in making templates from engineering drawings and blueprints."

"I'll do my best. Where do you want me to go?" Stefan asked.

"Here's a list of manufacturing companies. The largest companies have their own machine shops and some of those shops might want to subcontract some of their work. Find out what they need and the quantity they need. I'll calculate my cost and give you a written estimate to present to them. If they haven't called back in a couple of days, call them. If they haven't given us the job, find out why and try to negotiate," Ivan said.

At first, Ivan went with Stefan to help him answer technical questions and listened while Stefan pitched the machine shop. Stefan was a good salesman, but competing with established machine shops was difficult. Ivan cut his prices to bare bones just to get contracts. He wanted his customers to see how good he was, letting the finished product speak for itself. His customers were satisfied, but the problem was the lack of jobs. All the independent shops were fighting for the same contracts, and many were going out of business.

Ivan predicted there would be a conflict in Europe led by the Nazis and there would be a need for machinery. However, the need had not surfaced yet, for the war was in the smoldering stage. Milan and Joe were impatient and wanted to see some return on their investment. Ivan informed them he barely made enough money to cover his expenses. They had to wait a few months longer to see if the shop could make a profit.

The old building where the machine shop was located had many offices and half were empty. The man, who rented the room on the second floor directly above Ivan's shop, raised chickens. He complained to Ivan about the meager sum he was getting for his chickens and eggs. "Heck," he said, "My income is not enough to pay for rent and feed. I'm thinking of closing down and donating the chickens to a shantytown."

"I'm not doing much better," Ivan said.

About a year after Ivan had opened his shop, the phone rang in his apartment, waking him up in the middle of the night. He looked at the clock. No one called at three in the morning unless it was an emergency or unless it was some quack. He was groggy when he said, "Hello."

"Your machine shop is burning." The voice said.

"What? Who is this?" Ivan asked.

The phone clicked off and Ivan was wide awake.

Beth asked in a sleepy voice, "What's going on?"

"Someone told me the shop is on fire. I hope this is a joke. I'd better check and see." Ivan pulled on his clothes and went out the door. Jacky started to whimper, and Beth got out of bed to tend to her.

It was no joke. Ivan could see smoke for several blocks coming from the direction of his shop. When he arrived, the building was engulfed in flames and two firefighters were spraying water on the roaring fire. The floor above had crashed down onto the first floor and the building resembled a crushed box of cereal. The chicken man stood next to Ivan, "That building needed burning."

"Don't talk like that. It sounds like you set the fire," Ivan said.

"I didn't. Accidents happen." The chicken man said.

The fire department determined the fire started on the second floor above the machine shop. The insurance company questioned all the tenants separately. The chicken man said, "I know the custodian smokes cigarettes. If he left a live stub on the floor, the kerosene in the brooder stove would've caught fire."

"The custodian says he was home sick in bed. His wife verified this. Where were you when the fire started?" The insurance agent asked.

"I was home in bed. I got a phone call in the middle of the night telling me about the fire, so I rushed to the building," The chicken man said.

"Who was the man that phoned you?" The agent asked.

"I don't know. I think the same person phoned Ivan Poncek."

"He's the next name on my list."

Beth and Ivan welcomed the suited insurance agent into the apartment. The agent did not waste time in getting to his questions. "My company knows you were watching the building burn. How were you informed about the fire?" He asked Ivan.

"I got a call at three in the morning that woke me up." Ivan said.

"Who was it?" The agent asked.

"I didn't recognize the man's voice and he didn't identify himself. He said my shop was burning. At first, I thought he was joking, but his voice was serious so I rushed to my shop," Ivan said.

"Your business wasn't doing well. Did you destroy it to get insurance money?"

"No, I didn't! The building is old and faulty wiring could have started the fire," Ivan said.

When Stefan was interrogated, he said. "I'm the sales rep. I only go to the shop to talk with my brother. I have no idea how the fire started."

The agent's job was interesting to Stefan. Although his polka band was popular, the group never had enough gigs to bring in a decent income. He needed a steady income.

"You have to take educational courses to learn about the insurance business. I'll give you a phone number to register for the classes," the insurance agent said.

Unable to prove arson, the insurance company had to pay those who had fire insurance, like Ivan who paid back Milan and Joe their investment. He paid the money owed on the destroyed equipment and had a small sum left over. If only Ivan had waited another year to open his shop, he would have succeeded, for his prediction of war in Europe came true.

MISCHIEF

Beth wasn't sorry the machine shop burned down. Keeping the business afloat was time-consuming and a struggle for Ivan. She spent many weekends and nights without him. It was nice having her husband home, playing with Jacky, fixing things in the apartment, when he wasn't looking for a job. Their second child was due in a few weeks. It was during Monday night dinner when Beth asked, "If we have a boy, shouldn't we name him Ivan Jr?"

"I think that's a great idea. What if we have another girl?" Ivan said.

"I haven't thought of a girl's name," Beth said.

Jacky had a good appetite and finished her plate of food before climbing onto Ivan's lap. Beth took second place when Ivan was near. "Why don't we go to Katja's house so Jacky can play with Ben," Ivan said.

Beth no longer babysat baby Ben and Jacky missed her playmate. After six months of therapy, Katja was tuberculosis free and dismissed from the hospital. Beth decorated Aunt Bea's house with balloons and confetti to celebrate the homecoming. Shouts of joy greeted Katja when she arrived. The first thing she did was search the crowd for her little Ben. She spied him holding onto Aunt Bea's skirt. The toddler looked frightened when Katja held her arms open to him and clung to Aunt Bea.

"He's forgotten me," Katja said.

"Don't be upset, it'll take time for Ben to get used to you again. You've been gone six months and that's a lifetime to a child." Beth said.

Husband Benny put his good arm around Katja, "You look good, kid. You've gained weight and you got color in your face." Benny still limped and had limited use of his right arm.

Katja's smile came back and she said, "You've gained a few pounds too." She poked Benny's stomach and laughed.

Beth was gaining weight too, her slim face becoming round due to her pregnancy. Still wanting to look attractive, she let her hair grow long and wrapped it in a coil around her head in the new style. Curves were in, but she'd have to wait a few months after the baby was born to cinch her waist. This baby was not as active in the womb as Jacky had been during the last three months. This birth experience would not be as traumatic as the first, for this baby was going to be born in the hospital.

After weeks of frustration hunting for a job, Ivan applied for one with the Works Progress Administration, a relief measure for the unemployed initiated by the Roosevelt Administration. W.P.A. workers repaired buildings, improved the city zoo and parks, and helped build the first segment of highway I-90. Ivan also applied for another New Deal program, the Federal Writers Project. He did not qualify, for he needed to be an unemployed educator. Much to the relief of Beth, Ivan's W.P.A. application was accepted and the young family had an income.

While this was happening Jacky blossomed and had a large vocabulary for a two and a half year old. "Why are you so big Mommy?" Jacky pointed to Beth's enlarged abdomen.

Beth placed Jacky's hand on her tummy and said, "A baby is growing inside. Soon it will come out and you will have a playmate."

"It will be my doll," Jacky said.

"The baby will be very small at first and has to grow bigger before she can become your playmate," Beth said.

Jacky was a curious child and one day while visiting Grandma Louiza, she ran out the front door, when no one was looking, and wandered down the street lined with houses toward the busy boulevard. Fritzy happened to be on her front porch when she saw the child and grabbed her. Both Louiza and Beth were rushing toward Fritzy, relieved to see Jacky retrieved.

"I'm going to buy a harness for that child. She wanders off the first chance she gets," Beth said.

"She is not a dog. That would be awful. You just have to keep an eye on her at all times." Louiza said.

"How could I watch her at all times at your house," Beth said.

"You'll have to visit with Jacky." Louiza said.

"Okay." Beth did not want to argue with her Mother-in-Law.

Baby Rose was born in the Cuyahoga County Hospital and her birth was easy. Jacky was holding Ivan's hand, when Beth, sitting in a wheel chair pushed by a nurse, came out of the hospital doors holding a bundle in her arms. Jacky squealed seeing Baby Rose's head, barely visible, above the blanket wrapped around her.

Jacky's large brown eyes widened as Beth kissed her oldest daughter and let her view the newborn. "She's so small!" Jacky said.

"You are a big sister now and can help Mama care for her," Ivan said.

Jacky ignored the baby and pouted when her aunts, uncles, and grandparents cooed at the newborn. She was used to being the center of attention and baby Rose had replaced her. After three days of watching the fuss, she said to Beth, "Mama, take baby back to the hospital."

"No, we have to keep her. Soon she'll be big enough to play with you," Beth said.

Baby Rose was docile, loved to sleep and was a poor eater, so opposite of her energetic sister. The sisters were not alike. Jacky was an adorable, alert little girl with large expressive eyes and an abundance of dark curly hair. Baby Rose was bald, listless and skinny. Beth worried and took her to Dr. Parme.

"Rose is underweight and needs more nutrition," Dr. Parme said.

"Rose never is hungry and seems full after nursing for just a few minutes. All she wants to do is sleep." Beth said.

"Feed her as often as possible. She needs to put weight on," Dr. Parme advised.

"I've tried that. I don't know what to do." Beth said.

"Here is a sample of cod liver oil. It will strengthen her. Put it at the back of her mouth with an eyedropper. Keep nursing her and start giving her cow's milk Maybe that will fatten her up."

Beth did as Dr. Parme instructed and baby Rose gained little weight, spitting up most of the cow's milk she couldn't digest. Jacky was beginning to accept Rose and stopped insisting she should go back to the hospital. Jacky often went into the nursery to see if Rose was growing and couldn't understand why she slept so much.

Beth caught Jacky poking her. "Why are you doing that?"

"I want her to wake up to play with me," Jacky said.

"Baby needs sleep. If I catch you poking her again, I will spank you," Rose said

After that incident, Beth took Jacky to Grandma Louize'a house and to Katja's house as often as possible. Jacky was a social child, happy to be at Grandma's house playing with her Aunts and Uncles and happy at Aunt Bea's house playing with Ben.

Aunt Bea was never home when Beth visited Katja. She was off traveling, since her brother Ted, a childless man, died and bequeathed his only sister all his assets. Bea sold the clothing store and became a wealthy woman. She paid Katja and Benny to take care of the house while she vacationed in Canada, Mexico and the states.

One afternoon, while Beth was chatting with Katja in the kitchen, baby Rose was sleeping in her playpen and Jacky and Ben were clanging pots and pans in the living room.

Katja hollered, "Stop that noise. You'll wake up the baby and your Father!" It seemed Rose and Benny was always napping.

"You look sad today, Katja. What is wrong?" Beth said.

"I've been thinking about your wedding," Katja said.

"You were so sick that day. You looked green," Beth said.

"Besides being sick, I had hurt feelings too. Why didn't you ask me, your own sister, to be your Matron of Honor?" Katja said.

"I didn't think you'd make it down the aisle," Beth said.

"You could have asked me anyway. I think you had Theresa as Maid of Honor because you felt obligated to Louiza," Katja said.

"I guess so. I'm sorry I hurt you. I do love you, you do know that," Beth said and put her arms around Katja.

While the sisters were having their intense conversation, Jacky and Ben stopped playing in the living room and opened the door to the hall closet. They found a bunch of hanging coats and a shoe box behind some old boots. Inside the box were brushes, cloths and two cans of polish. The children opened each of the cans. Jacky took a gob of brown polish and streaked the wax into her hair. Then she put a handful of the black polish into Ben's blond hair. The children giggled and laughed as they painted each other's clothes. This was more fun than coloring with crayons. When the polish was gone, Jacky said, "Let's show our Mamas," and the children skipped into the kitchen.

The mothers had been engrossed in their conversation and unaware of what their children were doing. The sisters stopped talking as the children came into the kitchen and twirled around to show off their wild creations. They displayed brown and black shoe polish all over their skin, clothes, and hair. The surprised mothers stared at their decorated offspring.

"Aren't we pretty, Mama," Jacky said.

"Oh, honey. How am I going to get you clean?" Beth said.

"You have to admit they are colorful," Katja remarked.

The children were not so happy when their mothers scrubbed and rubbed them to remove the stubborn wax. Katja shaved Ben's head and Beth cut off Jacky's lovely curls. They threw away the black and brown streaked clothes. The children's skin returned to normal after several months of dermal sloughing.

A Passage

Louiza was talking about the family as she sat with Ivan on the swing in the gazebo. "Poor Jacky, her skin is so red from scrubbing that polish off. I bet she'll never do that again. It's too bad Beth had to cut most of her hair, but it will grow back. I suppose we'll have more grandchildren now that Theresa is married. Our girls don't want to baby-sit any more for Beth and Ivan, they're more interested in school and dating. Jacky loves playing in their room while they preen in their mirrors."

"Ja," Anton said.

The sun was shining, wisps of clouds drifted in the blue sky and the Linden tree was budding. Soon the yellow flowers would be in full bloom.

"I hope our girls get married soon." Louiza said.

"Ja," Anton said. When his youngest daughters went on dates on Saturday nights, he sat in his red chair in the parlor, looking like a king sitting on his throne. He interrogated the young men waiting for his daughters, who were always late. He asked the nervous males questions, trying to impress him with their answers. The suitors looked relieved when the young women finally came down the stairs. Staying awake, to make sure his daughters were home by mid night, was never successful, for Anton was snoring in his red chair by that time

Louiza kept talking, "I don't think Boris is ever going to marry. He shies away from women. I often wonder if he likes females."

"Sure he does. He goes to the burlesque every week." Anton said.

"Stefan has finished his classes. I know he'll sell lots of insurance. Have you noticed how often Stefan mentions a girl named Majda?"

"Ja," Anton said.

"Stefan has had many girlfriends, but he really likes this one. He says, 'Majda is smart, Majda is pretty, Majda has a nice figure.' I said I've heard enough about Majda. Now I want to meet her. Do you think Stefan will marry Majda?"

"Ja," Anton said.

"Josip and his family will be visiting us soon."

"Ja. Josip is a good man," Anton said.

"Andrew writes that he feels good in California. He likes the weather and casual life-style. He never mentions a girlfriend. Eddi got promoted to manager at Grant's Department Store in Van Nuys and his wife is pregnant. You know California has earthquakes and no seasons. I like the fall when leaves are colorful and the spring, when everything is fresh and new again, just like Slovenia. Nothing is more beautiful than the Julian Alps in winter," Louiza said.

"Lake Bled is beautiful too," Anton said in a shaky voice.

"Europe's borders are not the same since the war. Slovenia is now a part of Yugoslavia. We cannot call ourselves Austrian and we aren't Yugoslavian.

"We are Americans." Anton said.

"Ja, we are Americans. I think it's nice you planted the Linden tree in honor of our parents. I wish my mother had lived long enough to see her grandchildren." Louiza said.

"Ja," Anton said.

Anton had seen his last days at the blacksmith shop, for the company was using trucks for transportation instead of horses. His partner Wolf retired several years ago and was never replaced. When Anton decided to retire too, the blacksmith shop closed. After working for the gas company for thirty years, Anton was given a gold watch and a monthly pension. His company was one of the first businesses in the United States to give their employees a retirement benefit. He filled his days napping and taking sips from a whiskey bottle he kept under the bed. He also liked sitting in the gazebo looking at his yard and thinking about the past.

A few months into his retirement and while watching Louiza pick yellow flowers from the Linden tree to make tea, Anton felt a severe pain in his chest. "I'm going into the house," he told her. Feeling weak, he made his way to the basement to ease the pain with a large tumbler of wine. It did help, but not enough. With labored breathing, he climbed back up the two sets of stairs to his bedroom, and did not show up at the dinner table. The family was used to eating without him.

Anton felt worse the next day and Louiza begged him to see Dr. Parme. The doctor told him, "Your liver is damaged from too much liquor. You're risking your life if you continue to drink." The doctor talked to Louiza privately, "Your husband is destroying himself; try to help him stop his alcohol addiction."

Anton stopped drinking for a day, resulting in sweating and nausea. That night he hallucinated in his sleep, believing he was protecting his mother from a strange man. He was punching and beating his pillow, and yelling. Louiza calmed him by cradling his head in her lap and stroking him. In the morning, Anton went to the basement and took a few swigs of wine. He felt much better.

A few days later, Louiza was sitting with Anton in the Gazebo. She stopped talking when Anton's face paled and his body started to shake. He was shivering, though the weather was quite mild and he wore a wool sweater.

"I'll get you a blanket." Louiza said.

"No, I'm going to bed. I'm tired," Anton said.

Louiza helped Anton get up the stairs to their bedroom. Louiza covered him with the afghan that Mati made so long ago. Anton began to snore. She closed the door to the bedroom and wondered if she should call Dr. Parme.

Louiza decided to wait, for Anton would feel better after he napped a while. She concentrated on making a large pot of stuffed cabbage. Theresa and her new husband had returned from their honeymoon and were coming to dinner. Ivan and his family were coming too. They all arrived at once and after the excitement died down, Theresa started talking about the Roosevelt administration's New Deal programs.

"They are successful. People are working," Theresa said.

"It's a form of socialism, I tell you," her husband answered.

"Maybe, but it's getting our people back to work." Theresa responded.

Ivan interrupted. "The programs are effective to a degree, but the war rumblings in Europe will give our economy the impetus it needs."

"That's what the Plain Dealer said in its editorial." Beth said, while holding baby Rose.

Louiza didn't want to debate politics and changed the subject by asking the newlyweds about their honeymoon. "Niagara Falls was stunning," Theresa said. Jacky was sitting in Ivan's lap while he listened to Theresa describe the beauty of the falls.

"You and Josip went there once, remember?" Louiza said.

"I almost forgot we went there Ma, it was a long time ago. I'm sure Theresa will show you her pictures." Ivan did not want to expose the lie he told many years ago.

"The pictures aren't developed yet," Theresa said.

Ivan breathed a sigh of relief that the discussion of Niagara had ended.

Louiza went up to the bedroom to see if Anton felt like eating. He was lying motionless with his eyes open.

"Oh, no!" Louiza cried out and fainted.

Boris heard Louiza scream and then a thud. The girls were laughing and talking so loudly in the kitchen, they didn't hear their mother. Boris ran upstairs, saw Ivan dead in bed and Louiza lying on the floor. He jumped down the down the stairs, almost tripped and yelled, "C-c-come, come. It's aw-awful."

Liquor had a stranglehold on Anton and squeezed life out of him at age fifty-five. His death was unexpected, even though the family was aware of his illness. They loved him, in spite of all his faults. As a young father, Anton played games with his children, took them on trolley rides and had them sit on his lap.

It was Ivan's duty as the eldest son, to guide the family in its funeral decisions. Anton was to be buried in one of the plots he bought many years ago in the Rest in Peace cemetery. Ivan designated his sisters to call the church and arrange the funeral. Stefan assignment was to buy a casket spray and floral stands for the church altar. Louiza and Ivan chose Ivan's burial clothes and casket.

"Does everyone understand their job?" Ivan asked.

The sad faces nodded.

When the hour-long funeral service was over, Anton's casket was loaded into a black hearse and taken to the cemetery. After the burial and graveside prayers, the spray flowers were distributed among the mourners. Ivan invited everyone to a reception at the Poncek home.

The Ponceks had occupied their house for twenty-five years and well known in their community. Friends and relatives gathered under the Linden tree, hugged, cried, drank, and ate. They were celebrating Anton's passage and their own lives.

Beth sat in the parlor, holding sleepy Rose while Jacky was sitting on her Aunt Theresa's lap greeting everyone. The guests patted her head or tweaked her cheeks and said she was pretty and cute. Josip came from Pennsylvania to pay his last respects to his father's friend, who let him live in his house without ever asking for a penny. He would be forever grateful to Anton. The house was filled with flowers and the family was given many gifts of cash. Tony Novak was generous by providing liquor for the reception. The Slovene Ladies Guild and the neighbors brought all the food.

By late afternoon, people started to leave, each of them telling Louiza she could count on them if she ever needed anything. By seven o'clock, only a few family members were in the house. Beth had gone home earlier because Jacky had missed her nap and was fussy. Theresa and her new husband were saying goodbye, when a stranger came to the door.

"My name is Jako. I knew Anton in Slovenia. May I come in?"

"Ja, ja, come in. Please, sit down. Can I get you something to drink or eat?" Louiza asked.

"Ne, hvala (No, thank you.)" Jako sat down, looking tired.

Ivan introduced himself, "I'm Ivan, Anton's oldest son."

"I want to talk to you alone," Jako said.

"I need to go to bed. Lachka noc (Good night,)" Louiza said. The girls went to their rooms and Stefan and Boris went to the kitchen. Ivan and Jako were alone.

"I have heart trouble. My days on this earth are few. My Priest advised me to clear my conscience before I die."

"You have my attention," Ivan said.

"You see, I was in love with the same young woman engaged to your father. Anton was about to be discharged from the army and I was starting my conscription. He saw me at the army camp and asked me about Agnes, his fiancé. You see, Agnes and I are from the same village. I led him to believe she was having an affair with another man. He was furious. Do you know why he never doubted my story?"

"No. Why?" Ivan's curiosity about his father's past was about to be satisfied. .

"Your grandmother, Anton's mother, was a beautiful woman with many suitors. She was lively and vivacious, warm and friendly, too friendly. She got involved with a man and became pregnant with your father. He was born out of wedlock. She was the topic of gossip in the village and when Anton was old enough to go to school, he suffered taunts by his peers for being a bastard.

"Your father was six years old, when a man from a neighboring village fell in love with his mother, your grandmother. Anton witnessed his mother's wedding and felt shame, for his half brother was already in his mother's womb. His half-brother, Boris, was born a few months after the marriage. Anton's trust in women was forever ruined and he was suspicious of all of them. Now you know why he believed my story about Agnes."

Ivan had a new understanding of his father's behavior toward his mother. His poor father had to carry the stigma of being a bastard in his youth. Ivan dwelled on his wedding night with Beth. Was she telling the truth about the slat ruining her virginity?

Jako continued, "There's one more thing. After your father left Slovenia, I asked Agnes to marry me, but she refused. She was devastated when your father rebuked her. The Priests helped her cope with her broken heart. She entered the convent as a novice and I saw her radiant face as she took her final vows."

"Did she wind up in a convent in Chicago?" Ivan asked.

"Ja," Jako said.

"I think Pa went to see her after he shot a man. He was different when he returned, like a weight had been taken off of his shoulders."

"It was me he shot in the leg. It was only a flesh wound. Somehow, he discovered I had deceived him about Agnes. When he saw me at Novak's Tavern he became enraged, attacked me and shot me with his gun."

Jako paused and with great emotion he said, "He only grazed my leg, but I faked a limp to make everyone think he crippled me. After your father returned from Chicago, he sent me money every month for a year. Here is what is left of the money your father sent to me." As

Ivan took the wad of money handed to him and Jako walked out of the house.

Ivan, stunned by the little man's revelations, sat in the parlor after shutting all the lights out. Jako had been cruel to his father and it took courage for him to confess the awful things he did. He felt sad that his father suffered so and still angry over the way he treated his mother. His father was a victim and his mother was a victim too. Yet his father had qualities he admired, his honesty and loyalty. When Anton was young, he had taught him how to do many things, like build a gazebo.

The old house seemed empty, even though Boris and his two youngest sisters occupied it with his mother. His sisters were pretty and sweet, and it wouldn't be long before they married and moved out. The pungent odor of decaying flowers permeated the air. Ivan gathered up the wilting flowers and threw them in a trashcan. He put the can outside, and locked the doors before he walked to his apartment with Jako's words vibrating in his head.

The money Jako gave him belonged to his mother. How much of his father's past should he tell her and how would it affect her? Maybe his mother already knew most of it. By the time Ivan got home, he decided to tell his mother the whole story.

He checked on his daughters sound asleep in their beds and entered his bedroom. Beth was lying on her side, her curvy figure outlined by the blanket tucked around her, little puffs coming from her slightly open mouth. Her face was relaxed, her skin had a rosy glow, and her thick brown hair spread over the pillow. Ivan loved Beth. He was jealous of the way men looked at her and the way she responded to their attention, laughing and joking with them. Maybe his father's attitude toward women had justification.

EPILOGUE

It had been a year since Anton died and Europe was in a turmoil in March of 1938. Adolf Hitler's German Nazi army occupied Austria without resistance and marched on to engulf Czechoslovakia in September. The following year Nazi troops stormed into Poland and killed many of its citizens and soldiers during the invasion. Britain and France, fearing Hitler would attack all of Europe, declared war on Germany. World War II had begun and it was the largest, deadliest war in history.

The United States wanted to be neutral, but sided with the Allies by allowing them to purchase arms to defend themselves against the Axis aggression led by Germany. The American people went to work making products for the war, thereby ending the Great Depression. The Fisher Body Manufacturing company of Ohio had been making cars since 1908. Because of the need for armament in the European conflict, the company converted their assembly lines to make jeeps, tanks, and airplanes. Machinists were in demand and Ivan was hired by National Acme to make parts for airplanes, such as the B-17, called the flying fortress. Ivan worked twelve-hour days, seven days a week, as did all the men with machining skills.

The unprovoked attack by Japan on Pearl Harbor in Honolulu, Hawaii on December 7, 1941, shocked the nation. The Imperial Japanese Navy surprised the United States' naval fleet, anchored in the harbor, early in the morning. The Japanese planes were launched from six aircraft carriers and came in two waves. They dropped bombs that sank or damaged twelve ships, including four battleships and one hundred eighty-eight U.S. aircraft.

They killed over two thousand four hundred service personnel. Franklin D. Roosevelt said it was, "A day that would live in infamy," and the United States Congress declared war on Japan. A few days later Germany supported Japan, their Axis partner, by declaring war on the United States. Thousands of American men volunteered and were drafted into the armed forces, and the whole nation became involved in the war effort. Women replaced men in the home workforce, rolled bandages for the Red Cross, sold war bonds, planted victory gardens, and Americans used government ration stamps for scarce commodities such as sugar, meat and gasoline. Most of the drafted men were young and single. Men with families did what they could toward the war effort at home. Stefan and his band entertained the service men in USO (United Service Organization) halls. The fight against the Axis alliance consumed the nation, and yet, the rhythm of life went on.

In spite of the fear that Japan might try to invade the western coast, Andrew and Eddi were doing well. Andrew owned several acres of land in the San Fernando Valley. His first love, Anchka, contacted him after her husband Hans died of a heart attack. With the help of the underground, she snuck out of Nazi controlled Vienna with her son and joined Andrew in California. Eddi was drafted and fought the Germans in North Africa where he was shot in the arm. He recovered and was honorably discharged from the army. Eddi was in his second marriage and owned an outdoor mall in North Hollywood.

Stefan married Majda. Theresa and husband had a child and another was due soon. Josip and his family lived in Johnstown and owned a grocery store. Anton's half brother, Boris, was still a bachelor and still living with Louiza. Her youngest daughters married their fiancés after the men received their draft notices. Katja and Benny inherited Aunt Bea's house and money, after she fell from an embankment and died on one of her trips. Beth and Ivan moved to a small house a few blocks from Louiza, and visited often. Jacky was old enough to walk by herself to her Grandma Louiza's house and loved reading her books to her.

Since the Normandy Invasion of Europe on June sixth, 1945 the allies had pushed toward Berlin, liberating countries and concentration camps. The pictures of dead bodies and emaciated prisoners in the camps were horrifying. The atrocities of the Nazi's were undeniably cruel. The Atomic Bombs dropped on Hiroshima and Nagasaki forced Japan to surrender and saved thousands of soldier and civilian lives. Louiza was sad that President Roosevelt could not see the conclusion of the four-year war he worked so hard to end. Two weeks after Roosefelt died, Adolf Hitler committed suicide in Berlin while allied troops were taking control of Germany. Between fifty to seventy million people were tortured, injured, or killed during the war.

The Axis armies of Italy and Germany had occupied Yugoslavia and the people suffered greatly. Louiza's sister, Maria, and family managed to survive in Gora due to its location. It was amazing that her husband Erich lived through the strife, for he was a member of the underground Partisans and helped blow up Nazi supply trains. He was a brave man, as were all those who fought for freedom in a war that cost millions of lives and millions of dollars. World War II had ended and Louiza's birthday was nearing. She was happy none of her kin were hurt or died in the war. She wanted to celebrate her good fortune and her birthday, by having a family party on Labor Day.

Louiza sat on the swing in the gazebo, looking at the Linden tree blooming with yellow flowers, while hearing the operatic voices of Jeannette McDonald, and Nelson Eddy sing, "I am calling you, oo-oo-oo, oo-oo-oo." The Victrola was plugged near the open window of the kitchen so she could listen to her favorite singers in the gazebo.

A sharp pain beginning on her right side radiated toward her navel. This pain occurred often after eating. Dr. Parme said she had gallstones and her gallbladder needed to be removed.. She scheduled the operation in the middle of September, after her birthday party. She was excited her family would gather under the Linden tree once again, the witness of many generations.